D1374528

The TAO of TRAVEL

Enlightenments
from Lives on
the Road

PAUL THEROUX

HAMISH HAMILTON
an imprint of
PENGUIN BOOKS

HAMISH HAMILTON

Published by the Penguin Group
Penguin Books Ltd, 80 Strand, London WC2R 0RL, England
Penguin Group (USA) Inc., 375 Hudson Street, New York, New York 10014, USA
Penguin Group (Canada), 90 Eglinton Avenue East, Suite 700, Toronto, Ontario, Canada M4P 2Y3
(a division of Pearson Penguin Canada Inc.)
Penguin Ireland, 25 St Stephen's Green, Dublin 2, Ireland (a division of Penguin Books Ltd)
Penguin Group (Australia), 250 Camberwell Road, Camberwell, Victoria 3124, Australia
(a division of Pearson Australia Group Pty Ltd)
Penguin Books India Pvt Ltd, 11 Community Centre, Panchsheel Park, New Delhi – 110 017, India
Penguin Group (NZ), 67 Apollo Drive, Rosedale, Auckland 0632, New Zealand
(a division of Pearson New Zealand Ltd)
Penguin Books (South Africa) (Pty) Ltd, 24 Sturdee Avenue, Rosebank,
Johannesburg 2196, South Africa

Penguin Books Ltd, Registered Offices: 80 Strand, London WC2R 0RL, England

www.penguin.com

First published in the United States of America by Houghton Mifflin Harcourt 2011
First published in Great Britain by Hamish Hamilton 2011
1

The permissions and credits on pages 286–7 constitute an extension of this copyright page

Set in Miller
Printed in Great Britain by Clays Ltd, St Ives plc

A CIP catalogue record for this book is available from the British Library

ISBN: 978-0-241-14464-0

www.greenpenguin.co.uk

MIX
Paper from
responsible sources
FSC
www.fsc.org   FSC™ C018179

Penguin Books is committed to a sustainable
future for our business, our readers and our
planet. This book is made from paper certified
by the Forest Stewardship Council.

Contents

Preface:
The Importance of Elsewhere

As a child, yearning to leave home and go far away, the image in my mind was of flight — my little self hurrying off alone. The word "travel" did not occur to me, nor did the word "transformation", which was my unspoken but enduring wish. I wanted to find a new self in a distant place, and new things to care about. The importance of elsewhere was something I took on faith. Elsewhere was the place I wanted to be. Too young to go, I read about elsewheres, fantasizing about my freedom. Books were my road. And then, when I was old enough to go, the roads I travelled became the obsessive subject in my own books. Eventually I saw that the most passionate travellers have always also been passionate readers and writers. And that is how this book came about.

The wish to travel seems to me characteristically human: the desire to move, to satisfy your curiosity or ease your fears, to change the circumstances of your life, to be a stranger, to make a friend, to experience an exotic landscape, to risk the unknown, to bear witness to the consequences, tragic or comic, of people possessed by the narcissism of minor differences. Chekhov said, "If you're afraid of loneliness, don't marry." I would say, if you're afraid of loneliness, don't travel. The literature of travel shows the effects of solitude, sometimes mournful, more often enriching, now and then unexpectedly spiritual.

All my travelling life I have been asked the maddening and oversimplifying question "What is your favourite travel book?" How to answer it? I have been on the road for almost fifty years and writing about my travels for more than forty years. One of the first books my father read to me at bedtime when I was small was *Donn Fendler: Lost on a Mountain in Maine*. This 1930s as-told-to account described how a twelve-year-old boy survived eight days on Mount Katahdin. Donn suffered, but he made it out of the Maine woods. The book taught me lessons in wilderness survival, including the basic one: "Always follow a river or a creek in the direction the water is flowing." I have read many travel books since, and I have made journeys on every continent except Antarctica, which I have recounted in eight books and hundreds of essays. I have felt renewed inspiration in the thought of little Donn making it safely down the high mountain.

The travel narrative is the oldest in the world, the story the wanderer tells to the folk gathered around the fire after his or her return from a journey. "This is what I saw" — news from the wider world; the odd, the strange, the shocking, tales of beasts or of other people. "They're just like us!" or "They're not like us at all!" The traveller's tale is always in the nature of a report. And it is the origin of narrative fiction too, the traveller enlivening a dozing group with invented details, embroidering on experience. It's how the first novel in English got written. Daniel Defoe based *Robinson Crusoe* on the actual experience of the castaway Alexander Selkirk, though he enlarged the story, turning Selkirk's four and a half years on a remote Pacific Island into twenty-eight years on a Caribbean island, adding Friday, the cannibals, and tropical exotica.

The storyteller's intention is always to hold the listener with a glittering eye and riveting tale. I think of the travel writer as idealized in the lines of the ghost of Hamlet's father at the beginning of the play:

> I could a tale unfold whose lightest word
> Would harrow up thy soul, freeze thy young blood,
> Make thy two eyes, like stars, start from their spheres,
> Thy knotted and combined locks to part
> And each particular hair to stand on end

But most are anecdotal, amusing, instructional, farcical, boastful, mock-heroic, occasionally hair-raising, warnings to the curious, or else they ring bells like mad and seem familiar. At their best, they are examples of what is most human in travel.

In the course of my wandering life, travel has changed, not only in speed and efficiency, but because of the altered circumstances of the world — much of it connected and known. This conceit of Internet-inspired omniscience has produced the arrogant delusion that the physical effort of travel is superfluous. Yet there are many parts of the world that are little known and worth visiting, and there was a time in my travelling when some parts of the earth offered any traveller the Columbus or Crusoe thrill of discovery.

As an adult travelling alone in remote and cut-off places, I learned a great deal about the world and myself: the strangeness, the joy, the liberation and truth of travel, the way loneliness — such a trial at home — is the condition of a traveller. But in travel, as Philip Larkin says in his poem "The Importance of Elsewhere", strangeness makes sense.

Travel in dreams, for Freud, symbolized death. That the journey – an essay into the unknown — can be risky, even fatal, was a natural conclusion for Freud to reach, since he suffered from self-diagnosed *Reiseangst*, travel anxiety. He was so fearful of missing a train that he appeared at railway stations two hours ahead of time, and when the train appeared at the platform he usually panicked. He wrote in *Introductory Lectures on Psycho-Analysis*, "Dying is replaced in dreams by departure, by a train journey."

This has not been my experience; I associate my happiest travelling days with sitting on trains. Some travel is more of a nuisance than a hardship, but travel is always a mental challenge, and even at its most difficult, travel can be an enlightenment.

The joy of travel, and reading about it, is the theme of this collection — and perhaps the misery too; but even remembered misery can produce lyrical nostalgia. As I was rereading some of the books quoted here I realized how dated they were, and how important as historical documents — the dramas as well as the romance of an earlier time. Yet a lot of the old-fangledness of travel ended very recently.

This book of insights, a distillation of travellers' visions and pleasures, observations from my work and others', is based on many decades of my reading travel books and travelling the earth. It is also intended as a guidebook, a how-to, a miscellany, a vade mecum, a reading list, a reminiscence. And because the notion of travel is often a metaphor for living a life, many travellers, expressing a simple notion of a trip, have written something accidentally philosophical, even metaphysical. In the spirit of Buddha's dictum "You cannot travel the path before you have become the path itself", I hope that this collection shows, in its approaches to travel, ways of living and thinking too.

ABBREVIATIONS OF BOOK TITLES

GRB	*The Great Railway Bazaar*
OPE	*The Old Patagonian Express*
KBS	*The Kingdom by the Sea*
SWS	*Sunrise with Seamonsters*
RIR	*Riding the Iron Rooster*
TEE	*To the Ends of the Earth*
HIO	*The Happy Isles of Oceania*
POH	*The Pillars of Hercules*
FAF	*Fresh Air Fiend*
DSS	*Dark Star Safari*
GTES	*Ghost Train to the Eastern Star*
WE	*World's End*

Travel in Brief

The Necessity to Move

Comes over one an absolute necessity to move. And what is more, to move in some particular direction. A double necessity then: to get on the move, and to know whither.

— D. H. Lawrence, *Sea and Sardinia* (1921)

Homesickness is a feeling that many know and suffer from; I on the other hand feel a pain less known, and its name is "Out-sickness". When the snow melts, the stork arrives, and the first steamships race off, then I feel the painful travel unrest.

— Hans Christian Andersen, letter, 1856, quoted in Jens Andersen, *Hans Christian Andersen* (2005)

The Road Is Life

Our battered suitcases were piled on the sidewalk again; we had longer ways to go. But no matter, the road is life.

— Jack Kerouac, *On the Road* (1958)

But to look back from the stony plain along the road which led one to that place is not at all the same thing as walking along the road; the perspective, to say the least, changes only with the journey; only when the road has, all abruptly and treacherously, and with the absoluteness that permits no argument, turned or dropped or risen is one able to see all that one could not have seen from any other place.

— James Baldwin, *Go Tell It on the Mountain* (1953)

You go away for a long time and return a different person — you never come all the way back. — DSS

A painful part of travel, the most emotional for me in many respects, is the sight of people leading ordinary lives, especially people at work or with their families; or ones in uniform, or laden with equipment, or shopping for food, or paying bills. — POH

Travel is a state of mind. It has nothing to do with existence or the exotic. It is almost entirely an inner experience. — FAF

The exotic dream, not always outlandish, is a dream of what we lack and so crave. And in the world of the exotic, which is always an old world peopled by the young or ageless, time stands still. — SWS

It is sometimes the way in travel, when travel becomes its opposite: you roll and roll and then dawdle to a halt in the middle of nowhere. Rather than making a conscious decision, you simply stop rolling. — GTES

Whatever else travel is, it is also an occasion to dream and remember. You sit in an alien landscape and you are visited by all the people who have been awful to you. You have nightmares in strange beds. You recall episodes that you have not thought of for years, and but for that noise from the street or that powerful odour of jasmine you might have forgotten. — FAF

Because travel is often a sad and partly masochistic pleasure, the arrival in obscure and picturesquely awful places is one of the delights of the traveller. — POH

In travel, as in many other experiences in life, once is usually enough. — POH

In travel you meet people who try to lay hold of you, who take charge like parents, and criticize. Another of travel's pleasures was turning your back on them and leaving and never having to explain. — KBS

Travel is flight and pursuit in equal parts. — GRB

All travel is circular . . . After all, the grand tour is just the inspired man's way of heading home. — GRB

It is almost axiomatic that as soon as a place gets a reputation for being paradise it goes to hell. — HIO

No one has ever described the place where I have just arrived: this is the emotion that makes me want to travel. It is one of the greatest reasons to go anywhere. — POH

It might be said that a great unstated reason for travel is to find places that exemplify where one has been happiest. Looking for idealized versions of home — indeed, looking for the perfect memory. — FAF

When strangers asked me where I was going I often replied, "Nowhere." Vagueness can become a habit, and travel a form of idleness. — OPE

Travel holds the magical possibility of reinvention: that you might find a place you love, to begin a new life and never go home. — GTES

One of the happier and more helpful delusions of travel is that one is on a quest. —GTES

I had gotten to Lower Egypt and was heading south in my usual travelling mood — hoping for the picturesque, expecting misery, braced for the appalling. Happiness was unthinkable, for although happiness is desirable it is a banal subject for travel; therefore, Africa seemed a perfect place for a long journey. —DSS

Invention in travel accords with Jorge Luis Borges's view, floated beautifully through his poem "Happiness" (LA DICHA), that in our encounters with the world, "everything happens for the first time." Just as "whoever embraces a woman is Adam", and "whoever lights a match in the dark is inventing fire", anyone's first view of the Sphinx sees it new: "In the desert I saw the young Sphinx, which has just been sculpted . . . Everything happens for the first time but in a way that is eternal." —DSS

Travelling is one of the saddest pleasures of life.

> —Madame de Staël, *Corinne, ou l'Italie* (1807)

Two Paradoxes of Travel

It is a curious emotion, this certain homesickness I have in mind. With Americans, it is a national trait, as native to us as the roller-coaster or the jukebox. It is no simple longing for the hometown or country of our birth. The emotion is Janus-faced: we are torn between a nostalgia for the familiar and an urge for the foreign and strange. As often as not, we are homesick most for the places we have never known.

> —Carson McCullers, "Look Homeward, Americans", *Vogue* (1940)

To a greater or lesser extent there goes on in every person a struggle between two forces: the longing for privacy and the urge to go places: introversion, that is, interest directed within oneself toward one's own inner life of vigorous thought and fancy; and extroversion, interest directed outward, toward the external world of people and tangible values.

— Vladimir Nabokov, *Lectures on Russian Literature* (1982)

Solitary Travel

Solitary Travellers: Neither sleepy nor deaf men are fit to travel quite alone. It is remarkable how often the qualities of wakefulness and watchfulness stand every party in good stead.

— Sir Francis Galton, *The Art of Travel* (1855)

Travel is at its best a solitary enterprise: to see, to examine, to assess, you have to be alone and unencumbered. Other people can mislead you; they crowd your meandering impressions with their own; if they are companionable they obstruct your view, and if they are boring they corrupt the silence with non-sequiturs, shattering your concentration with "Oh, look, it's raining" and "You see a lot of trees here."

It is hard to see clearly or to think straight in the company of other people. What is required is the lucidity of loneliness to capture that vision which, however banal, seems in your private mood to be special and worthy of interest. — OPE

In the best travel, disconnection is a necessity. Concentrate on where you are; do no back-home business; take no assignments; remain incommunicado; be scarce. It is a good thing that people don't know where you are or how to find you. Keep in mind the country you are in. That's the theory. — GTES

Travel is a vanishing act, a solitary trip down a pinched line of geography to oblivion. — OPE

The whole point of travelling is to arrive alone, like a spectre, in a strange country at nightfall, not in the brightly lit capital but

by the back door, in the wooded countryside, hundreds of miles from the metropolis, where, typically, people didn't see many strangers and were hospitable and do not instantly think of you as money on two legs. Arriving in the hinterland with only the vaguest plans is a liberating event. It can be a solemn occasion for discovery, or more like an irresponsible and random haunting of another planet. — GTES

In the best travel books the word "alone" is implied on every exciting page, as subtle and ineradicable as a watermark. The conceit of this, the idea of being able to report it — for I had deliberately set out to write a book, hadn't I? — made up for the discomfort. Alone, alone: it was like proof of my success. I had had to travel very far to arrive at this solitary condition. — OPE

There was no concept of solitariness among the Pacific islanders I travelled among that did not also imply misery or mental decline. Reading as a recreation was not indulged in much on these islands either — for that same reason, because you did it alone. Illiteracy had nothing to do with it, and there were plenty of schools. They knew from experience that a person who cut himself off, who was frequently seen alone — reading books, away from the hut, walking on the beach, on his own — was sunk in MUSU, *the condition of deep melancholy, and was either contemplating murder or suicide, probably both.* — HIO

All travellers are like ageing women, now homely beauties; the strange land flirts, then jilts and makes a fool of the stranger. There was no hell like a stranger's Sunday. — WE

Anonymity in Travel

On the days when I did not speak to anyone I felt I had lost thirty pounds, and if I did not talk for two days in a row I had the alarming impression that I was about to vanish. Silence made me

feel invisible. Yet to be anonymous and travelling in an interesting place is an intoxication. — KBS

Being invisible — the usual condition of the older traveller, is much more useful than being obvious. — GTES

The temporariness of travel often intensifies friendship and turns it into intimacy. But this is fatal for someone with a train to catch. I could handle strangers, but friends required attention and made me feel conspicuous. It was easier to travel in solitary anonymity, twirling my moustache, puffing my pipe, shipping out of town at dawn. — OPE

Travellers' Conceits

One traveller's conceit is that he is heading into the unknown. The best travel is a leap in the dark. If the destination were familiar and friendly what would be the point in going there? — DSS

Another traveller's conceit is that barbarism is something singular and foreign, to be encountered halfway round the world in some pinched and parochial backwater. The traveller journeys to this remote place and it seems to be so: he is offered a glimpse of the worst atrocities that can be served up by a sadistic government. And then, to his shame, he realizes that they are identical to ones advocated and diligently applied by his own government. As for the sanctimony of people who seem blind to the fact that mass murder is still an annual event, look at Cambodia, Rwanda, Darfur, Tibet, Burma and elsewhere — the truer shout is not "Never again", but "Again and again". — GTES

Yet another traveller's conceit is that no one will see what he has seen; his trip displaces the landscape, and his version of events is all that matters. He is certainly kidding himself in this, but if he didn't kid himself a little he would never go anywhere. — KBS

Strangers in Travel

Travel means living among strangers, their characteristic stinks and sour perfumes, eating their food, listening to their dramas, enduring their opinions, often with no language in common, being always on the move toward an uncertain destination, creating an itinerary that is continually shifting, sleeping alone, improvising the trip. — GTES

Most travel, and certainly the rewarding kind, involves depending on the kindness of strangers, putting yourself into the hands of people you don't know and trusting them with your life. — GTES

Cities and Travel

One of the pitfalls of long journeys is the tendency of the traveller to miniaturize a big city — not out of malice or frivolity, but for his or her own peace of mind. — RIR

My ideal of travel is just to show up and head for the bush, because most big cities are snake pits. In the bush there is always somewhere to pitch your tent. — FAF

Big cities seem to me like destinations, walled-in stopping places, with nothing beyond their monumental look of finality breathing You've arrived *to the traveller.* — POH

"Athens is a four-hour city," one man said, meaning that was all the time you needed to see it in its entirety. That hourly rate seemed to me a helpful index for judging cities. — POH

Adventure

Adventure travel seems to imply a far-off destination, but a nearby destination can be scarier, for no place is more

8

*frightening than one near home that people you trust have
warned you against.* — FAF

*For me the best sort of travel always involves a degree of trespass.
The risk is both a challenge and an invitation. Selling adventure
seems to be a theme in the travel industry, and trips have become
trophies.* — FAF

Travel and Optimism

*It was the poor person's way of going abroad — standing at the
seaside and staring at the ocean. All travellers are optimists, I
thought. Travel itself is a sort of optimism in action.* — KBS

*Travel, its very motion, ought to suggest hope. Despair is the
armchair; it is indifference and glazed, incurious eyes. I think
travellers are essentially optimists, or else they would never go
anywhere.* — FAF

*Travel is at its most rewarding when it ceases to be about your
reaching a destination and becomes indistinguishable from living
your life.* — GTES

Travel and Tradition

*Villages endure destitution better than towns, and rural poverty
can perversely seem almost picturesque.* — POH

*All places, no matter where, no matter what, are worth visiting.
But seldom-visited places where people were still living settled traditional lives seemed to me the most worthwhile, because they were
the most coherent — they were readable and nearly always I felt
uplifted by them.* — POH

Observing local rituals while travelling is important, not for its dubious sanctity, but because the set of gestures in rituals reveals the inner state of the people involved and their subtle protocol. — GTES

Travel and Politics

Any country which displays more than one statue of the same living politician is a country which is headed for trouble. — POH

In countries where all the crooked politicians wear pin-striped suits, the best people are bare-assed. — DSS

Sightseeing is perfect for a dictatorship — China is surely not anything else, politically speaking. The tourist visits, sees the sights, and when they've all been seen, it's time to go. The non-sightseer lingers, ignores the museums, asks awkward questions, fills people with alarm and despondency, and has to be deported. — RIR

Travel and Porno

It seemed incontestable to me that a country's pornography was a glimpse into its subconscious mind, revealing its inner life, its fantasy, its guilts, its passions, even its child-rearing, not to say its marriages and courtship rituals. It was not the whole truth, but it contained many clues and even more warnings, especially of its men. — POH

Landscape in Travel

A landscape looks different when you know the names of things, and conversely, can look exceedingly inhospitable and alien when it seems nameless. — FAF

It is rare to find silence anywhere in a natural landscape. There is always the wind at least. The rustle of trees and grass, the

drone of insects, the squawk of birds, the whistle of bats. By the sea, silence — true silence — is almost unknown. But on my last day here in Palau's Rock Islands, there was not even the lap of water. The air was motionless. I could hear no insects, nor any birds. The fruit bats flew high, beating their wings in absolute quiet. It seemed simple and wonderful: the world as an enormous room. — FAF

Africa, seemingly incomplete and so empty, is a place for travellers to create personal myths and indulge themselves in fantasies of atonement and redemption, melodramas of suffering, of strength — binding up wounds, feeding the hungry, looking after refugees, making long journeys in expensive Land Rovers, re-creating stereotypes, even living out a whole cosmology of creation and destruction. That's why many travellers in Africa are determined to see it not as fifty-three countries but rather as a single troubled landscape. — DSS

The nearest thing to writing a novel is travelling in a strange landscape. — SWS

Travel as a Waste of Time

Travelling is a fool's paradise. Our first journeys discover to us the indifference of places. At home I dream that at Naples, at Rome, I can be intoxicated with beauty, and lose my sadness. I pack my trunk, embrace my friends, embark on the sea, and at last wake up in Naples, and there beside me is the stern fact, the sad self, unrelenting, identical, that I fled from. I seek the Vatican, and the palaces. I affect to be intoxicated with sights and suggestions, but I am not intoxicated. My giant goes with me wherever I go.

— Ralph Waldo Emerson, "Self-Reliance" (1841)

Now my mind is made up. The whole journey is a trap. Travel does not broaden you so much as make you sophisticated, "up-to-date", taken in by the superficial with that really stupid look of a fellow serving on a beauty prize jury.

The look of a go-getter also. Worth no more. You can just as easily find your truth staring for forty-eight hours at some old tapestry.

— Henri Michaux, *Ecuador* (1970)

Travel, indeed, struck him as a being a waste of time, since he believed that the imagination could provide a more-than-adequate substitute for the vulgar reality of actual experience . . . No doubt, for instance, that anyone can go on long voyages of exploration sitting by the fire, helping out his sluggish or refractory mind, if the need arises, by dipping into some book describing travels in distant lands.

— Duc Jean Floressas des Esseintes, in *Against Nature* by J.-K. Huysmans (1884), translated by Robert Baldick (1959)

You think of travellers as bold, but our guilty secret is that travel is one of the laziest ways on earth of passing the time. Travel is not merely the business of being bone-idle, but also an elaborate bumming evasion, allowing us to call attention to ourselves with our conspicuous absence while we intrude upon other people's privacy — being actively offensive as fugitive freeloaders. — GTES

The Traveller as a Voyeur

The traveller is the greediest kind of romantic voyeur, and in some well-hidden part of the traveller's personality is an unpickable knot of vanity, presumption and mythomania bordering on the pathological. This is why a traveller's worst nightmare is not the secret police or the witch doctors or malaria, but rather the prospect of meeting another traveller.

But there is curiosity. Even the most timid fantasists need the satisfaction of now and then enacting their fantasies. And sometimes you just have to clear out. Trespassing is a pleasure for some of us. As for idleness, "An aimless joy is a pure joy." — GTES

Travel as Intrusion

It is well known that curious men go prying into all sorts of places (where they have no business) and come out of them with all sorts of spoil. This story [*Heart of Darkness*], and one other . . . are all the spoil I brought out from the centre of Africa, where, really, I had no sort of business.　　　　— Joseph Conrad, Author's Note, *Youth, Heart of Darkness, The End of the Tether* (1902)

Travel as Transformation

Travel is fatal to prejudice, bigotry and narrow-mindedness and many of our people need it sorely on those accounts. Broad, wholesome, charitable views of men and things cannot be acquired by vegetating in one little corner of the earth all one's lifetime.

— Mark Twain, *Innocents Abroad* (1869)

There is a change that takes place in a man or a woman in transit. You see this at its most exaggerated on a ship when whole personalities change.

— John Steinbeck, letter, June 1960, in *Steinbeck: A Life in Letters* (1975)

The person who wrote these notes died upon stepping once again onto Argentine soil. The person who edits and polishes them, me, is no longer. At least I am not the person I was before. The vagabonding through our "America" has changed me more than I thought.

— Ernesto "Che" Guevara, *Notas de Viaje (The Motorcycle Diaries)*, in Jon Lee Anderson, *Che* (2010)

The Traveller Must Be Worthy

The traveller must be himself, in men's eyes, a man worthy to live under the bent of God's heaven, and were it without a religion: he is such who has a clean human heart and long-suffering under his bare

shirt; it is enough and though the way be full of harms, he may travel
to the end of the world.

— C. M. Doughty, *Travels in Arabia Deserta* (1888)

Travelling Makes One Modest

To go back to Kuchuk [a courtesan and dancer in Esna]. You and I are
thinking of her, but she is certainly not thinking of us. We are weaving an aesthetic around her, whereas this particular very interesting
tourist who was vouchsafed the honours of her couch has vanished
from her memory completely, like many others. Ah! Travelling makes
one modest — you see what a tiny place you occupy in the world.

— Gustave Flaubert, in *Flaubert in Egypt*,
translated by Francis Steegmuller (1972)

Travel Writing

Literature is made out of the misfortunes of others. A large number
of travel books fail simply because of the monotonous good luck of
their authors.

— V. S. Pritchett, *Complete Essays* (1991)

*Travel writing, which cannot but be droll at the outset, moves
from journalism to fiction, arriving as promptly as the Kodama
Echo at autobiography . . . The anonymous hotel room in a
strange city drives one into the confessional mode.* — GRB

*The difference between travel writing and fiction is the difference
between recording what the eye sees and discovering what the
imagination knows.* — GRB

*When something human is recorded, good travel writing
happens.* — TEE

Whatever else travel writing is, it is certainly different from writing a novel: fiction requires close concentration and intense imagining, a leap of faith, magic almost. But a travel book, I discovered, was more the work of my left hand, and it was a deliberate act — like the act of travel itself. It took health and strength and confidence. — TEE

On that trip it was my good fortune to be wrong; being mistaken is the essence of the traveller's tale. — RIR

One of the reasons we are still ignorant of what space travel or lunar exploration is like: no astronaut has shown any ability to convey the experience in writing. There has never been a Melville on the moon, or even an Updike. — FAF

Lawrence's journeys by post-bus or cold late train or on foot are in that great laborious tradition which produced genuine travel books — the eye slowly taking it all in, the aching feet imposing the leisure to observe the common people in the smoky inn kitchen.

— Anthony Burgess, Introduction, *Lawrence and Italy* (1972)

[Henry Miller's *Colossus of Maroussi*] has all the normal stigmata of the travel book, the fake intensities, the tendency to discover the "soul" of a town after spending two hours in it, the boring descriptions of conversations with taxi-drivers.

— George Orwell, in the weekly *Tribune*, December 4, 1942, in *Orwell: Complete Works* (1968)

The Speed of Travel

I came to realize that I travelled best when I travelled no faster than a dog could trot.   — Gardner McKay, *Journey Without a Map* (2009)

Time Travel

The best of travel seems to exist outside of time, as though the years of travel are not deducted from your life. — GTES

Travel is so often an experiment with time. In Third World countries I felt I had dropped into the past, and I had never accepted the notion of timelessness anywhere. Most countries had specific years. In Turkey it was always 1952, in Malaysia 1937; Afghanistan was 1910 and Bolivia 1949. It is twenty years ago in the Soviet Union, ten in Norway, five in France. It is always last year in Australia and next week in Japan. Britain and the United States were the present — but the present contains the future. — KBS

Travel, which is nearly always seen as an attempt to escape from the ego, is in my opinion the opposite. Nothing induces concentration or inspires memory like an alien landscape or a foreign culture. It is simply not possible (as romantics think) to lose yourself in an exotic place. Much more likely is an experience of intense nostalgia, a harking back to an earlier stage of your life, or seeing clearly a serious mistake. But this does not happen to the exclusion of the exotic present. What makes the whole experience vivid and sometimes thrilling is the juxtaposition of the present and the past. — HIO

A true journey is much more than a vivid or vacant interval of being away. The best travel was not a simple train trip or even a whole collection of them, but something lengthier and more complex: an experience of the fourth dimension, with stops and starts and longueurs, spells of illness and recovery, hurrying then having to wait, with the sudden phenomenon of happiness as an episodic reward. — GTES

Travelling in a Time of Trouble

A national crisis, a political convulsion, is an opportunity, a gift to the traveller; nothing is more revealing of a place to a stranger than trouble. Even if the crisis is incomprehensible, as it usually is, it lends drama to the day and transforms the traveller into an eyewitness. — GTES

Travel and Love

> *If one is loved and feels free and has gotten to know the world*
> *somewhat, travel is simpler and happier.* — GTES

Smell a Country to Understand It

> [Kipling's] gift is to make people see (for the first condition of right
> thought is right sensation, the first condition of understanding a for-
> eign country is to smell it).
>
> — T. S. Eliot, *A Choice of Kipling's Verse* (1943)

Travel as a Love Affair

> For if every true love affair can feel like a journey to a foreign coun-
> try, where you can't quite speak the language, and you don't know
> where you're going, and you're pulled ever deeper into the inviting
> darkness, every trip to a foreign country can be a love affair, where
> you're left puzzling over who you are and whom you've fallen in love
> with . . . All good trips are, like love, about being carried out of your-
> self and deposited in the midst of terror and wonder.
>
> — Pico Iyer, "Why We Travel", *Salon* (2000)

Tourism and Sightseeing

> The tourist is part of the landscape of our civilization, as the pilgrim
> was in the Middle Ages.
>
> — V. S. Pritchett, *The Spanish Temper* (1954)

> He did not think of himself as a tourist; he was a traveller. The dif-
> ference is partly one of time, he would explain. Whereas the tourist
> generally hurries back home at the end of a few weeks or months, the
> traveller, belonging no more to one place than to the next, moves slowly,
> over periods of years, from one part of the earth to another.
>
> — Paul Bowles, *The Sheltering Sky* (1949)

17

Tourists don't know where they've been, I thought. Travellers don't know where they're going. — HIO

In Mumbai: A tourist would have been in a temple or a museum. I had been in a slum. — GTES

Sightseeing is an activity that delights the truly idle because it seems so much like scholarship, gawping and eavesdropping on antiquity. — GRB

Sightseeing was a way of passing the time, but . . . it was activity very largely based on imaginative invention, like rehearsing your own play in stage sets from which all the actors had fled. — GRB

Sightseeing is one of the more doubtful aspects of travel . . . It has all the boredom and ritual of a pilgrimage and none of the spiritual benefits. — SWS

Only a fool blames his bad vacation on the rain. — TEE

Travel is not a vacation, and it is often the opposite of a rest. — OPE

Nothing is more bewildering to a foreigner than a nation's pleasures. — KBS

Luxury is the enemy of observation, a costly indulgence that induces such a good feeling that you notice nothing. Luxury spoils and infantilizes you and prevents you from knowing the world. That is its purpose, the reason why luxury cruises and great hotels are full of fatheads who, when they express an opinion, seem as though they are from another planet. It was also my experience that one of the worst aspects of travelling with wealthy people, apart from the fact that the rich never listen, is that they constantly groused about the high cost of living — indeed, the rich usually complained of being poor. — GTES

It is almost axiomatic that air travel has wished tourists on only the most moth-eaten countries in the world: tourism, never more energetically pursued than in static societies, is usually the mobile rich making a blind blundering visitation on the inert poor. — OPE

Tourists will believe almost anything as long as they are comfortable. — HIO

After a man has made a large amount of money he becomes a bad listener and an impatient tourist. — POH

She saw their travels in terms of adverts and a long talcum-white beach with the tropical breeze tossing the palms and her hair; he saw it in terms of forbidden foods, frittered-away time, and ghastly expenses.
— Vladimir Nabokov, *The Original of Laura* (2009)

Departures

There is nothing shocking about leaving home, but rather a slow feeling of gathering sadness as each familiar place flashes by the window, and disappears, and becomes part of the past. Time is made visible, and it moves as the landscape moves. I was shown each second passing as the train belted along, ticking off the buildings with a speed that made me melancholy. — OPE

Nothing is more suitable to a significant departure than bad weather. — GTES

Frontiers

A mushroom-and-dunghill relationship exists at the frontiers of many unequal countries. — OPE

In the matter of visas and border crossings, the smaller the country the bigger the fuss: like a small policeman directing traffic. — POH

A river is an appropriate frontier. Water is neutral and in its impartial winding makes the national boundary look like an act of God. — OPE

Looking across the river, I realized I was looking towards another continent, another country, another world. There were sounds there — music, and not only music but the pip and honk of voices and cars. The frontier was actual: people do things differently there, and looking hard I could see trees outlined by the neon beer signs, a traffic jam, the source of the music. No people, but cars and trucks were evidence of them. Beyond that, past the Mexican city of Nuevo Laredo, was a black slope, the featureless, night-haunted republics of Latin America. — OPE

A person who has not crossed an African border on foot has not really entered the country, for the airport in the capital is no more than a confidence trick; the distant border, what appears to be the edge, is the country's central reality. — DSS

Air Travel

There is not much to say about airplane journeys. Anything remarkable must be disastrous, so you define a good flight by negatives: you didn't get hijacked, you didn't crash, you didn't throw up, you weren't late, you weren't nauseated by the food. So you are grateful. The gratitude brings such relief your mind goes blank, which is appropriate, for the airplane passenger is a time traveller. He crawls into a carpeted tube that is reeking of disinfectant; he is strapped in to go home, or away. Time is truncated, or in any case warped: he leaves in one time zone and emerges in another. And from the moment he steps into the tube and braces his knees on the seat in front, uncomfortably upright — from the moment he departs, his mind is focused on arrival. That is, if he has any sense at all. If he looked out of the window he would see nothing but the tundra of the cloud layer, and above is empty space. Time

*is brilliantly blinded: there is nothing to see. This is the reason so
many people are apologetic about taking planes. They say, "What
I'd really like to do is forget these plastic jumbos and get a three-
masted schooner and just stand there on the poop deck with the
wind in my hair."* —OPE

*Airplanes have dulled and desensitized us; we are encumbered,
like lovers in a suit of armour.* — OPE

*Airplanes are a distortion of time and space. And you get
frisked.* — GTES

*Air travel is very simple and annoying and a cause of anxiety. It
is like being at the dentist's, even to the chairs.* — FAF

*A train journey is travel; everything else — planes especially — is
transfer, your journey beginning when the plane lands.* — GRB

The Return Journey

*In any kind of travel there is a good argument for going back
and verifying your impressions. Perhaps you were a little hasty
in judging the place? Perhaps you saw it in a good month?
Something in the weather might have sweetened your disposition?
In any case, travel is frequently a matter of seizing the moment.
And it is personal. Even if I were travelling with you, your trip
would not be mine.* — RIR

*Travel is a transition, and at its best is a journey that begins
with setting forth from home. I hated parachuting into a place. I
needed to be able to link one place to another. One of the problems
I had with travel in general was the ease with which a person
could be transported so swiftly from the familiar to the strange,
the moon shot whereby the New York office worker, say, is insinuated overnight into the middle of Africa to gape at gorillas. That*

was just a way of feeling foreign. The other way, going slowly, crossing national frontiers, scuttling past razor wire with my bag and my passport, was the best way of being reminded that there was a relationship between Here and There, and that a travel narrative was the story of There and Back. — DSS

One of the greatest rewards of travel is the return home to the reassurance of family and old friends, familiar sights and homely comforts and your own bed. — HIO

❧ 2 ❧
The Navel of the World

ON EASTER ISLAND, OR RAPA NUI, WHERE I WAS camping and paddling my kayak, travelling for my *Happy Isles of Oceania* book, an islander said to me, "This is the *pito*." I said, "Really?" The term is a cognate of the Hawaiian word (*piko*) for navel. The Easter Islander went on, "*Te Pito te Henua*", and explained: Navel of the World. ¶ Perhaps just the delusion you would entertain on a smallish windswept rock in the middle of a cold ocean, two thousand miles from the nearest land. But it seems that the name may have been derived from the birth of a child by a woman who had just arrived on the first canoe, guided by the way-finder Hotu-Matua, the original ancestor and discoverer of Rapa Nui. The ritual cutting of the baby's navel may have been the earliest human ritual performed on the island. The date of this is disputed, but it would have been somewhere around the year 500 — amazing when you consider the canoe-building and navigational skills required for such a voyage. W. J. Thomson, in his exhaustive ethnographic study of the island, *Te Pito te Henua*, claims that this was the name that Hotu-Matua gave to the island on encountering it. Seen from a distance, the singular volcanic formation, the dead cone of Rana Raraku, a lump of bare rock in an empty sea, certainly looks like a petrified belly button.

In Delphi, Greece, wandering for *The Pillars of Hercules*, I was shown a rock and told by a guide in a solemn voice that it was the Omphalos, the Navel of the World. This got me thinking about the belief that one's village or town is the centre of the world. I am from Boston, and from childhood heard Boston referred to locally as "the Hub" — usually by headline writers of the *Boston Globe*. The Hub is actually the short form of "the Hub of the Universe". This hyperbole derives from Oliver Wendell Holmes in *The Autocrat of the Breakfast-Table*, writing about a Bostonian who says, "Boston State House is the hub of the solar system."

It seems to me a harmless conceit. Here is a list of other earthly navels:

China: The Chinese called (and still call) their country Zhongguo, the Middle Kingdom, meaning the centre of the world.

Arizona: Baboquivari Peak, near Sasabe in Pima County. The Tohono O'odham people regard this mountain as the Navel of the World, the place where, after the great flood subsided, humans emerged to populate the earth.

Cuzco, Peru: In Creation myth the word "Qosqo", in Quechua, means "the Navel of the World", and Cuzco was regarded as such by the Inca.

Jerusalem: The Al Aqsa Mosque ("the Furthermost") is dome-shaped to reflect the belief that it marks the Navel of the World.

Mecca, Saudi Arabia: The Kaaba, the most sacred site in Islam, is also said to be the Navel of the World. An Islamic text: "Forty years before Allah created the heavens and earth, the Kaaba was a dry spot floating on water, and from it the world has been spread out" (quoted in Rivka Gonen, *Contested Holiness*, 2003).

Mexico: Pacanda Island, on Lake Pátzcuaro in Mexico, has made a claim to be the Navel of the World.

Colombia: To the Arhuaco and Kogi peoples, who call themselves the Elder Brothers of humanity, the Sierra Nevada de Santa Marta range is called the Centre of the World.

Faroe Islands: Tórshavn, the capital of the Faroe Islands, was often called the Navel of the World by its most famous local author, William Heinesen (1900–1991), whose passionate nationalism perhaps led him to this delusion. He spoke Faroese but wrote in Danish.

Ayutthaya, Thailand: Wat Phra Si San Phet, built in 1448 by King Boromtrilokanath in this ancient former capital (1350–1767) of Siam, was called the Centre of the World.

Bodh Gaya, India: It is said that this holy site is the place where the Buddha sat when he was enlightened, which is called Vajrasana, meaning Diamond Throne. It was believed that when the universe is finally destroyed, this will be the last place to disappear and the first place to re-form when the universe begins again.

Perm, Russia: Nine thousand Permians voted in an Internet poll to have a monument built on a spot to be designated Navel of the Earth.

⊷ 3 ⊷
The Pleasures of Railways

N O MODE OF TRANSPORTATION INSPIRES MORE
detailed observation than the railway train.
There is no literature of air travel, not much of
one for bus journeys, and cruise ships inspire social observation but little else. The train is effective because
anyone who cares to can write (as well as sleep and eat)
on a train. The soothing and unstressful trip leaves deep
impressions of the passing scene, and of the train itself.
Every airplane trip is the same; every railway journey is
different. The rail traveller is often companionable, talkative, even somewhat liberated. Perhaps that's because
he or she can walk around. This person, this mood, is
what psychologists call "untethered"—such strangers
are the best talkers, the best listeners.

Train Travel — the Main Line

Anything is possible on a train: a great meal, a binge, a visit from card players, an intrigue, a good night's sleep, and strangers' monologues framed like Russian short stories. Anything is possible, even the urge to get off. — GRB

There seemed to me nothing more perfect in travel than boarding a train just at nightfall and shutting the bedroom door on an icy riotous city and knowing that morning would show me a new latitude. I would leave anything behind, I thought, for a sleeper on a southbound express. — OPE

Half of jazz is railway music, and the motion and noise of the train itself has the rhythm of jazz. This is not surprising: the Jazz Age was also the Railway Age. Musicians travelled by train or not at all, and the pumping tempo and the clickety-clack and the lonesome whistle crept into the songs. So did the railway towns on the route: how else could Joplin or Kansas City be justified in a lyric? — OPE

Ghosts, as old people seem to the young, have all the time in the world, another pleasure of long-distance aimlessness — travelling at half speed on slow trains and procrastinating. — GTES

No good train ever goes far enough, just as no bad train ever reaches its destination soon enough. — OPE

I had been in Latin America long enough to know that there was a class stigma attached to the trains. Only the semi-destitute, the limpers, the barefoot ones, the Indians, and the half-cracked yokels took the trains, or knew anything about them. For this reason, it was a good introduction to the social miseries and scenic splendours of the continent. — OPE

The great challenge in travel is not arriving at the glamorous foreign city, but solving the departure problem, finding a way out of

27

it, without flying. Buses are usually nasty, and bus stations the world over are dens of thieves, cutpurses, intimidators, mountebanks and muggers. Hired cars are convenient but nearly always a ripoff, and who wants narration from the driver? The train is still the ideal — show up and hop on. — GTES

There were few pleasures in England that could beat the small three-coach branch-line train, like the one from St. Erth to St. Ives. And there was never any question that I was on a branch-line train, for it was only on these trains that the windows were brushed by the branches of the trees that grew close to the tracks. Branch-line trains usually went through the woods. It was possible to tell from the sounds at the windows — the branches pushed at the glass like mops and brooms — what kind of train it was. You knew a branch line with your eyes shut. — KBS

The nostalgia of railway buffs is dangerous, since they hanker for the past and are never happier than when they are able to turn an old train into a toy. — KBS

The best story about Cairo Railway Station, told to me by a man who witnessed it unfold, does not concern a luminary but rather a person delayed in the third-class ticket line. When this fussed and furious man at last got to the window he expressed his exasperation to the clerk, saying, "Do you know who I am?" The clerk looked him up and down and, without missing a beat, said, "In that shabby suit, with a watermelon under your arm, and a third-class ticket to El Minya, who could you possibly be?" — DSS

A train isn't a vehicle. A train is part of the country. It's a place. — RIR

The train offers the maximum of opportunity with the minimum of risk. — GRB

Ever since childhood, when I lived within earshot of the Boston and Maine, I have seldom heard a train go by and not wished I were on it. Those whistles sing bewitchment: railways are irresistible bazaars, snaking along perfectly level no matter what the landscape, improving your mood with speed, and never upsetting your drink. The train can reassure you in awful places — a far cry from the anxious sweats of doom airplanes inspire, or the nauseating gas-sickness of the long-distance bus, or the paralysis that afflicts the car passenger. If a train is large and comfortable you don't even need a destination; a corner seat is enough, and you can be one of those travellers who stay in motion, straddling the tracks, and never arrive or feel they ought to. — GRB

Trains do not depart: they set out, and move at a pace to enhance the landscape, and aggrandize the land they traverse.

— William Gaddis, *The Recognitions* (1957)

Talking on Trains

The conversation, like many others I had with people on trains, derived an easy candour from the shared journey, the comfort of the dining car, and the certain knowledge that neither of us would see each other again. — GRB

The Romance of the Sleeping Car

The romance associated with the sleeping car derives from its extreme privacy, combining the best features of a cupboard with forward movement. Whatever drama is being enacted in this moving bedroom is heightened by the landscape passing the window: a swell of hills, the surprise of mountains, the loud metal bridge, or the melancholy sight of people standing under yellow lamps. And the notion of travel as a continuous vision, a grand tour's succession of memorable images across a curved earth — with none of the distorting emptiness of air or sea — is possible only on a train. A train is a vehicle that allows residence: dinner in the diner, nothing could be finer. — GRB

In my eyes [the berth] is the perfect thing, perfect in conception and execution, this small green hole in the dark moving night, this soft warren in a hard world.

— E. B. White, "Progress and Change", *One Man's Meat* (1944)

Trains Contain the Paraphernalia of a Culture

The state railway of Thailand is comfortable and expertly run, and now I knew enough of rail travel in Southeast Asia to avoid the air-conditioned sleeping cars, which are freezing cold and have none of the advantages of the wooden sleepers: wide berths and a shower room. There is not another train in the world that has a tall stone jar in the bath compartment, where, before dinner, one can stand naked, sluicing oneself with scoops of water. Thai trains have the shower jar with the glazed dragon on its side, Sri Lankan ones the car reserved for Buddhist monks, Indian ones a vegetarian kitchen and six classes, Iranian ones prayer mats, Malaysian ones a noodle stall, Vietnamese ones bulletproof glass on the locomotive, and on every carriage of a Russian train there is a samovar. The railway bazaar, with its gadgets and passengers, represented the society so completely that to board it was to be challenged by the national character. — GRB

Years before, I had noticed how trains accurately represented the culture of a country: the seedy distressed country has seedy distressed railway trains, the proud efficient nation is similarly reflected in its rolling stock, as Japan is. There is hope in India because the trains are considered vastly more important than the monkey wagons some Indians drive. Dining cars, I found, told the whole story (and if there were no dining cars the country was beneath consideration). The noodle stall in the Malaysian

train, the borscht and bad manners on the Trans-Siberian, the
kippers and fried bread on the Flying Scotsman. And here on
Amtrak's Lake Shore Limited I scrutinized the breakfast menu
and discovered that it was possible for me to order a Bloody Mary
or a Screwdriver: "a morning pick-me-up", as that injection of
vodka into my system was described. There is not another train
in the world where one can order a stiff drink at that hour of the
morning. — OPE

Particular Train Journeys

SOMERSET MAUGHAM IN THAILAND: WHY GET OFF THE TRAIN?

The train arrived at Ayudhya. I was content to satisfy my curiosity
about this historic place by a view of the railway station (after all, if
a man of science can reconstruct a prehistoric animal from its thigh
bone why cannot a writer get as many emotions as he wants from a
railway station? In the Pennsylvania Depot is all the mystery of New
York and in Victoria Station the grim, weary vastness of London).

— *The Gentleman in the Parlour* (1930)

PAUL MORAND ON THE ORIENT EXPRESS: PARIS TO CONSTANTINOPLE IN TWO PARAGRAPHS

The Simplon-Orient dragged its triweekly public through the gloom
as usual. The usual French dressmakers and, less elderly, milliners
were returning to Constantinople with a new lot of models; at La-
roche the perfume of Paris began to fade and the tenacious Oriental
odours, rose and peppery bergamot, reasserted themselves. Officials'
wives flitted in the corridors with six infant children who wouldn't
be properly put to bed this side of Bombay. Officers of the État-ma-
jor, in police caps, strode up the station platforms during the stops,
stretching their short, authoritative legs. French hearts are wholly
hidden by the multitude of their decorations. The English slept late,
whistled in the conveniences, where they stayed in relays until the
water and towels ran out. The Israelite-Spanish families from Sa-
lonika, returning after clarifying their complexions at Vichy, kept to

their bunks all day with their clothes on, stretched on the unmade bedding, between swaying flasks of Chianti hung from the electric light fixtures. Then after a tedium they and the rest of us slept to the rattle of the axles and the steel castanet springs. Snores. We beat on the mahogany panels to drive back the bedbugs. The conductor snoozed at the end of the corridor, on a cushion stuffed with contraband lire, dinars, drachmas, Rumanian leis and pounds, his alpaca tunic stuffed also with little folded papers full of jewels.

The train shook the loose glass of Gothic Swiss railway stations. For twenty-nine minutes the Simplon offered its large iron symphony. Then the banked roads and rice fields of the Piedmont. Then a station leading off into nothing, a great cistern of silence and shadows that was Venice. In the morning a zinc-coloured north wind overbent the Croatian corn in the plains. Pigs, striped black and white as with racing colours, betrayed the presence of Serbia; they were apparently devouring the corpse, or rather the wheels and an alarm signal, of a car which lay still derailed in a ditch. After rivers came yet other rivers that we crossed on rickety trestles beside the ruined piers of older bridges which had been destroyed in retreats. At Vinkovci we got rid of the velvet Rumanians, velvet eyes, velvet moustaches, daughters in undershirts plaiting their hair in the gelid darkness by the glimmer of half-frozen candles. After Sofia, pimentos hung drying across the house fronts. Oriental sun beat upon the Bulgar plains, ox-ploughs obtruded a symbolic prosperity as depicted upon the Bulgars' postage stamps and their money. At last, after the desert of Thrace, under a sky full of constellations lacking a polestar, with the disfigured Bear no longer recognizable at the low edge of the horizon, the Sea of Marmara stretched before us through a breach in the Byzantine wall.

— "Turkish Night", *Fancy Goods — Open All Night* (1922), translated by Ezra Pound

REBECCA WEST EN ROUTE TO YUGOSLAVIA

I raised myself on my elbow and called [to my husband] through the open door into the other wagon-lit: "My dear, I know I have inconvenienced you terribly by making you take your holiday now, and I know you did not really want to come to Yugoslavia at all. But when you get there you will see why it was so important that we should make this journey, and that we should make it now, at Easter. It will all be quite clear, once we are in Yugoslavia."

There was, however, no reply. My husband had gone to sleep. It was perhaps as well. I could not have gone on to justify my certainty that this train was taking us to a land where everything was comprehensible, where the mode of life was so honest that it put an end to perplexity. — *Black Lamb and Grey Falcon* (1941)

JEAN COCTEAU SUFFERING FROM BOMBAY TO CALCUTTA

Intolerable porters demand additional tips. Passepartout [Cocteau's lover, Marcel Khill] threatens them. They run off but return and glue their faces at the windows of the dining car, where one can just manage to collapse — it's the only word — into the seats one each side of the table.

I had no idea that such heat existed and that people could live in this cursed zone. The train starts off, and as we move out, I can recognize the old cannon on which Kim sat astride at the beginning of the book. [The cannon, Zamzama, was actually in Lahore, but this is a detail.]

The fire in India burns the glass, metal and coachwork to a white heat, raises the temperature of the atmosphere till you feel sick despite the electric fans which whip up its sticky paste.

Not having been warned against this torture, we leave the windows open. We doze off and wake up covered with a grey crust and our mouths, ears, lungs, hair full of the ashes of the fire which surrounds our journey. This inferno with insignificant interruptions of douches of cold water which quickly turn into boiling water, and lumps of ice that melt and become hot water, was to be the only knowledge of India vouchsafed to Mr. Fogg and Passepartout . . .

Nothing stirs. Corn, paddy fields, mud village, agricultural labour of the damned souls in this hell. Turquoise blue and black jays, occasional coconut palms and trees with fine luscious shadows begin to reappear. Sometimes a deodar stands alone in the desert dealing justice.

Stations. Shirts with tails hanging loose. Umbrellas. Workmen washing and massaging themselves with their fists. Then they stamp on their linen robes and wring them. And the never-ending procession of women beasts of burden. Blind men led by children. The heat is becoming less intolerable. By night it is almost cool. Tomorrow the inferno will be redoubled.

— *Mon Premier Voyage* (1937), published in English as *My Journey Around the World*, translated by W. J. Strachan (1959)

GUSTAVE FLAUBERT LEAVING HOME: "AT EVERY STATION I WAS ON THE POINT OF GETTING OFF"

From Nogent to Paris. What a ride! I closed the windows (I was alone in the compartment), held my handkerchief to my mouth, and wept. After a time, the sound of my own voice . . . brought me to myself, then the sobs began again. At one point my head was spinning so that I was afraid. "Calm down! Calm down!" I opened the window; the moon, surrounded by a halo of mist, was shining in puddles; it was cold. I thought of my mother, her face all contracted from weeping, the droop at the corners of her mouth . . .

At Montereau I went into the station restaurant and drank three or four glasses of rum, not to try to forget things, but just to do something, anything.

Then my misery took another form: I thought of returning. (At every station I was on the point of getting off; only the fear of being a coward prevented me.) I imagined the voice of Eugenie, crying, "Madame! It's Monsieur Gustave!" I could give my mother this tremendous joy at once; it was up to me entirely. I lulled myself with this idea: I was exhausted, and it relaxed me.

— *Flaubert in Egypt*, translated by Francis Steegmuller (1972)

VLADIMIR NABOKOV IN 1909: "INFORMAL CONTACT BETWEEN TRAIN AND CITY"

When, on such journeys as these, the train changed its pace to a dignified amble and all but grazed house fronts and shop signs, as we passed through some big German town, I used to feel a two-fold excitement, which terminal stations could not provide. I saw a city with its toylike trams, linden trees, and brick walls enter the compartment, hobnob with the mirrors, and fill to the brim the windows on the corridor side. This informal contact between train and city was one part of the thrill. The other was putting myself in the place of some passerby who, I imagined, was moved as I would be moved myself to see the long, romantic, auburn cars, with their intervestibular connecting curtains as black as bat wings and their metal lettering copper-bright in the low sun, unhurriedly negotiate an iron bridge across an everyday thoroughfare and then turn, with all windows suddenly ablaze, around a last block of houses.

— "First Love", *Nabokov's Dozen* (1958)

V. S. PRITCHETT: "LARGE THICK COLD OMELETTES"

Usually I travelled second or third class on the Spanish trains, for there the Spanish crowd came in and were good company. Often the women travelled with a pet bird in a cage: everyone took their shoes off and when they unpacked their large thick cold omelettes, they were careful to offer it first to everyone in the carriage. At the stations, which were often a couple of miles from the towns they served, water sellers calling out "Agua fresca" walked up and down in the red dust of the south and the pale dust of Castile.

— *The Spanish Temper* (1954)

EVELYN WAUGH ON THE TRAIN TO NAIROBI: "MY ILL TEMPER GRADUALLY COOLED"

But my ill temper gradually cooled as the train, with periodic derailments (three, to be exact, between Mombasa and Nairobi), climbed up from the coast into the highlands. In the restaurant car that evening I sat opposite a young lady who was on her way to be married. She told me that she had worked for two years in Scotland Yard and that had coarsened her mind; but since then she had refined it again in a bank at Dar-es-Salaam. She was glad to be getting married as it was impossible to obtain fresh butter in Dar-es-Salaam.

I awoke during the night to draw up my blanket. It was a novel

sensation, after so many weeks, not to be sweating. Next morning
I changed from white drill to grey flannel. We arrived in Nairobi a
little before lunch time.   —*Remote People* (1931)

CLAUDE LÉVI-STRAUSS: A MOSLEM FAMILY IN THE COMPARTMENT

At the foot of the Kashmir mountains, between Rawalpindi and Peshawar, the archaeological site of Taxila lies a few kilometres from
the railway line. I went there by train, which led to my being the
involuntary cause of a minor drama. There was only one first-class
compartment of a fairly old type — sleep four, seat six — simultaneously reminiscent of a cattle truck, a drawing room and — because of
the protective bars on the windows — a prison. A Moslem family was
already in possession, when I got in: a husband, with his wife and
two children. The lady was in purdah: although she made an attempt
to isolate herself by crouching down on her bunk wrapped in her *bur-
kah* and with her back obstinately turned towards me, the promiscu-
ity eventually appeared too shocking and the family had to split up.
The wife and children went off to the "Ladies Only" compartment,
while the husband continued to occupy the reserved seats and to
glare at me. I managed to take a philosophical view of the incident.

— *Tristes Tropiques* (1955), translated by John and Doreen Weightman

SIMENON: THE MAN WHO WATCHED TRAINS GO BY

That feeling about trains, for instance. Of course he had long out-
grown the boyish glamour of the steam engine. Yet there was something that had an appeal for him in trains, especially in night trains,
which always put queer, vaguely improper notions into his head.

— *The Man Who Watched Trains Go By* (1938),
translated by Marc Romano and D. Thin

GABRIEL GARCÍA MÁRQUEZ: TO ARACATACA WITH HIS MOTHER

We were the only passengers, perhaps in the entire train, and so far
nothing had been of any real interest to me. I sank into the lethargy
of *Light in August*, smoking without pause, but with occasional,

rapid glances to identify the places we were leaving behind. With a long whistle the train crossed the salt marshes of the swamp and raced at top speed along a bone-shaking corridor of bright red rock, where the deafening noise of the cars became intolerable. But after about fifteen minutes it slowed down and entered the shadowy coolness of the plantations with discreet silence, and the atmosphere grew denser and the ocean breeze was not felt again. I did not have to interrupt my reading to know we had entered the hermetic realm of the banana region.

The world changed. Stretching away on both sides of the track were the symmetrical, interminable avenues of the plantations, along which oxcarts loaded with green stalks of bananas were moving. In uncultivated spaces were sudden red brick camps, offices with burlap at the windows and fans hanging from the ceilings, and a solitary hospital in a field of poppies. Each river had its village and its iron bridge that the train crossed with a blast of its whistle, and the girls bathing in the icy water leaped like shad as it passed, unsettling travellers with their fleeting breasts.

— *Living to Tell the Tale* (2004), translated by Edith Grossman

JAN MORRIS: ALTERCATION ON THE ZEPHYR

I had pleasant companions at breakfast on the California Zephyr — a girl from Fresno who had never been on a train before, and two railroad buffs who kept me informed about the state of the track. However, I did have one altercation in the dining car. My ticket, I had been told, entitled me to anything I liked on the menu, but when I asked for cornflakes and scrambled eggs I was told that I was entitled to one or the other but not both. I called for the supervisor to expostulate, but I did not get far. I had got it wrong, the functionary said, not unkindly, and I quote him word for word: "You're not from this country. You don't understand the lingo." But the girl from Fresno thought the man had been rather rude, and one of the train buffs offered to share his scrambled eggs with me — only fair, really, because I had already urged upon him some of my Cooper's Oxford Marmalade.

— *Contact! A Book of Encounters* (2010)

❧ Travel Wisdom of ❧
HENRY FIELDING

In terms of travel, Henry Fielding was, as a youth, a student at the University of Leiden, and after he earned a law degree in London he became a circuit judge. His life (1707–1754) was short and turbulent, but he was productive, first as a writer of satirical plays, and after these were declared unlawful he wrote political pamphlets and the great novels *Joseph Andrews* (1742) and *Tom Jones* (1749). His ill health burdened him: he suffered from asthma, liver disease, gout, and dropsy (oedema), which he refers to repeatedly in his *Voyage to Lisbon*. I feel that his illnesses heightened his sensibilities and contributed to his close observation and the bite of his satire. He set sail for Lisbon looking for health, but the meandering voyage sickened him further and he died soon after he arrived. These paragraphs are from his *Voyage to Lisbon*, which was published the year after his death.

◆

There would not, perhaps, be a more pleasant, or profitable study, among those which have their principal end in amusement, than that of travels or voyages, if they were writ, as they might be, and ought to be, with a joint view to the entertainment and information of mankind. If the conversation of travellers be so eagerly sought after as it is, we may believe their books will be still more agreeable company, as they will, in general, be more instructive and more entertaining.

———•———

If the customs and manners of men were everywhere the same, there would be no office so dull as that of a traveller: for the difference of hills, valleys, rivers; in short, the various views in which we may see the face of the earth, would scarce afford him a pleasure worthy of his labour . . .

———•———

To make a traveller an agreeable companion to a man of sense, it is necessary, not only that he should have seen much, but that he should have overlooked much of what he hath seen. Nature is not, any more than a great genius, always admirable in her productions, and therefore the traveller, who may be called her commentator, should not expect to find everywhere subjects worthy of his notice.

❦ 4 ❧
Murphy's Rules of Travel

TRAVELLER I HAVE ADMIRED FOR MOST OF my travelling life is the writer Dervla Murphy, who was born in 1931 in Lismore, Ireland, where she still lives. I began reading her in the 1960s, with her first book, *Full Tilt* (1965). In Singapore in 1969, I met an Englishman who claimed to have met her. He had asked her how she'd managed, as a woman, to travel through Ethiopia, for her book *In Ethiopia with a Mule* (1968). She replied, "It was simple. I went as a man." ¶ Self-educated (she dropped out of school at the age of fourteen to look after her ailing mother), she mentions in her early memoir, *Wheels Within Wheels*, that at fifteen she was able to levitate herself. This fascinated me. But when I asked her about it, she told me that many people have written to her to relate similar experiences of levitation. As she grew older she lost this magical gift. And when her mother died, she set off on her *Full Tilt* journey, riding a bicycle from Ireland to India, suffering many dangers and indignities — snow, near drowning, being stoned by mullahs in Iran.

"By the time I arrived at the Afghan frontier," she writes in that book, "it seemed quite natural, before a meal, to scrape the dried mud off the bread, pick the hairs out of the cheese and remove the bugs from the sugar. I had also stopped registering the presence of fleas, the absence of cutlery, and the fact that I hadn't taken off my clothes or slept in a bed for ten days."

In India, after enduring these hardships — but being Dervla — she worked in a home for Tibetan refugees.

Though she has never married, she had a daughter, Rachel, whom she raised alone and took everywhere, including India, Baltistan, South America, and Madagascar. She writes, "A child's presence emphasizes your trust in the community's goodwill."

She has written twenty-three travel books, including books about England and Ulster. All her travel has been arduous, mainly solitary, and terrestrial, her preferred mode of travel an inexpensive bicycle. She never complains, never satirizes herself or the people she is among, and though her writing often contains infelicities, it reflects the woman herself: downright, patient, truthful, reliable, never looking for comfort but always the rougher experiences of the road; a wanderer in the oldest tradition. I find her admirable in every way, and her advice to travellers, "to facilitate escapism", is full of the wisdom of a life of journeying:

CHOOSE YOUR COUNTRY, USE GUIDEBOOKS TO IDENTIFY THE AREAS MOST FREQUENTED BY FOREIGNERS — AND THEN GO IN THE OPPOSITE DIRECTION.

This advice reeks of political incorrectness; it's "snobbish" to draw a clear distinction between travellers and tourists. Yet it's also realistic. The escapist traveller needs space, solitude, silence. Tragically, during my lifetime, roads have drastically depleted that natural habitat. Ads for phony "adventure tours" make me grind my few remaining teeth. For example,

"England to Kenya by truck! Overland adventure! See five countries in six weeks!" Who in their right mind wants to see five countries in six weeks? How not to escape ... I always try to get off the beaten track. One favourite place where I did so was a trek from Asmara to Addis Ababa. Things are different now, but most people I encountered then had never seen a white person before. Even on more recent trips, in Russia and Romania — where I took fairly obvious routes that certainly weren't uncharted land — I always stayed away from the tourist trails.

MUG UP ON HISTORY.
To travel in ignorance of a region's history leaves you unable to understand the "why" of anything or anyone. For instance, Castro's Cuba [the subject of Murphy's book *The Island That Dared: Journeys in Cuba,* 2008] must baffle visitors uninformed about the five-hundred-year lead-up to Fidel's revolution. Heavy sociological or political research is unnecessary, although if you happen to fancy that sort of thing it will add an extra dimension to your journey. Otherwise, enough of current politics will be revealed as you go along. And in those happy lands where domestic politics don't matter to the locals, you can forget about them.

Before your trip, learn as much as possible about religious and social taboos and then scrupulously respect them. Where gifts of money are inappropriate, find out what substitutes to carry. In Muslim countries such as Afghanistan, a code of conduct toward travellers prevents acceptance of money from guests, so I often buy gifts for children at the local bazaar.

TRAVEL ALONE OR WITH JUST ONE PREPUBESCENT CHILD.
In some countries two adults travelling together may be perceived as providing mutual support, making acceptance by the locals less spontaneous and complete. But a child's presence emphasizes your trust in the community's goodwill. And because children pay little attention to racial or cultural differences, junior companions rapidly demolish barriers of shyness or apprehension often raised when foreigners unexpectedly approach a remote village. I found this to be the case in all my travels with my young daughter, especially when we travelled through Kodagu in southern India.

DON'T OVERPLAN.

At sunrise, it's not necessary, or even desirable, to know where you are going to be at sunset. In sparsely inhabited areas carry a lightweight tent and sleeping bag. Elsewhere, rely on fate to provide shelter: dependence on those you meet en route greatly enhances escapism, and villagers are unfailingly hospitable to those who trust them. I have been welcomed into villagers' homes everywhere I've cycled or walked, and was always grateful for what was typically a space on the floor. "Trust" is a key word for relaxed travelling among people whose different way of life may demand adaptability but should prompt no unease or suspicion.

BE SELF-PROPELLED, OR BUY A PACK ANIMAL.

For long treks far from roads and towns, buy a pack animal to carry food, camping gear, kerosene for your stove if firewood is scarce — and of course your child, should he or she be too small to walk all day.

When organizing such a trek, allow for spending a week or ten days at your starting point, inquiring about the best source of pack animals. Take care to find a reliable adviser as well as a horse trader — preferably an adviser unconnected to the trader. In Ethiopia in 1966, I was lucky to be advised by Princess Aida, granddaughter of the then emperor, Haile Selassie, and half a dozen mules were paraded around the courtyard of a royal palace for my inspection. A decade or so later, in Baltistan, I bought a retired polo pony to carry Rachel, my six-year-old daughter, and our camping gear and supplies, including two sacks of flour, because in mid-winter in the Karakorum, the villagers have no spare food. In Peru, as a nine-year-old, Rachel rode a mule named Juana for the first six hundred miles from Cajamarca, but a fodder shortage necessitated her walking the remaining nine hundred miles to Cuzco: poor Juana had become so debilitated that she could carry only our gear.

It's important to travel light. At least 75 per cent of the equipment sold nowadays in camping shops — travel clothes lines, roll-up camping mats, lightweight hair dryers — is superfluous. My primary basics, although it depends on the journey, are a lightweight tent, a sleeping bag suitable for the country's climate, and a portable stove.

*IF ASSISTED BY A PACK ANIMAL, GET DETAILED LOCAL
ADVICE ABOUT THE TERRAIN AHEAD.*

And remember, a campsite suitable for you may be a disaster area for a
hungry horse or mule. Then you must press on, often to a site hardly fit
for humans but providing adequate grazing. People can do the mind-
over-matter bit, and resolve never again to let supplies run so low, but
an equine helper doesn't have that sort of mind. If there's no fodder at
six P.M., the mule cannot have consoling thoughts about stuffing it in at
six P.M. the next day. And there is nothing more guilt-provoking than
seeing a pack animal who has worked hard for you all day going without
sustenance.

CYBERSPACE INTERCOURSE VITIATES GENUINE ESCAPISM.

Abandon your mobile phone, laptop, iPod, and all such links to family,
friends, and work colleagues. Concentrate on where you are and derive
your entertainment from immediate stimuli, the tangible world around
you. Increasingly, in hostels and guesthouses one sees "independent"
travellers eagerly settling down in front of computers instead of conversing with fellow travellers. They seem only partially "abroad", unable to cut
their links with home. Evidently the nanny state — and the concomitant
trend among parents to overprotect offspring — has alarmingly diminished the younger generation's self-reliance. And who is to blame for this
entrapment in cyberspace? The fussy folk back at base, awaiting the daily
(or twice daily) e-mail of reassurance.

DON'T BE INHIBITED BY THE LANGUAGE BARRIER.

Although ignorance of the local language thwarts exchanges of ideas,
it's unimportant on a practical level. I've wandered around four continents using only English and a few courtesy phrases of Tibetan, Amharic, Quechua, Albanian, or whatever. Our basic needs — sleeping,
eating, drinking — can always be indicated by signs or globally understood noises.

Even on the emotional level, the language barrier is quite porous.
People's features, particularly their eyes, are wonderfully eloquent. In

our everyday lives, the extent to which we wordlessly communicate is taken for granted. In "far-flungery", where nobody within a hundred miles speaks a word of any European language, one fully appreciates the range of moods and subtle feelings that may be conveyed visually.

BE CAUTIOUS — BUT NOT TIMID.

The assumption that only brave or reckless people undertake solo journeys off the beaten track is without foundation. In fact, escapists are ultracautious: that's one of their hallmarks and an essential component of their survival mechanisms. Before departure, they suss out likely dangers and either change their route — should these seem excessive — or prepare to deal with any reasonable hazards.

Granted, there's a temperamental issue here: is a bottle half empty or half full? Why should your bones break abroad rather than at home? Optimists don't believe in disasters until they happen, and therefore are not fearful, which is the opposite of being brave.

INVEST IN THE BEST AVAILABLE MAPS.

And whatever you do, don't forget your compass.

෧ 5 ෨

Travellers on Their Own Books

T HE WRITING OF A TRAVEL BOOK IS, LIKE THE trip itself, a conscious decision, requiring a gift for description, an ear for dialogue, a great deal of patience, and the stomach for retracing one's steps. It is very different from fiction, the inner journey, which is an imaginative process of discovery. In the travel book, the writer knows exactly how the story will end; there are no surprises. The privations of the road become the privations of the desk. Because the travel book is a recounting of the journey, there is always the chance that the traveller will embroider, for effect or merely to stay awake. ¶ In a fit of candour or self-consciousness, many travel writers have felt the need to explain how or why they wrote their books, and in doing so they reveal a great deal about themselves. Here are some travellers reflecting on their work.

HENRY FIELDING: "IGNORANT, UNLEARNED, AND FRESH-WATER CRITICS"

Now from both these faults [plagiarism and hyperbole] we have endeavoured to steer clear in the following narrative: which, however the contrary may be insinuated by ignorant, unlearned, and fresh-water critics, who have never travelled either in books or ships, I do solemnly declare doth, in my own impartial opinion, deviate less from truth than any other voyage extant; my Lord Anson's alone being, perhaps, excepted.   — *Voyage to Lisbon* (1755)

SAMUEL JOHNSON: AN HOUR SPENT HATCHING THE IDEA OF A BOOK

I sat down on a bank, such as a writer of Romance might have delighted to feign. I had indeed no trees to whisper over my head, but a clear rivulet streamed at my feet. The day was calm, the air soft, and all was rudeness, silence, and solitude. Before me, and on either side, were high hills, which by hindering the eye from ranging, forced the mind to find entertainment for itself. Whether I spent the hour well I know not; for here I first conceived the thought of this narration.
                    — *A Journey to the Western Islands of Scotland* (1775)

C. M. DOUGHTY: "THE SEEING OF AN HUNGRY MAN"

We set but a name upon the ship, that our hands have built (with incessant labour) in a decenium, in what day she is launched forth to the great waters; and few words are needful in this place. The book is not milk for babes: it might be likened to a mirror. Wherein is set forth faithfully some parcel of the soil of Arabia smelling of *sámn* [clarified butter] and camels . . . And I rise now, from a long labour accomplished, with grateful mind and giving thanks to those learned men who have helped me, chiefly in the comparison — no light task — of my Arabic words, written from the lips of the people of Nejd, with the literal Arabic . . .

As for me who write, I pray that nothing be looked on in this book but the seeing of an hungry man and the telling of a most weary man; for the rest the sun made me an Arab, but never warped me to Orientalism.   — *Travels in Arabia Deserta* (1888)

DAVID LIVINGSTONE: "IT IS FAR EASIER TO TRAVEL THAN TO WRITE ABOUT IT"

As to those literary qualifications which are acquired by habits of writing, and which are so important to an author, my African life has not been favourable to the growth of such accomplishments but quite the reverse; it has made composition irksome and laborious. I think I would rather cross the African continent again than write another book. It is far easier to travel than to write about it.

— from the original Introduction to
Missionary Travels in South Africa (1857)

PAUL DU CHAILLU: "IT IS MUCH EASIER TO HUNT GORILLAS THAN TO WRITE ABOUT THEM"

The long and tedious labour of preparing this book for the press leaves me with the conviction that it is much easier to hunt gorillas than to write about them — to explore new countries than to describe them. During the twenty months which I have passed in the process of writing out my journals since my return to the United States, I have often wished myself back in the African wilds. I can only think that the reader, when he closes the book, will not think this labour wasted.

— Preface, *Explorations and Adventures in Equatorial
Africa* (1861); these lines were probably inspired by Livingstone
(see above), whom he acknowledges in the text of his book

ANTHONY TROLLOPE ON HOW HE WROTE THE WEST INDIES AND THE SPANISH MAIN: "PREPARATION . . . THERE WAS NONE"

Preparation, indeed, there was none. The descriptions and opinions came hot on the paper from their causes. I will not say that this is the best way of writing a book intended to give accurate information. But it is the best way of producing to the eye of the reader, and to his ear, that which the eye of the writer has seen and his ear heard.

— quoted in James Pope-Hennessy, *Anthony Trollope* (1971)

MARK TWAIN ON ROUGHING IT*: "VARIEGATED VAGABONDIZING"*

This book is merely a personal narrative, and not a pretentious history or a philosophical dissertation. It is a record of several years of variegated vagabondizing, and its object is rather to help the resting reader while away an idle hour than afflict him with metaphysics, or goad him with science. Still, there is information in the volume; information concerning an interesting episode in the history of the Far West, about which no books have been written by persons who were on the ground in person, and saw the happenings of the time with their own eyes. I allude to the rise, growth and culmination of the silver-mining fever in Nevada — a curious episode, in some respects; the only one, of its peculiar kind, that has occurred in the land; and the only one, indeed, that is likely to occur in it.

Yes, take it all around, there is quite a good deal of information in the book. I regret this very much; but really it could not be helped: information appears to stew out of me naturally, like the precious ottar of roses out of the otter. Sometimes it has seemed to me that I would give worlds if I could retain my facts; but it cannot be. The more I calk up the sources, and the tighter I get, the more I leak wisdom. Therefore, I can only claim indulgence at the hands of the reader, not justification.

— *Roughing It* (1872)

JOHN STEINBECK ON TRAVELS WITH CHARLEY*: "ANT-HILL ACTIVITY"*

It's a formless, shapeless, aimless thing and it is even pointless. For this reason it may be the sharpest realism, because what I see around me is aimless and pointless — ant-hill activity.

— letter, July 1961, in *Steinbeck: A Life in Letters* (1975)

VALERIAN ALBANOV ON HIS ARCTIC DEATH MARCH: "I SEE THIS DIARY . . . THROUGH A VEIL"

Fog all day long, with that dull light that makes one's eyes so terribly painful. At the moment mine hurt so much that I see this diary only as through a veil, and hot tears run down my cheeks. From time to time I have to stop writing and bury my head in my *malitsa* [a heavy, sacklike reindeer-hide sleeping bag]. Only in complete darkness does the pain gradually abate, allowing me to open my eyes again.

— *In the Land of White Death* (1917), first published in English in 2000, translated by Alison Anderson

APSLEY CHERRY-GARRARD: "I NEVER MEANT TO WRITE A BOOK"

When I went South I never meant to write a book: I rather despised those who did so as being of an inferior brand to those who did things and said nothing about them. But that they say nothing is too often due to the fact that they have nothing to say, or are too idle or too busy to learn how to say it. Everyone who has been through such an extraordinary experience has much to say if he has any faculty that way.

— Preface, *The Worst Journey in the World* (1922)

D. H. LAWRENCE: "MAKING LITTLE MARKS ON PAPER"

One says Mexico: one means, after all, one little town away South in the Republic: and in this little town, one rather crumbly adobe house built round two sides of a garden patio: and of this house, one spot on the deep shady veranda facing inwards to the trees, where there are an onyx table and three rocking chairs and one little wooden chair, a pot with carnations, and a person with a pen. We talk so grandly, in capital letters, of Morning in Mexico. All it amounts to is one little individual looking at a bit of sky and trees, then looking down at the page of his exercise book.

It is a pity we don't always remember this. When books come out with grand titles, like *The Future of America* or *The European Situation*, it's a pity we don't immediately visualize a thin or fat person, in a chair or in a bed, dictating to a bob-haired stenographer or making little marks on paper with a fountain pen.

—Mornings in Mexico (1927)

HENRI MICHAUX: "HE IS SUDDENLY AFRAID"

Preface: A man who knows neither how to travel nor how to keep a journal has put together this travel journal. But at the moment of signing he is suddenly afraid. So he casts the first stone. Here.

—Ecuador (1928)

FREYA STARK: "I TRAVELLED SINGLE-MINDEDLY FOR FUN"

I came to the conclusion that some more ascetic reason than mere enjoyment should be found if one wishes to travel in peace: to do things for fun smacks of levity, immorality almost, in our utilitarian world. And though personally I think the world is wrong, and I know that in my heart of hearts that it is a most excellent reason to do things merely because one likes the doing of them, I would advise all those who wish to see unwrinkled brows in passport offices to start out ready labelled as entomologists, anthropologists, or whatever other -ology they think suitable and propitious.

But as this book is intended for the Public, and is therefore necessarily truthful, I must admit that for my own part I travelled single-mindedly for fun. *— The Valleys of the Assassins* (1934)

GERALD BRENAN: "THE GIRL WITH THE UNFORGETTABLE FACE"

All I have aimed at is to entertain a few armchair travellers, who may enjoy whiling away a rainy night in reading of how people live in remote mountain villages in the serene climate of the South Mediterranean. One flies over these villages in the air, one sees their strange names on the map, one may even, if one leaves the main road, bump past them in a car, but their life remains as mysterious as that of the girl with the unforgettable face one caught sight of for a moment through the window of a railway carriage. Here is a description of one of those villages. *—South from Granada* (1957)

V. S. PRITCHETT: "STAMPING OUT HIS ANXIETIES WITH HIS HEAVY BOOTS"

How did writers and painters manage to live and keep their independence? . . . The thing to do was to write an original book of travel . . . I decided to take ship for Lisbon for economy's sake and walk from Badajoz to Vigo, through a part of Spain that was little known and, in patches, was notorious for poverty . . .

I have described it all in *Marching Spain* — note the deliberately ungrammatical, protesting, affected title. Though I have a tenderness for the book and think some pages are rather good, I am glad it has been out of print for forty years . . . It has a touching but shocking first chapter of exhibitionist prose; but despite the baroque writing of the rest, the mistakes of fact, and the declamations, it is original and has vigour. It is the work of a young man worried almost to illness by lack of money and by the future for a lot of the time. As he tramped along he was doing his accounts and stamping out his anxieties with his heavy boots.   — *Midnight Oil* (1970)

PAUL BOWLES: "THE CONFLICT BETWEEN WRITER AND PLACE"

What is a travel book? For me it is the story of what happened to one person in a particular place, and nothing more than that; it does not contain hotel and highway information, lists of useful phrases, statistics, or hints as to what kind of clothing is to be needed by the intending visitor. It may be that such books form a category which is doomed to extinction. I hope not, because there is nothing I enjoy more than reading an accurate account by an intelligent writer of what happened to him away from home.

The subject matter of the best travel books is the conflict between writer and place. It is not important which of them carries the day, so long as the struggle is faithfully recorded. It takes a writer with a gift for describing a situation to do this well, which is perhaps the reason why so many of the travel books that remain in the memory have been produced by writers expert at the fashioning of novels. One remembers Evelyn Waugh's indignation in Ethiopia, Graham

Greene deadpanning through West Africa, Aldous Huxley letting Mexico get him down, Gide discovering his social conscience in the Congo, long after other equally accurate travel accounts have blurred and vanished. Given the novelistic skill of these particular writers it is perhaps perverse of me to prefer their few travel pieces to their novels, but I do.

— "The Challenge to Identity" (1958), published in *Travels* (2010)

6

How Long Did the Traveller Spend Travelling?

AN INTENSE TRAVEL EXPERIENCE IS NOT AL-
ways a long one. D. H. Lawrence spent ten days
with his wife in Sardinia and wrote a lengthy
book about it. Kipling was ashore a few hours in Rangoon and never went to Mandalay, the subject of his famous poem. Ibn Battuta travelled all over the Muslim
world of the fourteenth century, rambling for twenty-
nine years, and Marco Polo was twenty-six years in
China. Is a long trip necessary to the vividness of the
experience? ¶ I am always curious to know how long
the traveller spent on the road. Sometimes the length of
the journey is plain in the title. *Ninety-two Days*, Evelyn

Waugh's 1932 book about his travels in Guiana and Brazil, says it all, and so does Isabella Bird's *Six Months in the Sandwich Islands*, and Heinrich Harrer's *Seven Years in Tibet*. But usually the length of the trip is not immediately apparent and has to be worked out from internal evidence — the mention of a date or a month, the passing of the seasons, or the research of a biographer.

The paradox of the passage of a traveller's time, and its meaning, was summed up beautifully by Doris Lessing in the first volume of her autobiography:

> Once I was making a mental list of all the places I had lived in, having moved about so much, and soon concluded that the commonsense or factual approach leads to nothing but error. You may live in a place for months, even years, and it does not touch you, but a weekend or a night in another, and you feel as if your whole being has been sprayed with an equivalent of a cosmic wind.
>
> — *Under My Skin* (1994)

Here are some notable sojourns, from the longest to the shortest:

Sir John Mandeville: Thirty-four years (1322–1356) travelling in Europe, Asia, and Africa. But Mandeville may not have existed, or if he did exist, as an English knight, he probably never left England. Although his *Travels* is full of incident and amazing sights, it is undoubtedly a massive example of literary cannibalism from the work of others: plagiarism, invention, legends, boasts, and tall tales culled from the works of travellers, borrowers, romancers, and other plagiarists.

Ibn Battuta: Twenty-nine years altogether (1325–1354). He went on the haj to Mecca in 1325 and kept going in Asia, Africa, and the Middle East. He was the only known medieval traveller who visited the countries of every Muslim ruler of his time, as well as such infidel places as Constantinople, Ceylon, and China. He described both Khan-Baliq (Beijing) and Timbuktu. Known in the Muslim world (and in particular his native Morocco), he came to prominence in English-speaking countries only after a translation of part of his *Travels* appeared in 1829. Called the greatest traveller the world has ever seen, Ibn Battuta's journeying has been estimated at about 75,000 miles.

He mistook the Niger for the Nile, but nevertheless received an enlightenment one day in 1352:

> I saw a crocodile in this part of the Nile [Niger], close to the bank; it looked just like a small boat. One day I went down to the river to satisfy a need, and lo, one of the blacks came and stood between me and the river. I was amazed at such lack of manners and decency on his part, and spoke of it to someone or other. He answered, "His purpose in doing that was solely to protect you from the crocodile, buy placing himself between you and it."

Marco Polo: Twenty-six years in total (1271–1297), seventeen of them in the service of Kublai Khan. In spite of this, Marco seems not to have noticed — certainly he never mentions — that the Chinese drink tea, use printing, and that they'd built the Great Wall.

"Marco Polo was not merely a traveller," Laurence Bergreen writes in *Marco Polo: From Venice to Xanadu*, "he was a participant in the history of his times." Bergreen identifies the reality behind some of the marvels (the humanlike "monkeys" in Sumatra were Pygmies, the dark unicorn a rhino, and so forth) and makes a case for Marco's omitting any mention of the Great Wall: "It was constructed during the Ming Dynasty (1368–1644), long after Marco Polo's day."

Marco does mention Buddhism and describes Buddha, calling him by his Mongol title, "Burkhan", the equivalent of "Enlightened". Nicknamed *Il Milione* for his reputation as a recounter of marvels (see Chapter 20, "Imaginary People"), he dictated his book to a well-known writer of romances, Rustichello (of Pisa), in 1298 while in prison for two years in Genoa. Rustichello may have overegged some of the events and descriptions, but the *Travels* (the first printed version appeared in Nuremberg in 1477) is still an astonishing eyewitness account of the then-known world and was regarded in Europe for centuries as a geography of Asia. Columbus carried an annotated copy with him on his voyages, which persuaded him in the Caribbean that he had reached the offshore islands of India, which is how the Indies got its name and why the natives of the hemisphere are known as Indians.

Xuanzang: Seventeen years (629–645). This Tang Dynasty monk, scholar, translator, and indefatigable traveller (his name is also rendered Hsüan-tsang), was twenty-seven when he set off on his journey to the West (the title of the Ming Dynasty novel that dramatized his travels), resulting in *The Great Tang Dynasty Record of the Western Regions.* This incomparable record of travel contains a precise account of distances, landscapes, commerce, and the numerous cultures, beliefs, and peoples along the Silk Road, to the edge of Persia, to what is now Afghanistan, Pakistan, India, and Nepal. Xuanzang's journey of thousands of miles is so well documented it enabled archaeologists of the nineteenth and twentieth centuries to find and excavate these ancient sites (see Chapter 13, "It Is Solved by Walking").

Lafcadio Hearn in Japan: The last fourteen years of his life, from 1890 to 1904. Hearn had travelled before this to the West Indies and elsewhere, and though he was not travelling the whole time he was in Japan, he lived as an alien, collecting grievances and insights into Japanese life, under his new name, Koizumi Yakumo.

William Bartram: Four years, 1773 to 1777, for his pioneering travels in the American South. There he botanized, gathered specimens, and studied the lives and habits of Native Americans for his groundbreaking and influential study of 1791, *Travels Through North and South Carolina, Georgia, East and West Florida, the Cherokee Country, the Extensive Territories of the Muscogulges or Creek Confederacy, and the Country of the Chactaws. Containing an Account of the Soil and Natural Productions of Those Regions; Together with Observations on the Manners of the Indians*, often called simply *Bartram's Travels*, a book read and praised by the Romantic poets Coleridge and Wordsworth.

Fanny Trollope in America: Almost four years (1827–1831). During that time she was in and out of the Nashoba settlement, an institution for the education of slaves who were hoping to be emancipated, but "one glance sufficed to convince me that every idea I had formed of the place was as far as possible from the truth. Desolation was the only feeling." She removed herself upriver to Cincinnati ("Porkopolis" — pigs in the street), where she put on "theatricals", and then built and opened a "bazaar," renting space to stallholders to sell "fancy goods". When this business failed, she did what many desperate people have done in search of solvency: she wrote a travel book, *The Domestic Manners of Americans* ("six hundred pages of griffonage" — scribblings), most of it trashing Americans as overfamiliar slobs and hypocrites who did nothing but spit. There is so much spitting in *Domestic Manners*, she could have called it *Great Expectorations*.

Yet this clearsighted book (greatly admired by Mark Twain) is not an account of city-haunting and sightseeing in America but a work "describing faithfully the daily aspect of ordinary life". She went on to write many more books, including a number of novels, and though her son Anthony (whom, at age twelve, she left in England) complained in his *Autobiography* that she was "much from home or too busy to be bothered", Fanny remained an inspiration to him and showed him the way to be a novelist and traveller. We would not have Anthony Trollope's great novels or his masterpiece of travel, *The West Indies and the Spanish Main*, were it not for his mother's bold example.

Fanny's conclusion about Americans: "I do not like them. I do not like their principles, I do not like their manners, I do not like their opinions."

Henry Morton Stanley crossing Africa: Three years, 1874 to 1877, for *Through the Dark Continent*. He travelled from east to west, Zanzibar to the heart of Africa and down the Congo River to Matadi and the Atlantic Ocean. A few years later he crossed Africa from west to east, a two-year trip.

Paul Du Chaillu in West Africa: Three years. Born in New Orleans (this is disputed; it might have been Paris) in 1835, he spent part of his youth in West Africa, where his father was a trader. He set off in 1855, when he was twenty years old. "I travelled — always on foot, and unaccompanied by other white men — about 8,000 miles. I shot, stuffed, and brought home over 2,000 birds, of which more than 60 are new species, and I killed up-wards of 1,000 quadrupeds, of which 200 were stuffed and brought home, with more than 60 hitherto unknown to science. I suffered fifty attacks of the African fever, taking, to cure myself, more than fourteen ounces of quinine. Of famine, long-continued exposures to the heavy tropical rains, and attacks of ferocious ants and venomous flies, it is not worth while to speak." He travelled in and around Gabon and halfway up the Ogowe (or Ogooue) River, 300 miles into the African interior, where he confirmed the existence of several species of gorilla (*Explorations and Adventures in Equatorial Africa*, 1861). On a later trip, for another book, he encountered various bands of Pygmies (*The Country of the Dwarfs*, 1871).

He inspired the travels of Mary Kingsley, H. M. Stanley, Jack London, and many others, and perhaps the fiction of Saul Bellow, whose *Henderson the Rain King* seems to echo the account of Du Chaillu's being made king of the Apingi in Gabon (see Chapter 21, "Writers and the Places They Never Visited").

Sir Ernest Shackleton's Endurance *Expedition:* Almost three years, 1914–1917. One of the most moving parts of *South* (1920), Shackleton's account of this heroic journey, is his sense that there was a mysterious fourth person with him on one of his marches:

> When I look back at those days I have no doubts that Providence guided us, not only across those snow fields, but across the storm-white sea that separated Elephant Island from our landing-place on South Georgia. I know that during that long and racking march of thirty-six hours over the unnamed mountains and glaciers of South Georgia it seemed to me often that we were four, not three. I said nothing to my companions on the point, but afterwards Worsley said to me, "Boss, I had a curious feeling on the march that there was another person with us." Crean confessed the same idea. One feels "the dearth of human words, the roughness of mortal speech" in trying to describe things intangible, but a record of our journeys would be incomplete without a reference to a subject very near to our hearts.

Without crediting it precisely, T. S. Eliot alludes to the phenomenon in a line of *The Waste Land:* "Who is the third who always walks beside you?" In a footnote Eliot writes that the line was "stimulated by the account of one of the Antarctic expeditions (I forget which but I think one of Shackleton's)".

Tobias Smollett in France and Italy: Two years, 1763–1765.

When a book reviewer criticizes a travel book for being negative, I always think of Smollett, who forcibly spoke his mind, as in this observation of the French character:

> If a Frenchman is admitted into your family, and distinguished by repeated marks of your friendship and regard, the first return he makes for your civilities is to make love to your wife, if she is handsome; if not, to your sister, or daughter, or niece. If he suffers a repulse from your wife, or attempts in vain to debauch your sister, or your daughter, or your niece, he will, rather than not play the traitor with his gallantry, make his addresses to your grandmother; and ten to one, but in one shape or another, he will find means to ruin the peace of a family, in which he has been so kindly entertained.
>
> — *Travels Through France and Italy* (1766)

C. M. Doughty in Arabia Deserta: Twenty-one months, 1876 to 1878, and it took him ten years to write his masterpiece, *Travels in Arabia Deserta* (1888).

T. E. Lawrence in Arabia: For *Seven Pillars of Wisdom,* one year, 1916 to 1917. He wrote the first version of the book in 1919, and lost it when he misplaced his briefcase at a railway station while changing trains. He wrote a second version in 1920, which he rewrote the following year. Eventually a much-shortened version was published in 1926.

This, like other great travel books, is not a travel book in any conventional sense. Subtitled "A Triumph", it is the record of Lawrence's involvement in the Arab revolt against the Ottoman Turks. But in the tradition of Doughty, whom Lawrence idolized, it describes the moods of the desert, the life of the Bedouin, and the subtleties of Islam, as well as military tactics. Lawrence's own contradictory character is a subject, and he is unsparing with himself.

"I was very conscious of the bundled powers and entities within me; it was their character which hid. There was my craving to be liked — so strong and nervous that never could I open myself friendly to another . . . There was a craving to be famous; and a horror of being known to like being known. Contempt for my passion for distinction made me refuse every offered honour." In this same section ("Myself") he adds, "I liked the things underneath me and took my pleasures and adventures downward. There seemed a certainty in degradation, a final safety. Man could rise to any height, but there was an animal level beneath which he could not fall."

Charles Dickens in Italy: Eleven months, to gather material for *Pictures from Italy*, 1844–45. He needed to get away from London because his sales of *Martin Chuzzlewit* were poor and casting a pall over his writing. He had been very discouraged by the negative, even hostile reviews of *American Notes* (1842). He witnessed a beheading in Rome and gave a detailed account of it, including this, the moment of truth:

> [The condemned man] immediately kneeled down, below the knife. His neck fitting into a hole, made for the purpose, in a cross plank, was shut down, by another plank above; exactly like the pillory. Immediately below him was a leathern bag. And into it his head rolled instantly.
>
> The executioner was holding it by the hair, and walking with it round the scaffold, showing it to the people, before one quite knew that the knife had fallen heavily, and with a rattling sound.
>
> When it had travelled round the four sides of the scaffold, it was set upon a pole in front — a little patch of black and white, for the long street to stare at, and the flies to settle on. The eyes were turned upward, as if he had avoided the sight of the leathern bag, and looked to the crucifix. Every tinge and hue of life had left it in that instant. It was dull, cold, livid, wax.

André Gide in Africa: Ten months, 1925–26, for *Travels in the Congo* (1929), the English edition of which includes *Voyage au Congo* and *Le Retour du Tchad.*

Gide had travelled at the official invitation of the French government, and yet this did not restrain him from criticizing colonial policies, or reporting on the many abuses of power against the African subjects (whippings, beatings, arson, intimidation), or the French colonial officers' taking advantage of Africans. It must be added that Gide, too, who fancied adolescent boys, indulged himself throughout the trip — and he was travelling with his much younger lover, Marc Allegret. Gide said to a friend that he was "very attracted, if I might dare to say, in a sensual way as well, by the Negro race".

To another correspondent he wrote — and this is true of a great deal of other travellers' experiences — "Everything that I expected to give me delight and which . . . persuaded me to undertake the journey has disappointed me — but out of that very disappointment . . . I have acquired an unexpected education."

W. Somerset Maugham in Burma: For *The Gentleman in the Parlour*, twenty-three days to Keng Tung, a few weeks more in Bangkok, but the whole trip, around the world from London, door to door, took nine months in 1922 and 1923.

Edward Abbey: About nine months, for *Desert Solitaire: A Season in the Wilderness* (1968). Not one season but two, in 1956 and 1957, "with adventures from in 1950, 1959 and 1965" (James Cahalan, *Edward Abbey*, 2001).

V. S. Naipaul in India: Nine months, for *An Area of Darkness: An Experience of India*, in which the Trinidad-born author, on his first-ever, 1962 trip to India, understands that he has no place in what he calls "the total Indian negation" and reasserts his feeling of "my own homelessness". He is frequently angry in the book, sometimes enraged, a condition he analyses after losing his temper. "It was brutal; it was ludicrous; it was pointless and infantile. But the moment of anger is a moment of exalted, shrinking lucidity, from which recovery is slow and shattering."

Richard Burton in Salt Lake City: About three weeks, though his entire North American trip took more than eight months. In Utah he wrote to a friend, "I'm travelling for my health which has suffered in Africa, enjoying the pure air of the prairies, and expecting to return in a state of renovation." Burton had sailed for Canada in April 1860, and after travelling across the United States by stagecoach and on horseback, he arrived in Salt Lake City toward the end of August. He wanted to know about Mormonism, particularly the practice of keeping plural wives. To this end, he spent time with Brigham Young, who had forty-nine wives at the time Burton met him. Burton had studied the practice of polygamy on his first trip to Africa and reached the conclusion that in countries where children had value and were a form of wealth, polygamy made sense. But he wrote in *The City of the Saints* (1861) that in the United States, "where the sexes are nearly equal, and where reproduction becomes a minor duty", it was inadvisable. His main objection to polygamy was that it was unromantic, merely an "unimpassioned domestic attachment". He went on, "Romance and reverence are transferred from Love and Liberty to Religion and the Church."

Joseph Conrad in the Congo: Six months in 1890, including twenty-eight days on the Congo River. Eventually this one-month river trip (published after his death as *Congo Diary*) would form the basis of the brilliant and evocative novella *Heart of Darkness*, which he wrote eight years after returning from the Congo, describing it as "experience pushed a little (and only very little) beyond the actual facts of the case".

Rebecca West in Yugoslavia: Three fairly short trips, about five months altogether. The first was on a British Council grant in the spring of 1936, but she was ill much of the time; then in spring 1937 for a few months, and a month in the early summer of 1938. The result was the 500,000-word *Black Lamb and Grey Falcon* (1941), regarded as the apotheosis of travel writing and self-analysis. One of my favourite passages, from the Epilogue, shows that a travel book can include anything, including — as here — an analysis of the divided self:

> Only part of us is sane: only part of us loves pleasure and the longer day of happiness, wants to live to our nineties and die in peace, in a house that we built, that shall shelter those who come after us. The other half is nearly mad. It prefers the disagreeable to the agree-

able, loves pain and its darker night despair, and wants to die in a catastrophe that will set back life to its beginnings and leave nothing of our house save its blackened foundations. Our bright natures fight in us with this yeasty darkness, and neither part is commonly quite victorious, for we are divided against ourselves and will not let either part be destroyed. This fight can be observed constantly in our personal lives. There is nothing rarer than a man who can be trusted never to throw away happiness, however eagerly he sometimes grasps it. In history we are as frequently interested in our own doom . . . We ignore this suicidal strain in history because we are consistently bad artists when we paint ourselves, when we prettify our wills and pretend they are not parti-coloured before the Lord.

Geoffrey Moorhouse in the Sahara: For *The Fearful Void*, four and a half months in 1972, travelling 3,600 miles, mainly on foot.

In an interview, Moorhouse said, "One reason I did this book is that all the books I've read about rough journeys, from Fuchs's *Crossing of Antarctica* to Thesiger's *Arabian Sands*, do tend to exclude the soft, weak, feeble, nasty sides we all have. They all seem to be bloody supermen. You think, Didn't they ever cry, or do something really shitty? As far as I can see, I'm a pretty ordinary bloke, and either they're very different from me, or they're excluding a part of themselves."

Bruce Chatwin: For *In Patagonia* (1977), four months, from mid-December 1974 to April 1975 (see Chapter 13, "It Is Solved by Walking").

Anton Chekhov in Sakhalin: Three and a half months in 1890, but the book, *Sakhakin Island* (translated by Brian Reeve), took him three years to write. He travelled from Moscow, by river steamer and horse-drawn coach, noting, "The Siberian highway is the longest, and, I should think, the ugliest road on earth." In an ingenious manner for a travel writer, to find out as much as he could about this remote penal settlement and this island of exile, he carried out his own detailed census, using a printed questionnaire.

"I am profoundly convinced that in fifty to a hundred years' time," he wrote, "they will regard the lifelong character of our penalties [exile, forced labour] with the same perplexity and sense of embarrassment with which we now look upon the slitting of nostrils or the amputation of fingers from the left hand."

And yet a hundred years after he wrote this, the Soviet government was exiling political prisoners to life sentences in the gulag and using them as forced labour. Russians on the outside were neither perplexed nor embarrassed, only afraid. I wrote about one of these prisons in *Ghost Train to the Eastern Star*, when I visited Perm 36. The prison was closed in 1992, a century after Chekhov's stay in Sakhalin.

The people who showed me around this prison in 2007, who knew it in its bad days, would have agreed with Chekhov's verdict in the Sakhalin settlement of Derbinskoye: "There were moments when it seemed to me that I was seeing the extreme and utmost degree of human degradation, lower than which it is simply impossible to go."

Ernest Hemingway in Africa: A little over three months, later writing *The Green Hills of Africa*. Hemingway reached Mombasa on December 6, 1933, and after his safari and travels up-country, left there in early March 1934.

W. H. Auden in Iceland: Three summer months in 1936, resulting in *Letters from Iceland* (1937), which he wrote with the poet Louis Mac-Neice, who spent one month there, liked the horseback rides, but hated the dried fish: "The tougher kind tastes like toe-nails, and the softer kind like the skin off the soles of one's feet." Because the book is more a scrapbook than a travel narrative, it is a mixture of poetic styles and observations.

William Least Heat-Moon: Three months (March–June 1978), 13,000 miles, on the back roads of America for *Blue Highways*. Before he set off he had an epiphany: "That night, as I lay wondering whether I would get sleep or explosion, I got the idea instead. A man who couldn't make things go right could at least go. He could quit trying to get out of the way of life. Chuck routine. Live the real jeopardy of circumstance. It was a question of dignity."

John Steinbeck, travelling with Charley: Three months in 1960.

D. H. Lawrence in Australia: Three months in 1922. He did not write a travel book but within a few weeks of arriving began a novel, *Kangaroo*, set in Australia, and finished it by the time he left.

Rockwell Kent's Greenland voyage: Three months in 1929, for *N by E* (1930). Nearing the coast of Greenland, his boat sank:

> The three men stand there looking at it all: at the mountains, at the smoking waterfall, at the dark green lake with the wind puffs silvering its plain, at the flowers that fringe the pebbly shore and star the banks. At last one of them speaks.
>
> "It's all right," he says, "that we should pay for beautiful things. And being here in this spot, now, is worth travelling a thousand miles for, and all that that has cost us. Maybe we have lived only to be here now."

Jean Cocteau: For *Mon Premier Voyage*, his trip around the world, eighty days in 1934. He had taken up the challenge of the *Paris-Soir* newspaper to duplicate the Jules Verne trip, and he succeeded, though unlike Verne's, his book is thin, patchy, and thrown together.

Bruce Chatwin in the Australian Outback: Nine weeks, for *The Songlines*, though he rattled around Sydney and Brisbane for four months.

George Gissing: For his travel book *On the Ionian Sea* (1901), two months in 1897. The book, well observed and diligent, is about the neglected south of Italy. But poor Gissing was a tormented man, with a weakness for drunken prostitutes, whom he tried to save — in the case of Nell, by stealing (and doing time for it) to support her. A key to his need for travel was a remark he made of himself: "I carry a desert with me."

Shiva Naipaul in Africa: For *North of South: An African Journey*, two months. At the end of this provocative book, published in 1979, Shiva Naipaul (brother of V. S.) concludes that the states of independent black

East and Central Africa are just as miserable and unjust as (then white-dominated) South Africa.

Eric Newby in Nuristan: For the trip recorded in *A Short Walk in the Hindu Kush* (1958), one month to get there and one month of hiking.

Toward the end of the trip, Newby and Hugh Carless encountered the explorer Wilfred Thesiger sauntering down a path on rope-soled shoes with some local guides. That evening, over a chicken dinner, Thesiger held court in the fading light.

> "England's going to pot," said Thesiger, as Hugh and I lay smoking the interpreter's king-size cigarettes, the first for a fortnight. "Look at this shirt, I've only had it three years, now it's splitting. Same with tailors; Gull and Croke made me a pair of whipcord trousers to go to the Atlas Mountains. Sixteen guineas — wore a hole in them in a fortnight. Bought half a dozen shotguns to give to my headmen, well-known make, twenty guineas apiece, absolute rubbish."
>
> He began to tell me about his Arabs.
>
> "I give them powders for worms and that sort of thing." I asked him about surgery. "I take off fingers and there's a lot of surgery to be done; they're frightened of their own doctors because they're not clean."
>
> "Do you do it? Cutting off fingers?"
>
> "Hundreds of them," he said dreamily, for it was very late. "Lord, yes. Why, the other day I took out an eye. I enjoyed that.
>
> "Let's turn in," he said.
>
> The ground was like iron with sharp rocks sticking up out of it. We started to blow up our airbeds. "God, you must be a couple of pansies," said Thesiger.

Peter Matthiessen in Nepal: For *The Snow Leopard*, two months in 1973 (see Chapter 13, "It Is Solved by Walking").

Jack London slumming in London, 1902: Seven weeks after arriving in England, Jack London had not only lived in, wandered around, and made notes about the poverty-stricken East End of London, but had also finished his account of the experience, *The People of the Abyss* (1903), a book of travel, socialist polemic, and farce, with a profusion of Cockney accents. London approached the experience as a travel writer rather than a muckraker, writing in his preface, "I went down into the underworld of London with an attitude of mind which I may best liken to that of the explorer."

Henry David Thoreau in Maine: Six or seven weeks. Between 1846 and 1857 Thoreau took three trips, of a few weeks apiece, to climb Mount Katahdin, to experience the wilderness, to learn about Indian life and language, and to gather information about the flora and fauna. He wrote three magazine articles for and gave lectures on the trips, and these pieces form the basis of his posthumous work *The Maine Woods.*

Graham Greene in Mexico: Six weeks, for *The Lawless Roads* (1939), and at the end of the trip he came to detest Mexico and Mexicans: "How one begins to hate these people — the intense slowness of that monolithic black-clothed old woman with the grey straggly hair . . . the hideous in-expressiveness of brown eyes . . . They just sit about."

Herman Melville in the Marquesas: One month, though he claimed it was four months, in the Typee Valley. En route to the Marquesas, in Honolulu, Melville was horrified by the behaviour of the missionaries:

> Not until I visited Honolulu was I aware of the fact that the small remnant of the natives had been civilized into draught-horses, and evangelized into beasts of burden. But so it is. They have been literally broken into the traces, and are harnessed to the vehicles of their spiritual instructors like so many dumb brutes!   — *Typee* (1846)

Some years later, he also travelled to Europe and the Holy Land. He wrote a mystical poem about the experience, as well as a diary in which he noted the behaviour of guides in Jerusalem, where he spent eighteen days:

> *Talk of the Guides:* "Here is the stone Christ leaned against, & here is the English Hotel. Yonder is the arch where Christ was shown to the people, & just by that open window is sold the best coffee in Jerusalem."   — *Journal of a Visit to Europe and the Levant* (1856–57)

Elias Canetti in Marrakesh: A month or so in 1954, when he joined some friends who were making a film in Marrakesh. He tagged along, immersed himself in the city, and made notes. He did not publish his book *Die Stimmen von Marrakesch* until 1967 (translated as *The Voices of Marrakesh*), because he thought that what he had to say about Morocco, and travel, was trivial. But the slim book is evocative, persuasive, and wise. For example, noticing a gathering of blind beggars chanting, and studying them, he reflects, "Travelling, one accepts everything; indignation stays at home. One looks, one listens, one is roused to enthusiasm by the most dreadful things because they are new. Good travellers are heartless."

Thoreau on Cape Cod: A little over three weeks, but in two trips, one in 1849, the other in 1855. *Cape Cod*, his account of the trip up "the bare and bended arm" of the Cape, from Sandwich to Provincetown, was published after his death, in 1865. Lines from the first chapter ("The Shipwreck") were appropriated and cannibalized by Robert Lowell for his poem "The Quaker Graveyard at Nantucket", and chapter 5, "The Wellfleet Oysterman", contains the first mention in print of broccoli being grown in the United States.

Graham Greene in Liberia: Twenty-three days. Greene's book *Journey Without Maps* (1936) is an ingeniously worked-up account of only a little over three weeks in the Liberian bush by an absolute beginner in Africa. Greene admits this early on: "I had never been out of Europe before; I was a complete amateur at travel in Africa." Amazingly, he brought his young female cousin Barbara along for company. "You poor innocents!" a stranger cried at them in Freetown. He didn't know the half of it.

Out of his element, Greene is gloomy, fidgety, nervous, and Barbara has no discernible skills. But the pitying man in Freetown can see from their helpless smiles and their lack of preparation that theirs is a leap in the dark — *Journey in the Dark* was one of the rejected titles for the book. How innocent was Greene? Here is an example. Just before arriving in Freetown to start his trip, he confides, "I could never properly remember the points of the compass." Can a traveller be more innocent than that?

Greene and his cousin are not deterred by their incompetence. They seek guidance. They hire porters and a cook. They board the train for the Liberian frontier and start walking around the back of the country. They have twenty-six poorly paid African porters carrying their food and equipment. They have a pistol, they have a tent (never to be used), they have a table and a portable bath and a stash of whisky. They even have trinkets to hand out to natives — but the natives prefer gifts of money or jolts of whisky to trinkets. The trip is eventful: the travellers suffer fatigue, Greene falls ill with a serious fever, there are misunderstandings and wrong turns. There is a great deal of foot dragging on the part of the porters. A little over a month after they set off, the Greenes are back on the coast, and in a matter of a week or so (the book skimps on dates) they are on a ship heading back to Britain.

Greene called this short but difficult trip "life-altering".

Thoreau on rivers: Travelling for *A Week on the Concord and Merrimac:* two weeks. This was one of the two books (*Walden* was the other) published in Thoreau's lifetime. The trip itself is a way of speculating on the natural world, the meaning of existence, urbanization, American history, and the nature of friendship. The book did not sell. In 1853, four years after publication, when the 706 unsold copies (of an edition of 1,000) were returned to him by the printer, Thoreau remarked wryly in a letter, "I now have a library of nearly nine hundred volumes, more than seven hundred of which I wrote myself."

D. H. Lawrence in Sardinia: Ten days. The travel book he wrote immediately afterward, *Sea and Sardinia*, is 355 pages long, and of course full of digressions.

He travelled throughout Italy at the same hectic pace. But Lawrence was so alert, even hypersensitive, he was able to sum up his travel experience with intense feeling, as here, in another travel book about Italy, where he is in Lago di Garda.

I went into the church. It was very dark, and impregnated with centuries of incense. It affected me like the lair of some enormous creature. My senses were roused, they sprang awake in the hot, spiced
darkness. My skin was expectant, as if it expected some contact,
some embrace, as if it were aware of the contiguity of the physical
world, the physical contact with the darkness and the heavy, sugges-
tive substance of the enclosure. It was a thick fierce darkness of the
senses. But my soul shrank.

I went out again. The pavemented threshold was clear as a jewel,
the marvelous clarity of sunshine that becomes blue in the height
seemed to distil me into itself.   — *Twilight in Italy* (1913)

Stephen Crane in "The Open Boat": A day and a half, from late afternoon on January 1 to noon on January 3, 1897, off the Florida coast.
Subtitled "A Tale Intended to Be After the Fact", this story is regarded
as a classic in ordeal literature. But the ordeal (Crane and three others
splashing fifteen miles to Daytona Beach in a dinghy after their ship, the
Cuba-bound *Commodore*, sank) is a landlubber's exercise in mythomania
and hyperbole. Though a literary critic was later emboldened to write,
"Captain Bligh's account of his small boat journey . . . seems tame in
comparison", it is a matter of record that Bligh's treacherous voyage of
four thousand miles in a small lifeboat took him six weeks, compared to
Crane's thirty-six hours.

Kipling in Mandalay: He never went there, though he was briefly in
Rangoon in 1889 and was impressed by the golden stupa of the Shwe
Dagon pagoda. "Briefly" meant a few hours, as he explained in *From Sea
to Sea* (1899):

> My own sojourn in Rangoon was countable by hours, so I may
> be forgiven when I pranced with impatience at the bottom of the
> staircase [of the pagoda] because I could not at once secure a full,
> complete and accurate idea of everything that was to be seen. The
> meaning of the guardian tigers, the inwardness of the main pagoda,
> and the countless little ones, was hidden from me. I could not un-
> derstand why the pretty girls with cheroots sold little sticks and

coloured candles to be used before the image of Buddha. Everything was incomprehensible to me.

There are obvious howlers in the poem "Mandalay" (written in 1890 and published in *Barrack-Room Ballads*): the old Moulmein pagoda is hundreds of miles from Mandalay, and the dawn does not come up "like thunder outer China 'crost the Bay," yet the poem is persuasively atmospheric, as in the last verse:

> Ship me somewheres east of Suez, where the best is like the worst,
> Where there aren't no Ten Commandments an' a man can raise a thirst;
> For the temple-bells are callin', an' it's there that I would be —
> By the old Moulmein Pagoda, looking lazy at the sea;
>> On the road to Mandalay,
>> Where the old Flotilla lay,
>> With our sick beneath the awnings when we went to Mandalay!
>> On the road to Mandalay,
>> Where the flyin'-fishes play,
>> An' the dawn comes up like thunder outer China 'crost the Bay!

❧ Travel Wisdom of ❧
SAMUEL JOHNSON

Some of the wittiest remarks on the subject of travel are Johnson's, and though he hated to leave London, he spoke about wanting to embark on voyages to Iceland and the West Indies; instead, he shuttled up and down England, made a long journey to Scotland in 1773, and a year later spent three months rattling around North Wales. He was one of the most passionate readers the world has known — his dictionary is proof of that. Born in 1709, he was a contemporary of Fielding, whom he called a "blockhead" (and remarked that *Tom Jones* was "corrupt" and "vicious"). ¶ Through his wide reading, Johnson knew the world much better than most of his contemporaries. He could talk easily about Abyssinia (he had translated Father Jerónimo Lobo's *Voyage to Abyssinia*, and his novel *Rasselas* is set there) and Corsica (Boswell introduced him to the Corsican patriot Pascal Paoli) and the classical Mediterranean. He discussed Tahiti with Boswell, who'd had dinner and discussed circumnavigation with Captain James Cook in London ("and felt a strong inclination to go with him on his next voyage"). Johnson had a neurological disorder that was probably Tourette's, with gout, and with melancholia, yet he stirred himself at the age of sixty-four to travel to the Western Isles of Scotland — far-off and strange — with Boswell, who also published his *Journal* of the trip.

———•———

In travelling; a man must carry knowledge with him, if he would bring home knowledge.

— Samuel Johnson, in James Boswell, *Life of Johnson*

———•———

He talked with an uncommon animation of travelling into distant countries; that the mind was enlarged by it, and that an acquisition of dignity of character was derived from it. He expressed a particular enthusiasm with respect to visiting the wall of China. I catched it for the moment, and said I really believed I should go and see the wall of China had I not children, of whom it was my duty to take care. "Sir, (said he,) by doing so, you would do what would be of importance in raising your children to eminence. There would be a lustre reflected upon them from your spirit and curiosity. They would be at all times regarded as the children of a man who had gone to view the wall of China. I am serious, Sir."

— *Life of Johnson*

———•———

It will be observed, that when giving me advice as to my travels, Dr. Johnson did not dwell upon cities, and palaces, and pictures, and shows, and Arcadian scenes. He was of Lord Essex's opinion, who advises his kinsman Roger Earl of Rutland, "rather to go an hundred miles to speak with one wise man, than five miles to see a fair town".

— *Life of Johnson*

———•———

Boswell: Is not the Giant's Causeway worth seeing?
Johnson: Worth seeing? Yes; but not worth going to see.
— *Life of Johnson*

Travel light

We found in the course of our journey the convenience of having dis-incumbered ourselves, by laying aside whatever we could spare; for it is not to be imagined without experience, how in climbing crags, and treading bogs, and winding through narrow and obstructed pas-sages, a little bulk will hinder, and a little weight will burthen; or how often a man that has pleased himself at home with his own resolution, will, in the hour of darkness and fatigue, be content to leave behind him everything but himself.

— *Journey to the Western Islands of Scotland*

The importance of seeing more at first hand

It will very readily occur, that this uniformity of barrenness can af-ford very little amusement to the traveller; that it is easy to sit at home and conceive rocks and heath, and waterfalls; and that these journeys are useless labours, which neither impregnate the imagina-tion, nor enlarge the understanding. It is true that of far the greater part of things, we must content ourselves with such knowledge as description may exhibit, or analogy supply; but it is true likewise, that these ideas are always incomplete, and that at least, till we have compared them with realities, we do not know them to be just. As we see more, we become possessed of more certainties, and conse-quently gain more principles of reasoning, and found a wider basis of analogy.

— *Journey to the Western Islands of Scotland*

7

The Things That They Carried

TRAVEL MAGAZINES ALWAYS MAKE A POINT of telling you the essential thing to carry on your trip, and it used to be a Swiss Army knife — that is, until air travellers were screened, x-rayed, patted down, and presented with a list of forbidden items. Now it is likely to be a cell phone, in my view one of the great impediments to a travel experience. I always take a small shortwave radio, to give me the news and weather of the place I'm in and to keep up with world events. The writer and traveller Pico Iyer says he never travels without a book to read; I am of the same mind. ¶ William Burroughs, a lifetime addict and also a traveller, never went anywhere without a drug of some kind, usually heroin. Kit Moresby, in Paul Bowles's novel *The Sheltering Sky*, carried evening gowns in her bag in the Sahara Desert. Bowles told me once that he travelled to India and South America in the old style, "with trunks, always with trunks". Bruce Chatwin, a self-described minimalist in travel, said that all he needed was his Mont Blanc fountain pen and his personal bag of muesli. But his biographer, Nicholas Shakespeare, claimed Chatwin always took much more. One of his friends, seeing Chatwin's typewriter and pyjamas and book bags on an Indian train, said, "It was like travelling with Garbo."

Edward Lear in Albania, 1848: "some rice, curry powder, and cayenne"

Previously to starting a certain supply of cooking utensils, tin plates, knives and forks, a basin etc., must absolutely be purchased, the stronger and plainer the better, for you go into lands where pots and pans are unknown, and all culinary processes are to be performed in strange localities, innocent of artificial means. A light mattress, some sheets and blankets, and a good supply of capotes and plaids should not be neglected; two or three books; some rice, curry powder, and cayenne; a world of drawing materials — if you be a hard sketcher; as little dress as possible, though you must have two sets of outer clothing — one for visiting consuls, pashas and dignitaries, the other for rough, everyday work; some quinine made into pills (rather leave all behind than this); a Boyourdi, or general order of introduction to governors or pashas; and your Teskere, or provincial passport for yourself and guide. All these are absolutely indispensable, and beyond these, the less you augment your impedimenta by luxuries the better.

— *Edward Lear in the Levant,* edited by Susan Hyman (1988)

Sir Richard Burton Heads for Mecca in Disguise: "certain necessaries for the way"

IN ADDITION TO his disguise as "Mirza Abdullah", he had "a Miswak, or tooth-stick" — a twig for cleaning his teeth; "a bit of soap and a comb, wooden, for bone and tortoiseshell are not, religiously speaking, correct". A change of clothing, a goat-skin water-bag, a "coarse Persian rug — which besides being couch, acted as chair, table and oratory", a pillow, a blanket, a large, bright yellow umbrella ("suggesting the idea of an overgrown marigold"), a "Housewife" (needles, thread, and buttons in a pouch), a dagger, a brass inkstand and penholder, "and a mighty rosary, which on occasion might have been converted into a weapon of defence". (*Personal Narrative of a Pilgrimage to Al-Madinah and Meccah*, 1855–56)

Paul Du Chaillu in Equatorial Africa: "white beads . . . small looking-glasses . . . and my guns"

I foresaw that, from the dread all the coast natives have of the cannibal tribes, I should have difficulty in carrying all my luggage. I therefore determined not to encumber myself with supplies of provisions or anything that could be spared. My outfit consisted only of the following articles: — A chest containing 100 fathoms of prints [cloth], 19 pounds of white beads, a quantity of small looking-glasses, fire-steels and flints, a quantity of leaf tobacco. In addition to which came my greatest dependence, viz, 80 pounds of shot and bullets, 20 pounds of powder, and my guns.

— *Explorations and Adventures in Equatorial Africa* (1861)

C. M. Doughty and Chaucer in Arabia Deserta

DOUGHTY CARRIED IN his camel's saddle bags a seventeenth-century edition of Chaucer's *Canterbury Tales*, and he wrote *Travels in Arabia Deserta* under the direct influence of Chaucer's style.

Henry Miller on Coast-to-Coast Travel: A Monkey Wrench

There's one thing I'd like to advise anyone thinking of making a transcontinental journey: see that you have a jack, a monkey wrench and a jimmy. You'll probably find that the wrench won't fit the nuts but that doesn't matter; while you're pretending to fiddle around with it someone will stop and lend you a helping hand.

— *The Air-Conditioned Nightmare* (1945)

Laurens van der Post: To Nyasaland with Sealing Wax

I have said nothing, though it is traditional on these occasions, about what I had packed in my suitcases . . . All I did was to add to my store of khaki clothing, to choose some books for the journey, because they can be difficult to find in Africa, and to lay in a small supply of sealing wax. I was doubtful whether I could get sealing wax at my destination, and I could not risk being without it as I needed it for making secure the samples I hoped to collect on my journey. But all in all I was taking so little that my friends, with their warm and affectionate concern for what is individual and eccentric, quickly created a legend among themselves. Would one believe it, they said, that I had gone off again to Central Africa with a stick of scarlet sealing wax in one hand and a copy of George Meredith's *Modern Love* in the other?

— *Venture to the Interior* (1951)

V. S. Naipaul Among the Believers: Smedley Roll-Neck, Exercise Pants

IN HIS BIOGRAPHY of Naipaul, *The World Is What It Is*, Patrick French writes, "Before leaving England for Indonesia, Vidia put together a 'travelling list'. In its care and restraint, in its honing, it reflected the man and the writer." And it was also a memo to his wife, Pat, to pack his bags so that he would be presentable when he met his mistress, Margaret, who was flying from Buenos Aires to Djakarta to meet him. A partial list: "*Suits & trousers and jackets:* Travel out in Simpson's grey; Pack — Simpson's beige lightweight; *Trousers:* M & S cotton, BHS cotton, Oscar Jacobson charcoal lightweight worsted; *Underclothes:* Pants 4 prs, *Socks* 4 prs, Pyjamas 1 pr, T-shirts, 2, Sleeveless vests 2. *Shirts:* 4 cotton (dress); M&S leisure 2, Smedley shirts 2, Smedley roll-neck 3. *Shorts:* Bathing trunks, Exercise pants, trainers 1 pr perhaps to be worn on journey . . ."

Freya Stark in Luristan: "a crumpled gown and a powder-puff"

My saddle-bags disclosed in their depths, a crumpled gown and a powder-puff, of which I made the best use I could, and finally emerged to meet my host more or less like a lady.

— *The Valleys of the Assassins* (1934)

Tapa Snim: A Buddhist Monk's Possessions

When I came back to the compartment, Tapa Snim was rummaging in his bag. I watched him take out an envelope, and then he began knotting the two strands that made this simple square of cotton cloth into a bag.

"Do you have another bag?" I asked, because the smallness of this one seemed an improbable size for a long-distance traveller.

"No. These are all my possessions."

Everything, not just for a year of travel, but everything he owned in the world, in a bag he easily slung under one arm. True, this was a warm climate, but the bag was smaller than a supermarket shopping bag.

"May I ask you what's inside?"

Tapa Snim, tugging the knot loose, gladly showed me the entire contents.

"My bowl, very important," he said, taking out the first item. It was a small black plastic soup bowl with a close-fitting lid. He used it for begging alms, but he also used it for rice.

In a small bag: a piece of soap in a container, sunglasses, a flashlight, a tube of mosquito repellent, a tin of aspirin.

In a small plastic box: a spool of grey thread, a pair of scissors, nail clippers, Q-tips, a thimble, needles, rubber bands, a two-inch mirror, a tube of cream to prevent foot fungus, ChapStick, nasal spray, and razor blades.

"Also very important," he said, showing me the razor blades. "I shave my head every fifteen days."

Neatly folded, one thin wool sweater, a shawl he called a *kasaya*, a change of clothes. In a document pouch, he had a notebook and some papers, a photograph showing him posed with a dozen other monks ("to introduce myself") and a large certificate in Chinese characters he called his *bikkhu* certificate, the official proof he was a monk, with signatures and seals and brushwork.

And a Sharp electronic dictionary that allowed him to translate from many languages, and a string of beads — 108 beads, the spiritual number.

As I was writing down the list, he said, "And this" — his straw hat — "and this" — his fan.

"Nothing else?"

"Nothing."

"What about money?"

"That's my secret."

And then carefully he placed it on the opened cloth and drew the cloth together into a sack, everything he owned on earth.

— GTES

Joe Polis, Thoreau's Abenaki Guide: "no change of clothing"

He wore a cotton shirt, originally white, a greenish flannel one over it, but no waistcoat, flannel drawers, a strong linen or duck pants, which had also been white, blue woollen stockings, cowhide boots, and a Kossuth hat. He carried no change of clothing, but putting on a stout thick jacket, which he laid aside in the canoe, and seizing a full-sized axe, his gun and ammunition, and a blanket, which would do for a sail or knapsack if wanted, and strapping on his belt, which contained a large sheath-knife, he walked off at once, ready to be gone all summer. — *The Maine Woods* (1864)

William Least Heat-Moon: Portable Toilet

FOR HIS 13,000-MILE *Blue Highways* road trip in his van called Ghost Dancing, Heat-Moon carried a sleeping bag and blanket, a Coleman cooker, a plastic basin and bucket, a portable toilet, a cookstove, utensils, a tool kit, writing materials, a camera, and a "U.S. Navy sea bag of clothes."

William Burroughs: Snakebite Serum and a Hammock

I took a few days to assemble my gear and dig the capital. For a jungle trip you need medicines: snake bite serum, penicillin, enterovioformo and aralen are essentials. A hammock, a blanket and a rubber bag known as a tula to carry your gear in.

— *The Yage Letters* (1963)

Pico Iyer: A Book

The most important thing always to have with me in my case is a book: no companion is likely to be richer, stranger, more alive and more eager to be intimate. Pens and notebooks, of course. Pieces of America to give away. A Lonely Planet guide to get angry with and bitterly repudiate. More novels and biographies for eight-hour waits.

I think I spend more time thinking about what I don't want to take with me: assumptions, iPods, cameras, plans, friends (in most cases), laptops, headphones, suntan lotion, résumés, expectations.

— in conversation with PT

❧ 8 ❧
Fears, Neuroses, and Other Conditions

"MEN WHO GO LOOKING FOR THE SOURCE of a river are merely looking for the source of something missing in themselves, and never finding it," Sir Richard Burton wrote, shrewdly summing up the mental state of the explorer. The great travellers are all sorts, of course. A large number have been depressives or bipolar types capable of serious gloom: Livingstone sulked in his tent for days, Vancouver locked himself in his cabin, Speke shot himself, Scott sometimes wept, Nansen was suicidal and so was Meriwether Lewis. Most suffered from gout. But at their best they are curious, contented, patient, courageous, and paragons of self-sufficiency. Their passion is visiting the unknown.

In the pathology of travel, many journeyers who seem in pursuit of a goal are driven by demons, attempting to flee, often unsuccessfully, some condition of the mind. Burton also said, "Travellers, like poets, are mostly an angry race."

Tobias Smollett is one of the more uproarious travellers, full of opinions and generalizations. I often think that the ill or afflicted traveller sometimes has an advantage, which is summed up by a character speaking in Smollett's comic novel *The Expedition of Humphry Clinker*: "People of experience and infirmity, my dear Letty, see with very different eyes from those that such as you and I make use of."

Tobias Smollett: Deep unhappiness, discontent, the epitome of the unhappy traveller. He travelled to the Continent not long after his young daughter died, and his grief shows in his rage. He also suffered from an intestinal disorder, which contributed to his death at the age of fifty.

> There is one in every boat train that leaves Victoria, in every liner that leaves New York, in every bar of every hotel all over the world: the unhappy traveller. He is travelling not for pleasure but for pain, not to broaden the mind but, if possible, to narrow it; to release the buried terrors and hatreds of a lifetime; or, if these have already had a good airing at home, to open up colonies of rage abroad. We listen to these martyrs, quarrelling with hotel keepers, insulting cooks, torturing waiters and porters, the scourges of the reserved seat and viragos of the sleeping car. And when they return from their mortifications it is to insult the people and the places they have visited, to fight the battle over the bill or the central heating, again and again, with the zest so sore that we conclude that travel for them is a continuation of domestic misery by other means . . .
>
> Of these Smollett is the only good example I can think of, and after 180 years, his rage still rings out.
>
> — V. S. Pritchett, *Complete Essays* (1991)

Lady Hester Stanhope: Merely restless, melancholic, and frustrated before she left England in 1810. But in the Middle East, where she spent the rest of her life, she became a megalomaniac — "I am the Queen of them all" — power hungry, imperious, and with a violent temper. Her boast was that no one could slap a servant's face harder than she.

Francis Parkman: Parkman was a physical wreck, from his earliest expedition, for *The Oregon Trail* (1849), and increasingly thereafter, in his travels and his writing, suffering nervous ailments, lameness, partial blindness, and severe headaches. This might have contributed to the detachment and pessimism in his historical works.

Richard Henry Dana: His eyesight was so poor that he was unable to attend Harvard and instead went on the voyage that resulted in *Two Years Before the Mast* (1840).

David Livingstone: A manic depressive obsessed with his bowels. He believed that constipation was the cause of most maladies in tropical Africa — headaches, muscular weakness, distraction, and much else. His advice to a prospective traveller in Africa: "With the change of climate there is often a peculiar condition of the bowels which makes the individual imagine all manner of things in others. Now I earnestly and most respectfully recommend you to try a little aperient medicine occasionally" (quoted in Timothy Holmes, *Journey to Livingstone,* 1993).

Sir Richard Burton: His explosive temper and pugnacity earned him the nicknames "Ruffian Dick" and "Dirty Dick". He had a morbid aversion to darkness, so his wife, Isabel, said: "He hated darkness so much that he would never have the blind down lest he might lose a glimpse of light from twilight to dawn."

Burton was also seriously lacking in social skills. "The fact was that though undeniably brilliant," his biographer Mary S. Lovell wrote in *A Rage to Live,* "Richard Burton had a blind spot in his social skills . . . He either lacked the patience, or he could not be bothered to pretend to like, or work with, people he did not like or respect, no matter what their station or influence. And to these individuals he gave deep offence without hesitation, frequently intentionally."

Captain George Vancouver: Fits of temper and depression, which may have been caused by tuberculosis or a thyroid condition. Prone to a paranoid melancholy, he was ashamed of his humble origins and had to suffer the contempt of snobbish senior officers. In *Driving Home*, Jonathan Raban convincingly argues that Vancouver "wrote his changing moods into the permanent nomenclature" of the Pacific Northwest coast. After a cheerful period in which he named Discovery Bay and Protection Island, Vancouver fell into "what now appears to have been clinical depression" in the spring of 1792, and saw the landscape as "dreary" and "dismal", and he applied names that reflected his low spirits — for example, the anchorage he named Desolation Sound.

Captain Robert Falcon Scott: Depressive, hypersensitive, lachrymose. Apsley Cherry-Garrard, on the Antarctic expedition, writes in *The Worst Journey in the World*: "[Scott] was sensitive, femininely sensitive, to a degree which might be considered a fault, and it will be clear that leadership to such a man may be almost a martyrdom . . . Temperamentally he was a weak man, and might easily have been an irritable autocrat. As it was he had moods and depressions which might last for weeks . . . He cried more easily than any man I have known."

Fridtjof Nansen: A great skier, Arctic explorer (he made the first crossing of Greenland, led the *Fram* expedition to the Arctic), oceanographer, zoologist (neuron theory), and diplomat, Nansen was a relentless womanizer and suffered from suicidal melancholia.

Jack London: Alcoholism from an early age (described in his "alcoholic memoir", *John Barleycorn*), as well as serious physical ailments, kidney disease, gastrointestinal problems, double fistula surgery. London was in pain during much of his travels for *Cruise of the Snark* and *The People of the Abyss*, and had frostbite while reporting the Russo-Japanese War. He took morphine and died from a morphine overdose at the age of forty.

William Burroughs: Drug addiction for the whole of his adult life did not stop him from travelling throughout the United States and Mexico, to Europe, Morocco, and elsewhere, including Colombia, Ecuador, and Peru, where he searched for the ultimate hallucinogen, ayahuasca, a trip recounted in *The Yage Letters*.

Graham Greene: Manic depression, a horror of spiders, and an irrational fear of birds.

Dr. Samuel Johnson: Tourette's-like disease, depression, sloth. In *Journal of a Tour to the Hebrides*, the account of a trip on which James Boswell spent three uninterrupted months travelling with Johnson, Boswell wrote, "He had a constitutional melancholy, the clouds of which darkened the brightness of his fancy, and gave a gloomy cast to his whole course of thinking." As for his physical ailments, "His head, and sometimes also his body, shook with a kind of motion like the effect of a palsy: he appeared to be frequently disturbed by cramps, or convulsive contractions, of the nature of that distemper called St. Vitus's dance." Johnson blamed his parents, telling Boswell that "we inherit dispositions from our parents. I inherited (said he) a vile melancholy from my father, which has made me mad all my life, at least not sober."

Henry Morton Stanley: "I was not sent into the world to be happy," Stanley wrote, "I was sent for special work." He succeeded in his exploration, fuelled by his inferiority complex, his deep feelings of rejection, his illegitimacy, his masochism and manic attacks. He was tormented by identity confusion, pretending to be American, the son of a wealthy man named Stanley from New Orleans, but in fact he was Welsh, named John Rowlands, a pauper raised in a workhouse in Denbigh. He denied this his whole life, leading him to abandon writing his autobiography.

Apsley Cherry-Garrard: Extreme myopia, clinical depression. Nevertheless, he endured the rigors of the Antarctic for two years, and after serving in battle in World War I wrote his masterpiece, *The Worst Journey in the World* (1922). Later, he was nagged by the thought that he might have saved the life of Captain Scott, and suffered self-reproach. "It was not till long afterwards that the thought of what he might have done — and the fantasy of what others were thinking and saying about him — became a little cloud on the margin of his mind that grew till it covered his whole sky" (George Seaver, Foreword, *Worst Journey*, 1965).

William Somerset Maugham: "Maugham was an unhappy child who evolved into a deeply melancholic man, 'violently pessimistic', as he characterized himself and . . . in later life suffered frequently from nightmares" (Selina Hastings, *The Secret Lives of Somerset Maugham*, 2009).

Gertrude Bell: Depression, despair over her long epistolary dalliance with a married man, a soldier who remained with his wife and died heroically at Gallipoli in 1915. Bell, who had threatened suicide in letters to the soldier, died of an overdose of barbiturates, an apparent suicide, after a series of family tragedies. She was fifty-eight.

Henry James: An almost permanent state of constipation, which drove him from spa to spa in Europe in search of relief throughout his adult life.

Geoffrey Moorhouse: Fear of solitude, empty spaces, and the unknown. He also had agoraphobia, which he sought to conquer in a crossing of the Sahara from west to east, an ordeal he recounted in his book *The Fearful Void* (see Chapter 10, "Travel as an Ordeal").

Evelyn Waugh: Paranoia and persecution mania on a voyage to Ceylon, which resulted in his novel *The Ordeal of Gilbert Pinfold*, an account of a man's paranoia and persecution mania.

Joshua Slocum: Subject to what he himself described as "mental lapses", one of which, when he was sixty-two, was the sexual assault of a twelve-year-old girl in New Jersey in 1906, for which he was arrested. He pleaded "no contest". Rape was not proven; it was assumed he exposed himself to her. After forty-two days in jail, he was released (see Chapter 14, "Travel Feats").

Freya Stark: At the age of thirteen, in a small town in Italy, where she was living with her single mother, her hair was caught in the flywheel of a weaving machine and she was seriously injured — a torn scalp, part of an ear ripped off. "A trauma of this order, both invasive and disfiguring, at an exquisitely vulnerable moment of adolescence, forever shaped her perception of herself. She was never able to overcome a dread that she might not be attractive to the opposite sex," one of her biographers, Jane Fletcher Geniesse, wrote (*Passionate Nomad: The Life of Freya Stark*). "Her parents' estrangement, her insecure childhood, and the injury that nearly killed her left Freya with a passion to conquer the fears and anxieties that plagued her and drove her to find personal validation through notable achievement." But Jonathan Raban, who travelled with her to the Euphrates in the 1970s, told me, "She had the kind of facial ugliness that eventually ages into monumental grandeur. Her intense egotism was a wonder to behold."

Bronislaw Malinowski: The great pioneering anthropologist in the Trobriand Islands suffered from depression, anxiety, rage, and feelings of rejection. He was seen in his work as objective and wholly focused, and for him the Trobrianders were (as his title depicted them) *Argonauts of the Western Pacific* (1922). But in his intimate *Diary in the Strict Sense of the Word*, published more than forty years later, another Malinowski was revealed. "The natives still irritate me, particularly Ginger, whom I would willingly beat to death," he wrote. "I understand all the German and Belgian atrocities." Or: "Unpleasant clash with Ginger . . . I was enraged and punched him in the jaw once or twice." Or: "I am in a world of lies here." In his scholarly work he wrote about Trobrianders as great navigators, canoe builders, and gardeners. But he confided in the diary "my dislike of them, my longing for civilization," and "the niggers were noisy . . . general aversion to niggers."

Edward Lear: As the last of twenty-one children, and raised by his much older sister Ann, Lear hardly knew his parents. He suffered frequent grand mal epileptic seizures from early in his life, frequent melancholia, and a depression he called "the morbids".

Jan Morris: Not a mental condition but a sex change, recounted in *Conundrum* (1974). James Morris climbed Everest and travelled and wrote about the United States, Oman, South Africa, Venice, Spain, and England. Then, after gender reassignment and surgery in 1972, the newly emergent Jan Morris continued to travel and write, about Wales, Hong Kong, Australia, and the great cities of the world. Rare among travellers, indeed among writers generally, for someone to write and travel as a man and then as a woman. After the operation, I believe her prose style became more breathless and bejewelled.

❧ 9 ❧

Travellers Who Never Went Alone

I HAVE ALWAYS TRAVELLED ALONE. WITH THE EX-
ception of large-scale expeditions involving a crew or
a team, every other kind of travel is diminished by the
presence of others. The experience is shared — someone
to help, buy tickets, make love to, pour out your heart to,
help set up the tent, do the driving, whatever. Although
they do not usually say so, many travellers have a companion. Such a person is a consolation, and inevitably a
distraction. "Look at that camel in front of the Lexus,
honey — hey, it's the old and the new!" ¶ A man who always travels alone, Jonathan Raban, has this to say on
the subject: "Travelling with a companion, with a wife,

with a girlfriend, always seems to me like birds in a glass dome, those Victorian glass things with stuffed birds inside. You are too much of a self-contained world for the rest of the world to be able to penetrate. You've got to go kind of naked into the world and make yourself vulnerable to it, in a way that you're never going to be sufficiently vulnerable if you're travelling with your nearest and dearest on your arm. You're never going to see anything; you're never going to meet anybody; you're never going to hear anything. Nothing is going to happen to you." (quoted in *A Sense of Place*, edited by Michael Shapiro, 2004). Raban has enlarged on this in his essay "Why Travel?" in his collection *Driving Home* (2010): "You are simply not lonely enough when you travel with companions . . . Spells of acute loneliness are an essential part of travel. Loneliness makes things happen."

Underlining this, Kipling wrote in "The Winners," a poem that serves as an epigraph to "The Story of the Gadsby" (1889):

> What the moral? Who rides may read.
> When the night is thick and the tracks are blind
> A friend at a pinch is a friend, indeed,
> But a fool to wait for the laggard behind.
> Down to Gehenna or up to the Throne,
> He travels the fastest who travels alone.

In an earlier echo of this, Thoreau was succinct on the subject in *Walden*: "The man who goes alone can start today; but he who travels with another must wait till that other is ready."

None of the following people agreed with this, and even Thoreau, who never travelled alone, did not follow his own advice.

Samuel Johnson and James Boswell

BOSWELL, WHOSE NAME is a byword for an amanuensis, travelled with Dr. Johnson to the Western Isles in the fall of 1775, and both men wrote books about the trip: Johnson's thoughtful *Journey to the Western Islands of Scotland* appeared in 1775, and Boswell's gossipy *Journal of a Tour to the Hebrides* in 1785, which, taken together, comprise a lively dialogue between two travellers, an inner and an outer journey. So toward the end of the trip, when his patience is wearing thin, Johnson remarks in his book, "The conversation of the Scots grows every day less unpleasing to the English; their peculiarities wear fast away." Around the same time, Boswell reports in his *Journal* how, after listening to a Scotsman talk ignorantly about the Church of England, Johnson says, "Sir, you know no more of our church than a Hottentot."

Henry David Thoreau and Friends

HE WALKED ACROSS Cape Cod with William Ellery Channing, who also boated with him down the Concord and Merrimack rivers; he traipsed and paddled through the Maine woods with his cousin George Thatcher and two Indian guides. He went from Concord, Massachusetts, to Staten Island, New York, alone, but then lived with a family there for two months, before becoming homesick and returning to Concord. He spent a week in Canada on a sort of package tour, on a train full of tourists going from Boston to Montreal (recounted in *A Yankee in Canada*).

And then there is *Walden*, the last word in solitude. Or is it all theoretical? Thoreau's cabin was only a mile and a half from his house in Concord, where his adoring mother waited, baking pies for him and doing his laundry; and throughout the Walden experience he went home most days. He had two chairs in the cabin, and as he says, he often went with a group of friends to pick huckleberries.

Sir Richard Burton, to Mecca with Mohammed

PART OF BURTON'S disguise to enter Mecca as the robed and bearded Afghan dervish "Mirza Abdullah" was to have an Arab servant and guide. This was the eighteen-year-old Mohammed El-Basyuni, who was headed to Mecca to see his mother. Burton liked his self-confidence, but the young man was watchful too. At the end of the trip Burton recounts that Mohammed suspected Burton might be an unbeliever. "'Now, I understand,' said the boy Mohammed to his fellow-servant, 'your master is a Sahib from India; he hath laughed at our beards.'"

But there might have been another cause for suspicion (so the Burton biographer Mary S. Lovell writes). It was rumoured that Burton, instead of squatting, had stood up to pee, something a good Muslim would never do. And it was also rumoured, because the argumentative Burton had many enemies, that he had killed Mohammed for knowing his secret.

Though it had not happened, Burton so enjoyed his image as a hell-raiser that he said he had indeed killed his travelling companion. "Oh, yes," he would say. "Why not? Do you suppose one can live in these countries as one lives in Pall Mall and Piccadilly?"

André Gide and His Lover

FOR HIS TEN-MONTH trip through the Congo and Chad in 1925–26, the fifty-six-year-old Gide brought along his twenty-six-year-old lover, Marc Allegret, who had done most of the preparation for the journey. Though they had been lovers for almost ten years, they were anything but monogamous. "Throughout the trip," writes Gide's biographer Alan Sheridan (*André Gide*, 1998), "sexual companions of both sexes were freely, abundantly available and Marc discovered his *penchant* for adolescent girls."

Redmond O'Hanlon and His "Small Column"

ONE OF THE greatest talkers, one of the most likeable of men, with a stomach for hard travel and a wonderful ear for dialogue (he is also an alert listener), O'Hanlon is anything but a loner. "Muko, at the head of our small column," he writes of one of the marches described in *Congo Journey* (1996). "Small column" just about sums up the O'Hanlon manner of travel. He is never alone. His is not conventional travel, and hardly solitary, but more in the nature of an expedition, the misery shared by many disillusioned friends, martyrs to companionship.

For the trip recounted in *Into the Heart of Borneo* (1983) he travelled with the poet James Fenton (the trip was Fenton's idea), and the book profits greatly from Fenton's wit. For his South American trip O'Hanlon asked Fenton whether he wished to go to the Amazon and visit the fierce

Yanomami people. In the book itself, *In Trouble Again* (1988), Fenton is quoted as saying, "I would not come with you to High Wycombe." And so O'Hanlon persuades Simon Stockton, a worldly-wise-guy Englishman who, halfway through the trip, maddened by the heat, the insects, the mud, and the hideous food, throws a wobbly and goes home.

On the *Congo Journey* quest to find a monstrous creature, perhaps a living dinosaur, Mokélé-mbembé, said to haunt a lake in a remote part of the Congolese jungle, O'Hanlon takes an American, Lary Shaffer, who sticks it out for most of the way but finally succumbs and heads home. These departures leave O'Hanlon with the guides and the bearers.

He thrives on conflict, adversity—much of the adversity in the form of insects. He suffers bad bouts of malaria and even a sort of dementia in places, and never fails to anatomize his ailments: "My penis had turned green. To the touch it felt like a hanging cluster of grapes. Swollen tapir ticks as big as the top of a thumb were feeding all down its stem. 'Keep calm,' I repeated out loud, and then I scrabbled at them" (*In Trouble Again*). And: "Ants, red-brown ants, about a quarter of an inch long, were running in manic bursts down my shirt-front, swinging left and right, conferring with their fellows, climbing over the hairs on my arms . . . a bagful of ants fastened on my genitals" (*Congo Journey*).

Gusto is O'Hanlon's watchword, though his hearty tone masks a scientific mind, a deep seriousness, and (so he says) a depressive spirit. Perhaps his fear of gloom is another reason why he travels with others. His books are often compared with those of Victorian adventurers, but in fact they are distinctly modern, sometimes hallucinatory, and depending almost entirely for their effect on dialogue. O'Hanlon uses his travelling companions and local guides as foils, for humour, and to extend the narrative.

V. S. Naipaul and His Women

IN THE PROLOGUE to *An Area of Darkness*, Naipaul mentions difficulties on his arrival in India—paperwork, red tape, and heat—and then says, "My companion fainted." In the U.S. edition of the book, this was changed to "My wife fainted." Patricia Naipaul accompanied him throughout his

THE TAO OF TRAVEL

travels in India, as well as for the three months he was resident in Kashmir, but she is mentioned only that one time. In *A Turn in the South*, Naipaul's mistress went with him and did all the driving and most of the arranging of hotels, as his biographer reported. This mistress also went with Naipaul on his *Among the Believers* tour through the Muslim world, though halfway through the *Beyond Belief* sequel she was replaced by Nadira Khannum Alvi, who later became his wife and uncredited travelling companion.

John McPhee, His Fellow Paddlers, and His Wife

IN SOME OF his travels, McPhee seems to be on his own — in *Looking for a Ship* (1990) he is the only landlubber on board. But halfway through *Coming into the Country*, about his travels throughout Alaska, he mentions his "increasing sense of entrapment", and then parenthetically, "(my wife was with me)". The earlier part of the book is full of his travelling companions, four or five of them.

Bruce Chatwin and Friends

CHATWIN, AS HIS letters show, was compulsively gregarious. His apparently solitary travels, for *In Patagonia* and *The Songlines*, were often made with a friend or a guide; other trips were made with a male lover or with his wife, Elizabeth. I once mentioned to him that in recounting travel experiences one had to come clean. Chatwin replied with a shrieking laugh, "I don't believe in coming clean!"

Colin McPhee and Jane

IN *A House in Bali* (1947), his enthusiastic account of living on that island, McPhee is a musicologist bewitched by Balinese music. He builds a house, makes friends, and studies the music. Many of his friends seem to be Balinese boys. In one passage, McPhee is swept into a turbulent stream. He is spotted by some boys onshore:

It was then that I noticed that one of the more boisterous [boys] threw himself into the water, swam to a boulder and jumped over to where I was struggling. He knew by heart every shallow and hollow in the river bed, for he quickly led me ashore . . . When we reached land, this naked dripping youngster and I stood facing one another. He was perhaps eight, unfed and skimpy, with eyes too large for his face . . . I offered him a cigarette, but he suddenly took fright and was off into the water before I could say a word.

The boy's name is Sampih. He becomes important to the narrative and to McPhee's life in Bali. McPhee adopts him and mentors him, though he does not mention that the whole time he spent there he was with his wife, Jane Belo, a lesbian, and an anthropologist, the author of a definitive study of hypnotic states in Bali (*Trance in Bali*), and that it was she who funded his trip.

Eric Newby and Wanda

IN *A Short Walk in the Hindu Kush*, Newby travelled with Hugh Carless. In *Slowly Down the Ganges*, *The Big Red Train Ride*, and *Through Ireland in Low Gear*, he took his wife, Wanda, and in these three books he continually describes her expostulating in her Slovenian accent, "Horrick, vye you are saying zat to me?" But he is often funny and has a sharp eye for detail.

Rudyard Kipling and Carrie

WIDELY TRAVELLED, NEVER alone. Known for his jingoism and his bombast, Kipling was, in fact, an enigmatic and melancholy figure. He was marked by his lonely childhood, spent in a cruel household ("the House of Desolation", he called it) in England, away from his parents in India (from the ages of five to eleven; see his story "Baa, Baa, Black Sheep"). He never mentions his wife, Carrie, who was American, a Vermonter, but she was always at his side. Much of his work is based on travel, especially in India, South Africa, and the United States, and his book of travel pieces, *From Sea to Sea* (1899), is superb.

Graham Greene and Companions

BEGINNING WITH HIS first travel book, *Journey Without Maps*, his long walk through the hinterland of Liberia, which he took (leaving his wife and children at home) with his cousin Barbara, Greene always had a travelling companion or a driver or a lover on board. He could not cook, drive a car, or use a typewriter, so he was helpless alone. Greene seemed to require the mateyness of another person — his friend Michael Meyer, who travelled with him through the Pacific, or later in his life the priest Father Duran, who appears in *Monsignor Quixote*. Greene claimed to be manic depressive, sometimes suicidal, and lonely. He had numerous love affairs, many of them passionate. He remained married to the same woman, Vivien Greene, the whole of his life, but never went anywhere with her.

D. H. Lawrence and Frieda

LAWRENCE ALWAYS TRAVELLED with his wife, Frieda von Richthofen (her cousin was the Red Baron), beginning with their elopement in 1912, two months after they met (she was then married to Ernest Weekly, a French professor). Although they quarrelled constantly, they lived in and travelled through Italy, the United States, Mexico, and Australia — and he wrote books based on his travels in all these places, notably *Mornings in Mexico* and *Sea and Sardinia*, sometimes mentioning Frieda, usually not.

Somerset Maugham and Lover

ON HIS LONGEST trips — to China, which yielded *On a Chinese Screen*, and to South-East Asia, which resulted in *The Gentleman in the Parlour* — Maugham travelled with his lover, Gerald Haxton, though he does not disclose the fact, largely because he was married to Syrie, who resented his two-timing her with this young American drunkard, and because at the time he was travelling, the 1920s and 1930s, homosexuality was a crime in Britain. But Maugham had a terrible stammer, and he needed someone to converse with locals and bring back colourful stories and dialogue for his books. "Master Hacky" was just the man to help. Also Maugham loved him deeply. After Haxton died, Maugham travelled with Alan Searle, a greedy young Londoner who had sent him fan letters and became his lover and literary executor.

Rebecca West and Henry

PROBABLY NO TRAVEL book is fuller of the expressions "My husband said . . ." or "My husband told me . . ." than *Black Lamb and Grey Falcon* (1941), Rebecca West's account of her various trips through Yugoslavia, and since it is a book of some 1,200 pages, the words "my husband" appear numerous times. He was a banker, named Henry Andrews, and full of theories and explanations, which she approvingly recounts in the book.

John Steinbeck and Elaine

STEINBECK TRAVELLED WITH his dog in *Travels with Charley*, as he said, but (though he never mentioned them) he had many conjugal visits en route: his wife, Elaine, met him every few weeks on the road to cheer him up. We know this from the letters that were published after his death; for example, on October 10, 1960: "I'm glad you came out and it was a good time, wasn't it? It took the blankness off a lot" (*Life in Letters*). This "blankness" he speaks of is never disclosed in the jolly book.

Patrick Leigh Fermor and Friends

AS A YOUNG man he travelled alone, walking across Europe from Holland to Turkey in 1933, a trip he described many years later in two books, *A Time of Gifts* (1977) and *Between the Woods and the Water* (1986). He is justly famous for having written one of the most evocative books about the Caribbean, *The Traveller's Tree* (1950) (see Chapter 23, "Classics of a Sense of Place"). He makes no bones about travelling in a group, and in fact has a felicitous way of describing this: "My companions, from beginning to end, were two friends: Joan, who's English, and Costa, who is Greek. Both of them, whittled now to shadows, are constantly present in the following pages."

Edward Abbey and Family

A GREAT HERO of loners and wanderers, high-plains drifters and monkey-wrenchers (eco-saboteurs), Abbey, a contradictory soul, craved the company of others, usually fellow boozers. But he had a way of pretending to have been solitary, being selective in the retelling of his experiences. In *Desert Solitaire,* where he celebrates solitude and his lonely communing with nature in southern Utah, he does not mention that for one five-month period he was living in a trailer with his third wife, Rita, and young son. Whole chapters of the book, such as "The Moon-Eyed Horse", "very likely never happened at all", his biographer, James Cahalan, wrote.

Wilfred Thesiger and Friends

OFTEN THOUGHT OF as the solitary nomad of the Empty Quarter, Thesiger could not bear to be alone. In his *Wilfred Thesiger: The Life of the Great Explorer,* Alexander Maitland writes, "As for Thesiger's pursuit of 'the peace that comes with solitude', by his own admission he found solitude unbearable. His friend John Verney [a painter] described him as someone who 'hates being left alone for more than a minute. He may travel in remote parts of the world, but always accompanied by a crowd of tribesmen, porters or whatever and has probably spent fewer hours in total solitude than, like most painters, I'm accustomed to spend in a week. By solitude, Thesiger appears to have meant something like the 'clean' space of desert undefiled by modern communications or modern transport, and the harmonious traditional life he found among the tribes who lived there." In later life Thesiger lived with an African family in northern Kenya. They demanded money, cars, and radios, and he paid up, not minding that he was being fleeced as long as they kept him company.

Jean Cocteau, Passepartout, and Charlie Chaplin

PART STUNT, PART challenge by *Paris-Soir*, but primarily a literary opportunity, Cocteau (1889–1963) claimed that he could travel at least as well as Phileas Fogg and make it around the world in eighty days. He set off in March 1946, accompanied by his lover and part-time secretary Marcel Khill, whom he called Passepartout in the book *Mon Premier Voyage* (1937). He had met Khill in 1932, when Cocteau was forty-three and Khill twenty (though he looked fifteen, Cocteau said). The book was translated as *My Journey Round the World*. In an introduction to a new edition, the actor and writer Simon Callow wrote: "[Khill] and Cocteau met at the house of a Toulon naval officer . . . who had 'discovered' him working on a chain gang; he was dispensing opium, thus uniting in his person two of Cocteau's keenest appetites."

The book, a breathless diary, was dedicated to André Gide. In the course of travelling through Malaya, Cocteau puns in French on the name Kuala Lumpur, calling it "Kuala l'impure", but it is clear that he is too bored, fatigued, and preoccupied to care much about the places he is breezing through, mere glimpses of Egypt, India, Burma, Malaya, and Singapore, with slapdash diary entries.

And then, on a ship from Hong Kong, the tone of the book rises to a new register: "Charlie Chaplin is on board. It is a staggering piece of news. Later on, Chaplin was to say, 'The real function of a person's work is to make it possible for friends like ourselves to cut out preliminaries. We have always known each other.'" Cocteau had never met Chaplin before, but he is dazzled, and after this encounter the book catches fire — not as a travel book but as the account of a new friendship between two stage-struck and bedazzled celebrities, both highly creative and eccentric — and libidinous (Chaplin was travelling with Paulette Goddard). It so happened that Chaplin and Cocteau were exactly the same age, born in 1889 and forty-seven at that point. Chaplin had just made *Modern Times*, and as a composer (he wrote the song "Smile," for example) he was just as versatile as Cocteau.

They meet often on the ship, drink together, talk often (with Khill translating for Cocteau), appraise Honolulu and San Francisco together, and when Cocteau arrives in Los Angeles, Chaplin puts him in touch with the film world's luminaries, and Cocteau is soon dropping the names King Vidor, Marlene Dietrich, and Gary Cooper. Cocteau won the bet, arriving back in Paris in eighty days. *My Journey* is a patchy and unsatisfying book, but a glimpse into the hectic life of this ball of fire.

Claude Lévi-Strauss and Wife

AUTHOR OF *Tristes Tropiques*, one of the great books of travel in the (at the time) hardly known parts of Brazil in the 1930s, Lévi-Strauss studied remote and isolated people. And for 362 pages of this book, one is astonished by his serenity, his resourcefulness, and his capacity to deal with the rigours of jungle travel. And then, on page 363, discussing an infectious eye disease, which caused temporary blindness among the Nambikwara people, he writes, "The disease spread to our group; the first person to catch it was my wife who had taken part in all my expeditions so far." Dina Dreyfus Lévi-Strauss had been with him every step of the way.

❧ Travel Wisdom of ❧
SIR FRANCIS GALTON

The eminent Victorian Galton (1822–1911) had a consuming interest in everything on earth. His bestseller *The Art of Travel*
(1855) was just one of his many books. A noted scientist ("polymath"
is usually attached to his name), he was an inventor, a meteorologist,
and an early student of anthropology, psychology, fingerprinting, and
human intelligence. His wrote extensively on the subject of heredity,
and it is probably his association with the pseudoscience of eugenics
(he coined the word) that dimmed his reputation and made him seem
a dangerous crank. ¶ As his book shows, Galton was widely read in the
travel literature of his time, citing Mungo Park, Livingstone, Burton,
Speke, and Samuel Baker on African exploration; Elisha Kane on the
Arctic; Leichhardt on Australia; and Dana's *Two Years Before the Mast*.
He mentions his cousin Charles Darwin when discussing the use of
animal bones as fuel when firewood is scarce. Along with this exten-

sive reading, in his twenties and early thirties he travelled all over — to Egypt, Turkey, down the Nile, through the Middle East, and just before writing this book, he ranged over what is now Namibia, making maps of the interior. ¶ *The Art of Travel* is exhaustive on the subject of old-fashioned exploration, and full of tips, such as this: "It is a great mistake to suppose that savages will give their labour or cattle in return for anything that is bright or new: they have their real wants and their fashions as much as we have." The book is also useful as a reference and collection of curiosa, such as how to bivouac on snow and how to patch a water bag. Always scrupulous with details, Galton advises on the best way to roll up shirtsleeves so they won't fall down: "the sleeves must be rolled up inwards, towards the arm, and not the reverse way."

———————•———————

Qualifications for a Traveller. — If you have health, a great craving for adventure, at least a moderate fortune, and can set your heart on a definite object, which old travellers do not think impracticable, then — travel by all means. If, in addition to these qualifications, you have scientific taste and knowledge, I believe that no career, in time of peace, can offer to you more advantages than that of a traveller. If you have not independent means, you may still turn travelling to excellent account; for experience shows it often leads to promotion, nay, some men support themselves by travel. They explore pasture land in Australia, they hunt for ivory in Africa, they collect specimens of natural history for sale, or they wander as artists.

———————•———————

Powerful men do not necessarily make the most eminent travellers; it is rather those who take the most interest in their work that succeed the best; as a huntsman says, "it is the nose that gives speed to the hound."

———————•———————

TRAVEL WISDOM OF SIR FRANCIS GALTON

Tedious journeys are apt to make companions irritable one to another; but under hard circumstances, a traveller does his duty best who doubles his kindliness of manner to those about him, and takes harsh words gently, and without retort. He should make it a point of duty to do so. It is at those times very superfluous to show too much punctiliousness about keeping up one's dignity, and so forth; since the difficulty lies not in taking up quarrels, but in avoiding them.

———•———

Advantages of Travel. — It is no slight advantage to a young man, to have the opportunity for distinction which travel affords. If he plans his journey among scenes and places likely to interest the stay-at-home public, he will probably achieve a reputation that might well be envied by wiser men who have not had his opportunities.

⋘ 10 ⋙

Travel as an Ordeal

I F A VACATION REPRESENTS A TRAVELLER'S DREAM, the ordeal is the traveller's nightmare. Yet the travel book that recounts an ordeal is the sort that interests me most, because it tests the elemental human qualities needed for survival: determination, calmness, rationality, physical and mental strength. Such books, with their torments, are also more fun: they were among the first travel books I read as a child. No ordeal book is without instances of near madness, hallucinatory episodes, weird fugues, and near-death experiences. ¶ When I was a boy, Donn Fendler was my role model. Later I was enthralled by the accounts of Moorhouse in the Sahara and Thesiger in Arabia, and I had a whole shelf of books about boat sinkings in the Pacific, disasters that ended in many days spent in a rubber dinghy. Dougal Robertson's is the best such account.

Some ordeals bring out the wit in a traveller. The last person you'd expect to find travelling on his own in the Colombian jungle is the needy, addicted, and urbane William Burroughs. But Burroughs was determined to go through hell to find the rare Amazonian drug ayahuasca (or yage), purported to be the ultimate high. He succeeded, as he recounted in *The Yage Letters*.

An instance or two of ordeal is an element in most great travel books. That is, having a bad time sets such a book apart from the jolly travel romp, giving it a seriousness and depth; as a consequence we begin to understand the person travelling, the real nature of the writer of the book, tested to his or her limit.

Geoffrey Moorhouse: The Fearful Void *(1974)*

NO ONE HAD ever crossed (or at least written about crossing) the Sahara from west to east, an almost four-thousand-mile journey from the Atlantic to the Nile. Moorhouse decided to do it, less to be the first person to achieve it than to examine "the bases of fear, to explore the extremity of human experience".

"I was a man who had lived with fear for nearly forty years," he writes. Fear of the unknown, of emptiness, of death. And he wants to find a way — a journey — to conquer it. "The Sahara fulfilled the required conditions perfectly. Not only did the hazards of the desert represent ultimate forms of my fears, but I was almost a stranger to it."

Setting off in October 1972, Moorhouse travelled with various nomad guides, but most dropped away or were exposed as rogues. His sextant broke, he became seriously ill, and death by thirst threatened when he missed an oasis in a sandstorm. With the help of his guide Sid'Ahmed, Moorhouse reached Tamanrasset, in Algeria, in March 1973, where, exhausted and sick, he abandoned the trip. He had travelled two thousand miles, most of it on foot, through sand and gravel and howling wind.

In the empty eastern desert in Mali he runs out of water. He recalls that twenty-four hours without water in severe temperatures is the limit of human endurance. Half a day passes — no water. Night falls — and twelve hours pass — no water. They set off at six A.M. and walk and ride most of the morning. Following some camel tracks, they come upon a group of nomads. Fainting with thirst and weakness, Moorhouse is offered a cooking pot.

"There was all manner of filth floating on top of that water; morsels of rice from the dirty pot, strands of hair from the guerba [waterbag], fragments of dung from the bottom of some well. But the water itself was clear, and I could sense the coolness of it even as its level tipped in the cooking pot before touching my lips. It was the most wonderful thing that had happened to me in my life."

After he wrote *The Fearful Void*, he told an English interviewer for the *Guardian*, "Doing this journey was a piece of propaganda in a way. It seems to me that every writer's a propagandist, in that he's trying to advance a point of view he believes; and my own point of view is that we're all essentially like each other. We all suffer the same things, we all laugh at the same things, and we all have to recognize this interdependence."

Valerian Albanov: In the Land of White Death *(1917)*

THE BOOK TELLS of the three-month ordeal in 1914 of Albanov and thirteen crewmen, who left the ice-bound ship *Saint Anna* in Franz Josef Land in the Arctic and travelled 235 miles, sledging across snow and ice and open water (in homemade kayaks). This is essentially Albanov's diary of the terrible journey. Frostbite, desertion, sudden death, attacks by walruses and polar bears (they shot forty-seven bears), near drownings, and hallucinations: "Aromas of tropical fruit fill the air with their fragrance. Peaches, oranges, apricots, raisins, cloves, and pepper all give off their wonderful scents."

Later: "We have not washed now for two months. Catching a chance glimpse of my face in the sextant's mirror the other day gave me a terrible fright. I am so disfigured that I am unrecognizable, covered as I am with a thick layer of filth. And we all look like this. We have tried to rub off some of this dirt, but without much success. As a result we look even more frightening, almost as if we were tattooed! Our underclothes and outer garments are unspeakable. And since these underclothes are swarming with 'game' [lice], I am sure that if we put one of our infested jerseys on the ground, it would crawl away all by itself!"

Dougal Robertson: Survive the Savage Sea *(1973)*

OF THE MANY accounts of sudden sinkings, and survival at sea in a raft, this book stands out as coolly observed, detailed, and eloquent in its stoicism. After a year of sailing, the *Lucette*, a well-made but fifty-year-old yacht, is rammed by a pod of killer whales just west of the Galápagos Islands. It sinks in a minute, and Captain Robertson has only enough time to launch a dinghy and an inflatable to save himself, his wife, their twin sons, their daughter, and a teenage friend.

This is the beginning of a 37-day, 750-mile voyage, and after the dinghy sinks, they are crammed into the leaky inflatable, living on rations for a short time and then on fish that they catch and the occasional turtle, battling storms and twenty-foot waves and huge ocean swells. The group also endures bickering between husband and wife, the fear and weakness of the children, sharks, sores, boils, heavy rain, and near capsizes. Robertson, who had been a farmer in rural England, is resourceful in fashioning tools and catching fish and turtles. Many pages describe the catching and butchering of turtles on the tiny raft; the drying and preparation of meat; the manner by which rainwater is trapped and kept.

One is convinced, before the book ends, that the Robertsons could have made it to land on their own — they were spotted by a Japanese fishing boat 290 miles off the coast of Costa Rica.

"'Our ordeal is over,' I said quietly. Lyn and the twins were crying with happiness . . . I put my arms about Lyn feeling the tears stinging my own eyes. 'We'll get these boys to land after all.' As we shared our happiness and watched the fishing boat close with us, death could have taken me quite easily just then, for I knew that I would never experience another such pinnacle of contentment."

Donn Fendler: Lost on a Mountain in Maine *(1939)*

HIKING WITH HIS family high on Maine's Mount Katahdin in the summer of 1939, twelve-year-old Donn Fendler became separated from the others, then lost in a low cloud. For the next nine days, until he stumbled upon some campers in a remote cabin, he wandered down the mountain, following the course of a stream. At one point he loses his shoes and has to continue barefoot. On the sixth day he faints in the middle of the day.

The next thing I knew I woke up and it was getting dark.

I was sitting on a rock looking at my feet. They didn't seem to belong to me at first. They were the feet of someone else. The toenails were all broken and bleeding and there were thorns in the middle of the soles. I cried a little as I tried to get out those thorns. They were in deep and broken off. I wondered why they didn't hurt more, but when I felt my toes, I knew — those toes were hard and stiff and hardly any feeling in them. The part next to the big toe was like leather. I tried to pinch it, but I couldn't feel anything.

My head ached and I didn't want to move, but night was falling and I had to go on, at least as far as some big tree. I got to my feet. Was that hard! I could scarcely bend my knees, and my head was so dizzy I staggered. I had to go across an open space to the stream, and as I went along I saw a big bear, just ahead of me. Christmas, he was big — big as a house, I thought — but I wasn't a bit scared — not a single bit. I was glad to see him.

Wilfred Thesiger: Arabian Sands *(1959)*

THESIGER, WHO DIED in 2003 at the age of ninety-three, is often thought to have been the last real explorer, someone who travelled in remote regions and made significant discoveries — in essence a mapmaker, in the spirit of Richard Burton and H. M. Stanley. Fluent in Arabic, a rider of camels, with a deep sympathy for traditional cultures, Thesiger fought in Ethiopia during World War II and after the war made scientific and personal expeditions in Arabia. He also lived for long periods among the Madan people in the marshes of southern Iraq, an experience he recounts in *The Marsh Arabs* (1964). That book has great historical value, because the people were displaced by Saddam Hussein in one of his persecutions. Even an average day among the Marsh Arabs seems like an ordeal, but nothing in Thesiger's work compares with his starving in the Empty Quarter of Arabia:

> I had almost persuaded myself that I was conditioned to starvation, indifferent to it. After all, I had been hungry for weeks . . . Certainly I thought and talked incessantly of food, but as a prisoner talks of freedom, for I realized that the joints of meat, the piles of rice, and the bowls of steaming gravy which tantalized me could have no reality outside my mind . . .
>
> For the first day my hunger was only a more insistent feeling of familiar emptiness; something which, like a toothache, I could partly overcome by an effort of will. I woke in the grey dawn craving for food, but by lying on my stomach and pressing down I could achieve a semblance of relief . . .
>
> I faced another night, and the nights were worse than the days. Now I was cold and could not even sleep except in snatches . . .
>
> In the morning I watched Mikhail turn the camels out to graze, and as they shuffled off, spared for a while from the toil which we imposed upon them, I found I could only think of them as food. I was glad when they were out of sight . . . I lay with my eyes shut, insisting to myself, "If I were in London I would give anything to be here" . . . No, I would rather be here starving as I was than sitting in a chair, replete with food, listening to the wireless, and dependent upon cars to take me through Arabia. I clung desperately to this conviction. It seemed infinitely important. Even to doubt it was to admit defeat, to forswear everything to which I held.

Apsley Cherry-Garrard: The Worst Journey in the World *(1922)*

CHERRY-GARRARD WAS ONLY twenty-four when he joined Robert Falcon Scott's Antarctic expedition in 1910. Scott and four of his men died on the way back from the pole. But before that, in the winter of 1911, Cherry-Garrard trudged through the polar darkness and cold (minus 79°F) to find a rookery of emperor penguins. This was "the Worst Journey". After returning to Britain Cherry-Garrard fought in World War I at the Battle of the Somme, where almost a million men died. But he said, "The Somme was a relative picnic compared to the Antarctic." He also said, "Exploration is the physical expression of the Intellectual Passion."

In this magnificent book, in a chapter titled "Never Again", he wrote:

> And I tell you, if you have the desire for knowledge and the power to give it physical expression, go out and explore. If you are a brave man you will do nothing; if you are fearful you may do much, for none but cowards have need to prove their bravery. Some will tell you that you are mad, and nearly all will say, "What's the use?" For we are a nation of shopkeepers, and no shopkeeper will look at research which does not promise him a financial return within a year. And so you will sledge nearly alone, but those with whom you sledge will not be shopkeepers: that is worth a good deal. If you march your Winter Journeys you will have your reward, so long as all you want is a penguin's egg.

Jon Krakauer: Into Thin Air *(1999)*

IN THE SPRING of 1996, Jon Krakauer, forty-two, on an assignment for *Outside* magazine, joined a guided expedition to Mount Everest. Just a story about guided climbing, but he found himself in the deadliest Everest season since climbing began there seventy-five years before, on Sagarmatha, Mother Goddess of the World.

Like all ordeal books, this one contains many lessons. The central issue is that you can buy your way up Everest, but to what extent is the hubristic motive in guided climbing an invitation to disaster? A person pays $70,000 (the going rate in 1996) to an expert, on the understanding that the client will successfully reach the summit. The client may be reasonably fit and experienced, or may be (as some clients Krakauer describes) first-timers at high altitudes, with a minimum of know-how. In the latter case, the client might be "short-roped" and yanked up the mountain, photographed at the top, and then dragged down.

Krakauer had dreamed from childhood of climbing Everest, yet was new to bottled oxygen, new to the Himalayas, and had never been anywhere near this height (29,000 feet). But he followed instructions, acclimatized himself, practised for weeks in workout climbs from base camp, and finally made it to the top. During his descent, he suffered from hypoxia, hallucinations, extreme fatigue, and cold.

The story could have ended there. But there were many others on the mountain (he lists sixteen teams, two of them with more than twenty guides, clients, and sherpas), impatient to get to the top. So Krakauer's difficult but successful climb was only the beginning of the ordeal.

As Krakauer descended, twenty people lined up to climb the narrow ridges that led to the summit. Like Krakauer, they were worn down by oxygen deprivation, disorientation, hunger, thirst, and fatigue — and a storm was approaching. The climbers, undeterred, running late, pushed for the top; and in the thunderstorm that hit, accompanied by lightning, high winds, and blinding snow, chaos ensued. In the cold and the blowing snow, climbers got lost, fell, froze, hesitated, and panicked. Some guides stood by their clients, others abandoned them.

"With enough determination, any bloody idiot can get up this hill," Rob Hall, one of the guides, had told his clients early on. "The trick is to get back down alive." Struggling to save a faltering client, Hall died on the mountain, and so did the client, and ten others.

Everest does not inspire prudent people to climb its flanks, Krakauer writes: "Unfortunately, the sort of individual who is programmed to ignore personal distress and keep pushing for the top is frequently programmed to disregard signs of grave and imminent danger as well. This forms the nub of a dilemma that every Everest climber eventually comes up against: in order to succeed you must be exceedingly driven, but if you are too driven, you're likely to die. Above 26,000 feet, moreover, the line between appropriate zeal and reckless summit fever becomes grievously thin. Thus the slopes of Everest are littered with corpses."

William Burroughs: The Yage Letters *(1963)*

DOES THE BURROUGHS book belong here? I think so, as the narrative of a comic ordeal. These funny, informative, even scabrous letters, written to Allen Ginsberg, his lover at the time, were sent from various places in Latin America — Panama, Colombia, and Peru — and seem to be dispatches from a distant land. But I see them as mad memoranda, the ordeal of a man going in ever-narrowing circles. Burroughs hates travel, he hates foreigners, he mocks them unmercifully. What he craves is the ultimate high, and hearing it is to be found in the drug ayahuasca, a potion made from a jungle vine, he goes in search of it and relates his findings in these letters.

The landscape is insignificant, and the details of the trip — the people, the places — are almost beneath notice. He wants to try this drug; he is a man who needs a particular fix. If there were a progression, a sense of time, a mounting idea of discovery, an episodic enlightenment, this might rank as one of the great books about a quest. But it is deflationary and self-mocking, and he makes light of his ordeal.

"The Upper Amazon jungle has fewer disagreeable features than the Mid-West stateside woods in the summer," Burroughs writes in a typically dismissive way. And later, "Sure you think it's romantic at first but wait til you sit there five days onna sore ass sleeping in Indian shacks and eating hoka and some hunka nameless meat like the smoked pancreas of a two-toed sloth."

Burroughs did find the ayahuasca, and he had his visions, but the rest of the time he was chasing boys, many of whom (he says) stole from him. He took it in stride. "Trouble is," he writes in this cheery anti-travel book, "I share with the late Father Flanagan — he of Boys Town — the deep conviction that there is no such thing as a bad boy."

11

English Travellers on Escaping England

MUCH HAS BEEN WRITTEN ABOUT ENGLISH travellers. Why so many? Why do they tend to seek out tropical regions, or the Costa del Sol, or anywhere but England? Even a short residence in England is enough to convince anyone that it is the class system that drives the English to places where class doesn't matter (as long as you're a bwana or a sahib). And for those who have status, it is the dreary climate that does the rest, sending the English looking for better weather. Generally, the history of English travel is the history of people in search of sunshine. D. H. Lawrence was unequivocal, and so was Robert Louis Stevenson, but the rest tend not to admit it.

At the beginning of her *Travels in West Africa* (1897), Mary Kingsley summed up the hypocrisy of such travellers: "If you were to take many of the men [in Africa] who most energetically assert that they wish they were home in England, 'and see if they would ever come to the etc., etc., place again', and if you were to bring them home, and let them stay there a little while, I am pretty sure that — in the absence of attractions other than those of merely being home in England, notwithstanding its glorious joys of omnibuses, underground railways, and evening newspapers — these same men, in terms varying with individual cases, will be found sneaking back apologetically to the [African] Coast."

Here are seven travellers who made no bones about it.

Lady Hester Stanhope: Toward the end of her life, in her house in Djoun (in present-day Lebanon, where she lived for twenty-three years), she was visited by the English painter William Bartlett, who wrote, "She conducted us to an arbour in the gardens, quite English in appearance. I made this observation, when she replied, 'Oh, don't say so; I hate everything English'" (James C. Simmons, *Passionate Pilgrims*, 1987).

D. H. Lawrence: From wartime Sussex, April 30, 1915: "How dark my soul is! I stumble and grope and don't get much further. I suppose it must be so. All the beauty and light of the days seems [*sic*] like a [*sic*] iridescence on a very black flood . . . I wish I were going to Thibet — or Kamschatka — or Tahiti — to the Ultima ultima ultima Thule. I feel sometimes, I shall go mad, because there is nowhere to go, no 'new world'. One of these days, unless I watch myself, I shall be departing in some rash fashion, to some foolish place" (*Letters*, vol. 2, 1913–1916, edited by George Zytaruk and James Boulton, 1981).

T. E. Lawrence: "We export two chief kinds of Englishmen," he wrote in the Introduction to Doughty's *Travels in Arabia Deserta,*

> who in foreign parts divide themselves into two opposed classes. Some feel deeply the influence of native people, and try to adjust themselves to its atmosphere and spirit. To fit themselves modestly into the picture they suppress all in them that would be discordant

with local habits and colours. They imitate the native, and so avoid friction in their daily life. However, they cannot avoid the consequences of imitation, a hollow, worthless thing. They are like the people but not of the people, and their half-perceptible differences give them a sham influence often greater than their merit. They urge the people among whom they live into strange, unnatural courses by imitating them so well that they are imitated back again.

The other class of Englishmen is the larger class. In the same circumstances of exile they reinforce their character by memories of the life they have left. In reaction against foreign surroundings they take refuge in the England that was theirs. They assert their aloofness, their immunity, the more vividly for their loneliness and weakness. They impress the peoples among whom they live by reaction, by giving them an ensample of the complete Englishman, the foreigner intact.

Doughty is a great member of the second, the cleaner class.

And T. E. Lawrence was a member of the first, the gone-native class.

W. Somerset Maugham: "To me England has been a country where I had obligations that I did not want to fulfil and responsibilities that irked me. I have never felt entirely myself till I had put at least the Channel between my native country and me" (*The Summing Up*, 1938).

W. H. Auden: "England is terribly provincial — it's all this family business. I know exactly why Guy Burgess went to Moscow. It wasn't enough to be queer and a drunk. He had to revolt still more to break away from it all. That's just what I've done by becoming an American citizen . . . I also find criticism in England very provincial. In the literary world in England, you have to know who's married to whom, and who's slept with whom and who hasn't. It's a tiny jungle. America's so much larger. Critics may live in New York, but the writers don't" (quoted in Charles Osborne, *W. H. Auden*, 1980).

Gerald Brenan: "It will naturally be asked how I came to make my home in such a remote spot" — the tiny village of Yegen, in the Sierra Nevada of Andalusia, Spain, in 1920. "The shortest explanation would be that I was rebelling against English middle-class life . . . The England I knew was petrified by class feeling and by rigid conventions, as well as, in my case, poisoned by memories of my public school, so that as soon as the war was over and I was out of uniform I set off to discover new and more breathable atmospheres" (*South from Granada*, 1957).

Bruce Chatwin: "I've decided to leave England. As Richard Burton said: 'The only country in which I do not feel at home'" (*Under the Sun: The Letters of Bruce Chatwin*, edited by Elizabeth Chatwin and Nicholas Shakespeare, 2010).

12
When You're Strange

ATRAVELLER IS A STRANGER. ONE OF THE DELU-sions of the tourist, usually buffered from real-ity, is that he or she is a friend and even perhaps a benefactor of the locals. "We're putting money into the economy," is a common tourist observation. The travel-ler, ever the outsider, always moving on, would never say that. "Tourism is a mortal sin," said the film director Werner Herzog. And yet it is the rough traveller, not the tidy tourist, who confronts — and needs the goodwill of — the native of the land. This is often a recapitulation of a recurrent human event in history that has always fascinated me — First Contact, meeting The Other. The most vivid examples come from the history of explora-tion and discovery. Usually, First Contact is construed as Columbus meeting his first Arawak and calling him an Indian, because Columbus believed he had reached the coast of India. But consider the opposite: the Arawak meeting a fat little Italian clutching a copy of Marco Polo's *Travels* on the deck of a caravel.

In the year of contact, 1778, the Hawaiians believed Captain James Cook to be the god Lono. The Aztecs, in 1517, took the Spaniards to be avatars of Quetzalcoatl, the Plumed Serpent, god of learning and of wind. The polar Inuit assumed that they were the only people in the world, so when they saw their first white stranger, the explorer Sir William Parry, in 1821, they said to him, "Are you from the sun or the moon?"

Until I went to live in Africa, I had not known that most people in the world believe that they are the People, and their language is the Word, and strangers are not fully human — at least not human in the way the People are — nor is a stranger's language anything but the gabbling of incoherent and inspissated felicities. In most languages, the name of a people means "the Original People", or simply "the People". "Inuit" means "the People", and most Native American names of so-called tribes mean "the People". For example, the Ojibwe, or Chippewa, call themselves Anishinaabe, "the Original People", and the Cherokee (the name is not theirs but a Creek word) call themselves Ani Yun Wiya, meaning "Real People", and Hawaiians refer to themselves as Kanaka Maoli, "Original People".

As recently as the 1930s, Australian gold prospectors and New Guinea Highlanders encountered each other for the first time. The grasping, world-weary Aussies took the Highlanders to be savages, while the Highlanders, assuming that the Aussies were the ghosts of their own dead ancestors, on a visit, felt a kinship and gave them food, thinking (as they reported later), "They are like people you see in a dream." But the Australians were looking for gold and killed the Highlanders who were uncooperative. The Lakota, who called white men *washichus*, Nathaniel Philbrick writes in *The Last Stand*, "believed that the first white men had come from the sea, which they called *mniwoncha*, meaning 'water all over.'" In an echo of this accurate characterization, and at about the same time, the historian Fernand Braudel tells us, "To West Africans, the white men were *murdele*, men from the sea."

Otherness can be like an illness; being a stranger can be analogous to experiencing a form of madness — those same intimations of the unreal and the irrational, when everything that has been familiar is stripped away.

It is hard to be a stranger. A traveller has no power, no influence, no known identity. That is why a traveller needs optimism and heart, because without confidence travel is misery. Generally, the traveller is anonymous, ignorant, easy to deceive, at the mercy of the people he or she travels among. The traveller might be known as "the American" or "the Foreigner", and there is no power in that.

A traveller is often conspicuous, and consequently is vulnerable. But in my travelling, I whistled in the dark and assumed all would be well. I depended on people being civil and observing a few basic rules. I did not expect preferential treatment. I did not care about power or respectability. This was the condition of a liberated soul, of course, but also the condition of a bum.

Among the Batelela in the Sankuru region of central Congo the word for stranger is *ongendagenda*. It is also one of the most common names for a male child. The reasoning is that when a child is born — and males matter most among the Batelela — he appears from nowhere and is unknown, so he is usually called Stranger, and this name stays with him throughout his life — Stranger is the "John" of the Sankuru region.

Bruce Chatwin, in *The Songlines*, quotes an Old English proverb: "The stranger, if he be not a trader, is an enemy." In *The Valleys of the Assassins*, Freya Stark wrote of the nomads in Luristan: "The laws of hospitality are based on the axiom that a stranger is an enemy until he has entered the sanctuary of someone's tent."

Some words for stranger have the meaning of a spirit, as in the case of the New Guinea Highlanders, who could not conceive of the white Australians as anything but spectral ancestors. In Swahili, the word *muzungu* (plural, *wazungu*) has its root in the word for ghost or spirit, and cognates of the word — *mzungu* in Chichewa and *murungu* in Shona and other Bantu languages — have the meaning of a powerful spirit, even a god. Foreigners had once seemed godlike when they first appeared in some places.

The word for foreigner in Easter Island, in Rapa Nui speech, is *popaa* — so I was told there. But this is a neologism. In an earlier time the Rapa Nui word for foreigner (according to William Churchill's *Easter Island*, 1915) was *etua*, which also means god or spirit. It is related to the Hawaiian word *atua*, though the Hawaiian word for stranger is *haole*, meaning "of another breath".

Here is a list of countries and languages and their words for stranger.

Maori—pakeha, white man, foreigner.

Fiji—kai valagi (pronounced *valangi*), white person, foreigner, "person from the sky", as opposed to *kai India* for Indians and *kai China* for Chinese.

Tonga—papalangi, a cognate of Samoan *palangi*, meaning "sky burster", a person who comes from the clouds, not a terrestrial creature.

Samoa—palangi, "from the sky", related to the Fijian *kai valangi*.

Trobriand Islands—dim-dim, for foreigner or white-skinned person; *koyakoya* for dark-skinned non-Trobriander. *Koya* is the word for mountain. But there are no mountains in the Trobriand Islands. So a *koyakoya* is a mountain person — that is, from mainland New Guinea, or simply an off-islander.

Hong Kong—gweilo, "ghost man", a prettier way of saying "foreign devil", since a ghost is menacing, something to fear.

Japan—gaijin. The word is composed of two characters, *gai*, meaning outside, and *jin*, person. This appears to be a contraction for *gai-kokujin*, "outside-country person", thus an outsider in the most literal sense — racially, ethnically, geographically.

China—wei-guo ren is the neutral term, a person from a foreign country. But *yanguize*, "foreign devil", is also common, and there are words for "red-haired devil", "white devil", and "big nose".

Arabic—ajnabi, "people to avoid"; also *ajami*, meaning foreigner, barbarian, bad Arabic speaker, Persian; also *gharib*, stranger, "from the west".

Kiribati—I-matang. Travelling by kayak within the huge atoll of Christmas Island (Kiritimati), I heard this word often. *I-matang* is generally used to mean foreigner (there were four such people on Christmas

Island), but etymologically it is "the person from Matang", said to be the ancestral home of the I-Kiribati, the original fatherland, a place of fair-skinned people. The word implies kinship. By the way, it is an actual place — Madang, on the northern coast of Papua New Guinea, thought by historians to be the origin of these Micronesian people.

Mexico—gringo. The word seems to have come from *griego*, a Spanish term for a Greek. The *Diccionario Castellano* (1787) defines *gringo* as a word used in Málaga for "anyone who spoke Spanish badly", and in Madrid for "the Irish". It implies gibberish. The many popular theories (among them, that it may be derived from hearing the disenchanted Irish soldiers who'd joined the Mexicans singing "Green Grow the Rushes Oh!" during the Mexican–American War in the mid-1840s) are fanciful and unconvincing. The earliest recorded use of *gringo* in print is in the *Western Journal* (1849–1850) of John Woodhouse Audubon (son of John James, and also an artist), who travelled by horseback through northern Mexico on his way from New York to witness the Gold Rush in California. In Cerro Gordo ("a miserable den of vagabonds") Audubon and his fellow travellers were abused: "We were hooted and shouted as we passed through, and called 'Gringoes' etc., but that did not prevent us from enjoying their delicious spring water."

Being Frank

I HEARD THE word *faranji*, for foreigner, in Ethiopia when I was on my *Dark Star Safari* trip, and remembered *farang* in Thailand, *ferangi* in Iran, and *firringhi* in India and Malaysia (though *orang-puteh*, for white person, is more common in Malaysia). What's the connection?

When Richard Burton took his first trip to Abyssinia — recounted in *First Footsteps in East Africa* — he wrote, "I heard frequently muttered by the red-headed spearmen the ominous term 'Faranj'." Burton went on to say that the Bedouin in Arabia "apply this term to all but themselves". In his time, even Indian traders in Africa were called *faranji* if they happened to be wearing trousers (*shalwar*), since trouser-wearing was associated with outsiders. In his *Personal Narrative of a Pilgrimage to Al-Madinah and Meccah* (1853), he wrote, "The convert [in Arabia] is always watched with Argus eyes, and men do not willingly give information to a 'new Moslem', especially a Frank."

In *The Valleys of the Assassins* (1934), Freya Stark says, "The aim of the Persian government is to have [the people of Luristan] dressed *à la Ferangi* in a year's time." Later on, in a valley "stood the castle of Nevisar Shah to which no Frank, so they told me, had ever climbed".

These words, all related to *farang*, are cognates of "Frank", though the people who use the word don't know beans about Franks. The Franks were a Germanic tribe who peregrinated western Europe in the third and fourth centuries. But the name, of which "French" is a cognate, probably gained currency from the Crusades of the twelfth century, when Europeans plundered Islamic holy sites and massacred Muslims in the name of God. In the Levant and ultimately as far as East Africa and South-East Asia, a Frank was any Westerner.

Even in Albania: "Immense crowds collected to witness the strange Frank and his doings," wrote Edward Lear about himself, in his Albanian journal in 1848. A form of *faranji*, the word *afrangi* is regarded as obsolete in Egypt, though it is still occasionally used, especially in combination. In Egypt, a *kabinet afrangi* is a Western, sit-down toilet.

Almost the entire time I spent in Harar, Ethiopia — where the poet Rimbaud had lived — I was followed by children chanting, "*Faranji! Faranji! Faranji!*" Sometimes older people bellowed it at me, and now and then as I was driving slowly down the road a crazed-looking Harari would rush from his doorstep to the window of my car and stand, spitting and screaming the word into my face.

❧ Travel Wisdom of ❧
ROBERT LOUIS STEVENSON

In spite of being weak and tubercular — wraithlike in his John Singer Sargent portrait — Stevenson travelled widely. Mostly he travelled for his health, searching for clement weather to ease his infected lungs, but also for the romance of the experience:

> I would like to rise and go
> Where the golden apples grow.

He rambled on the Continent, criss-crossed the United States, sailed around the Pacific, and ended up in Samoa, where he died (1894) and is buried. He was well read and undoubtedly knew Montaigne, who wrote in his essay "Of Vanity": "But, at such an age, you will never return from so long a journey. What care I for that? I neither undertake it to return, nor to finish it: my business is only to keep myself in motion, whilst motion pleases me; I only walk for the walk's sake." Stevenson seems to paraphrase this in his first quotation:

For my part, I travel not to go anywhere, but to go. I travel for travel's sake. The great affair is to move; to feel the needs and hitches of our life a little more nearly, to get down off this feather-bed of civilization, and to find the globe granite underfoot and strewn with cutting flints.

— *Travels with a Donkey in the Cevennes* (1879)

A voyage is a piece of autobiography at best.

— *The Cévennes Journal:*
Notes on a Journey Through the French Highlands (1978)

Little do ye know your own blessedness; for to travel hopefully is a better thing than to arrive, and the true success is to labour.

— "Virginibus Puerisque"

Herein, I think, is the chief attraction of railway travel. The speed is so easy, the train disturbs so little the scenes through which it takes us, that our heart becomes full of the placidity and stillness of the country; and while the body is being borne forward in the flying chain of carriages, the thoughts alight, as the humour moves them, at unfrequented stations.

— "Ordered South"

There lie scattered thickly various lengths of petrified trunk . . . It is very curious, of course, and ancient enough, if that were all. Doubtless,

the heart of the geologist beats quicker at the sight; but, for my part, I was mightily unmoved. Sightseeing is the art of disappointment.
— "The Silverado Squatters"

———•———

There's nothing under heaven so blue,
That's fairly worth the travelling to.
But, fortunately, Heaven rewards us with many agreeable
prospects and adventures by the way.
— "The Silverado Squatters"

∽⊙ 13 ⊙∼
It Is Solved by Walking

ALL SERIOUS PILGRIMS GO ON FOOT TO THEIR holy destination — Chaucer's Canterbury pilgrims stand for so many others. Walking is a spiritual act; walking on one's own induces meditation. The Chinese characters for pilgrimage mean "paying one's respect to a mountain" (*ch'ao-shan chin-hsiang*). As I saw on my *Riding the Iron Rooster* trip, many Taoists make a point of visiting the five holy mountains they regard as pillars of China, the cardinal compass points as well as the centre, separating Heaven and Earth. And there are four other mountains, sacred to Buddhism and associated with a particular bodhisattva. "Paying respect" means climbing the mountains — though this often involves walking up stairs, since steps have been cut into most of the mountainsides. Ambrose Bierce defined a pilgrim as "a traveller that is taken seriously".

In his essay "Walking", in the posthumous collection *Excursions* (1863), Thoreau spoke of the word "saunter" as having been derived from the French expression "going to the Holy Land": "I have met with but one or two persons in the course of my life who understood the art of Walking, that is, of taking walks, who had a genius, so to speak, for *sauntering*: which word is beautifully derived from idle people who roved about the country, in the Middle Ages, and asked charity, under pretence of going 'à la Sainte Terre', to the Holy Land, till the children exclaimed, 'There goes a *Sainte-Terrer*', a Saunterer, a Holy-Lander. They who never go to the Holy Land in their walks, as they pretend, are indeed mere idlers and vagabonds; but they who do go there are saunterers in the good sense, such as I mean." And later in this long paragraph he says, "For every walk is a sort of crusade, preached by some Peter the Hermit in us, to go forth and reconquer this Holy Land from the hands of the Infidels."

The Spanish word *sendereando*, for hiking, is compact and pretty (*sendero* is path), but the wisest phrase for this activity is the Latin *solvitur ambulando* ("it is solved by walking"), attributed to Saint Augustine. The phrase was mentioned by the long-distance walker Patrick Leigh Fermor to Bruce Chatwin. "Hearing it, immediately Bruce whipped out his notebook," Chatwin's biographer wrote. Walking to ease the mind is also an objective of the pilgrim. There is a spiritual dimension too: the walk itself is part of a process of purification. Walking is the age-old form of travel, the most fundamental, perhaps the most revealing.

Chatwin regarded walking in an almost mystical way. His predecessors, beginning with the great Japanese poet Bashō, felt the same. Walking inspired the poets Whitman and Wordsworth, and Rousseau based a series of philosophical essays on walks. Stanley walked across Africa twice. When David Livingstone wished to get into shape, and to invoke the travelling mood, he walked for weeks at a time in the African bush, "until my muscles were hard as boards".

Some walks are those of the *flâneur*, an almost untranslatable French word meaning stroller, saunterer, drifter — the essence of a traveller — but in this case usually one in a city, perhaps the very word to describe someone trying to solve a problem. Some walks by travellers border on stunts or bids for the record book — two obvious examples are Ewart Grogan tramping from Cape Town to Cairo in 1898, and more recently Ffyona Campbell, who in her way walked around the world (see Chapter 14, "Travel Feats").

But it is the committed walker, the thoughtful walker, who interests me the most.

Xuanzang (603-664): The Ultimate Pilgrim

A MONK AND a scholar, the young Xuanzang (Hsüan-tsang in some renderings) felt that the Buddhist texts in China were badly translated, debased versions of the originals, so he decided to travel to India to verify them and to bring back as many texts as possible. He hoped also to see the holy places associated with Buddha's life and enlightenment. In some old illustrations he is shown accompanied by a pony — he certainly brought back the manuscripts on packhorses. But in his account of his seventeen years of travels he frequently refers to walking on narrow and difficult trails, and he appears to have travelled alone.

"At a time when the country was most prosperous, and equipped with unparalleled virtue, he started his journey to the remote lands carrying his pewter staff and whisked the dust with his robes," wrote Yu Zhining, Duke of Yanguo, in the original preface to *The Great Tang Dynasty Record of the Western Regions*. In a postscript to the book, Xuanzang is eulogized: "With the prestige of the emperor, he made his way, and under the protection of deities, he travelled in solitude."

Xuanzang left from the Tang Dynasty capital, Changan — Xian today, site of the terracotta warriors, imperial tombs, and glorious pagodas — and kept going, through Qinghai and across Xingjiang to Bokhara, Samarkand, and into present-day Afghanistan. All the while he made notes on the state of Buddhism, the condition of monasteries, the number of monks. He was awestruck by the giant carved Buddha statues at Bamiyan (dynamited and destroyed by the Taliban in 2001, to the cries of "Allah is great!"). He crossed Peshawar and Taxila in what is now Pakistan, describing the ruins of Gandhara, where "there were more than a thousand monasteries but they are now dilapidated and deserted, and in desolate condition." He wandered all over India. The fastidiousness of the early manifestations of the caste system fascinated him: "Butchers, fishermen, harlots, actors, executioners, and scavengers mark their houses with banners and are not allowed to live inside the cities," he wrote of the walled towns of northern India.

Throughout, he chronicled the presence of dragons, some protective, others menacing. He succeeded in his mission to find copies of ancient Buddhist texts, to visit the sacred places associated with Buddha: Gaya, Sarnath, Lumpini Gardens, and at last Kushinagara, where Buddha died. He stayed for years at a time in monasteries, learned Sanskrit, kept travelling, and returned to China with 657 texts, carried by twenty packhorses. At the suggestion of the emperor, he dictated *The Great Tang Dynasty Record*, finishing it in 646. When it was translated into French and English in the nineteenth century, other travellers (Aurel Stein for one) were able to find the lost cities and forgotten ruins that Xuanzang had so meticulously described. A new edition of Xuanzang's travels appeared in 1996, translated by Li Rongxi.

Matsuo Bashō (1644–1694): Narrow Road to the Deep North

BASHŌ WAS A nickname — it means banana tree: one was planted at the hut of the poet by an admirer, and the poet adopted the name. Bashō is said to be one of the greatest writers of haiku, the highly distilled, rigorously syllabic, and allusive Japanese three-line poem.

A Zen practitioner, Bashō also wrote *haibun*, a compressed and sometimes staticky prose that resembles the starkness of haiku. An admirer of the mendicant monks, he spent his life alternating spells of meditative living, usually in a remote hut, with walks (occasionally resorting to horseback), some short, several of them quite lengthy, which he recounted in books that combined prose with poems. He acknowledged Kamo-no-Chōmei (see page 162) as an inspiration in the writing of travel journals. His first, a quest for spiritual wisdom, was *The Records of a Weather-Exposed Skeleton* (1685). One passage is heart-rending:

On a road along the Fuji River we came upon an abandoned child, about two years of age and crying pathetically. Apparently his parents, finding the waves of this floating world as uncontrollable as the turbulent rapids of this river, had decided to leave him there until his life vanished like a dewdrop. He looked like a tiny bush-clover blossom that would fall any time tonight or tomorrow beneath the blow of an autumn gust. I tossed him some food from my sleeve pocket, and mused as I passed by:

> Poets who sang of monkey's wailing:
> How would they feel about this child forsaken
> In the autumn wind?
> (translated by Makoto Ueda, *Matsuo Bashō*, 1977)

In 1689 Bashō took his most ambitious trip, nine months of walking that resulted in his best-known work, his masterpiece, *The Narrow Road to the Deep North* (or *Back Roads to Far Towns*), at the time a remote and forgotten part of Honshu, the main island of Japan. Bashō was accompanied by his friend Sora, and both dressed as pilgrims. On this long walk Bashō describes the enlightenment he seeks:

Spent night at Iizuka, bathed at hot-springs there, found lodgings but only thin mats over bare earth, ramshackle sort of place. No lamp, bedded down by shadowy light of fireplace and tried getting some rest. All night, thunder, pouring buckets, roof leaking, fleas, mosquitoes in droves: no sleep. To cap it off the usual trouble cropped up [illness], almost passed out. The short night sky at last broke, and again picked up and went on. But the night's traces dragged, mind balked. Hired horses, got to post town of Ko-ori. Future seemed farther off than ever, and recurring illness nagged, but what a pilgrimage to far places calls for: willingness to let world go, its momentariness to die on the road, human destiny, which lifted spirit a little, finding foot again here and there, crossing the Okido Barrier in Date.

> — *Back Roads to Far Towns*, translated by
> Cid Corman and Kamaike Susumu (1968)

The Nomadism of Bruce Chatwin

CHATWIN WAS DELIBERATELY enigmatic, but a relentless explainer in the excitable way of a self-taught and widely read person, fond of theorizing. His work has this same excitable, distracted quality, with flashes of true brilliance in description. He was greatly influenced by Robert Byron's *Road to Oxiana*, and this admiration shows in his own work, in his idealizing oddity of description and a love of the grotesque or unexpected. His self-assurance showed, as Augustus Hare said of Mrs. Grote in his autobiography, as the stating of every belief "with the manner and tone of one laying down the laws of Athens".

Chatwin was just as unambiguous in his belief in the value of walking. Walking defined him. And he felt that walking defined the human race — the best of it. His earliest work was on nomads; he lived his life on the move. Chatwin scoffed at the term "travel writer" and even "travel book". He claimed that much of what he wrote, sold as "travel", was fiction. "*The Songlines* is a novel," he said, though most readers regard it as Bruce's own adventures in the Australian outback. Some of *In Patagonia* was made up or fudged. He was contradictory, intense, unreliable, elusive, a compulsive exaggerator, almost a Munchausen, and also secretive. "Hate confessional mode," he wrote in one of his notebooks.

Chatwin could seem at times frivolous, or so intense and demanding as to be exhausting. But without question he was an imaginative writer and one of the great walkers in travel literature.

This is not plain in the text of *In Patagonia*, where a typical sentence is "I left the Rio Negro and went on south to Port Madryn" — a trek of two hundred miles, but he doesn't say how he got there. Or "I crossed over into Fireland" or "I passed through three boring towns" or "I went to the southernmost town in the world." He is an insubstantial presence in his books ("I am not interested in the traveller"), but in his letters home he was explicit. "Dying of tiredness. Have just walked 150 odd miles," he wrote to his wife.

The walker sees things clearly: the sun on the walker's head, the wind in the walker's face, the country under the walker's feet: "I walked out of town to the petrified forest," he wrote in *The Songlines*. "Wind pumps whirled insanely. A steel-blue heron lay paralysed under an electric cable. A dribble of blood ran along its beak. The tongue was missing. The trunks of extinct monkey-puzzles were broken clean as if in a sawmill."

If *The Songlines* is a novel, as Chatwin said, it is a very patchy piece of fiction. I think he meant that he invented much of it, and this may be true; but making things up in a travel book is not the same as writing a novel. *The Songlines* is a book arguing the case for nomadism: "The more I read, the more convinced I became that nomads had been the crankhandle of history, if for no other reason than the great monotheisms had, all of them, surfaced from the pastoral milieu."

This, on Chatwin's part, is bad history. The historian Fernand Braudel, in his study of global shifts in culture, *The Structure of Everyday Life*, writes that nomads were "horse- and camel-men" who "represented speed and surprise at a period when everything moved slowly". Chatwin seems not to have known this. Later in *The Songlines*, he asserts, "Natural Selection has designed us — from the structure of our brain cells to the structure of our big toe — for a career of seasonal journeys *on foot* through a blistering land of thorn-scrub or desert."

Chatwin spent some weeks in an SUV in Australia, visiting Aboriginals. But what one remembers of these visits, and the stops in the outback, are the many instances of racism and mindless abuse from Australian whites (he was travelling in the mid-1980s). When he is on foot his prose is sharper:

> I walked over a plateau of sandhills and crumbly red rock, broken by gulches which were difficult to cross. The bushes had been burnt for game-drives, and bright green shoots were sprouting from the stumps. [Then I climbed the plateau to find] Old Alex, naked, his spears along the ground and his velvet coat wrapped in a bundle. I nodded and he nodded.
>
> "Hello," I said. "What brings you here?"
>
> He smiled, bashful at his nakedness, and barely opening his lips, said, "Footwalking all the time all over the world."
>
> — *The Songlines*

Werner Herzog: Walking on Foot Is a Virtue

ON HIS DEATHBED, "Bruce summoned Herzog because he thought the director had healing powers," Nicholas Shakespeare wrote in his biography *Bruce Chatwin*. "When they first met in Melbourne in 1984 . . . their talks had begun with a discussion on the restorative powers of walking. 'He had an almost immediate rapport with me,' says Herzog, 'when I explained to him that tourism is a mortal sin, but walking on foot is a virtue, and that whatever went wrong and makes our civilization something doomed is the departure from the nomadic life.'"

Herzog's belief in *solvitur ambulando* is unshakeable. In an interview he said, "I personally would rather do the existentially essential things in life on foot. If you live in England and your girlfriend is in Sicily, and it is clear you want to marry her, then you should walk to Sicily to propose. For these things travel by car or aeroplane is not the right thing."

And he walked the walk. In 1974, hearing that the German film director Lotte Eisner was dying in Paris, Herzog decided to walk the five hundred miles there from Munich, "believing that she would stay alive if I came on foot." He added, as passionate walkers often do, "Besides, I wanted to be alone with myself." He was thirty-two. It was the winter of 1974. He described the journey in *Of Walking in Ice* (1980).

Herzog travelled almost as a mendicant. He rarely stayed in hotels, preferring to break into unoccupied houses and sleep in them, or sneak into barns and sleep in haystacks. He was frequently taken to be a tramp or an outlaw — he was indeed a trespasser, but that too is often the role of a walker. He was sent away from inns and restaurants for his sinister appearance.

His route was as the crow flies ("a direct imaginary line"), taking him through cities and slums and garbage dumps and past motorways; this is anything but pastoral, and yet his mood is reflective. His prose is cinematic, composed of heaped-up images, like a long panning shot of a young man trudging through snow and rain, across bleak landscapes, never making a friend, never ingratiating himself. His legs ache, his feet are so blistered and sore he limps. He writes, "Why is walking so full of woe?"

He records his dreams, he recalls his past, his childhood, and his prose becomes more and more hallucinatory. Nearer Paris, where he will find that Lotte Eisner has not died, he is strengthened by the sight of a rainbow: "A rainbow before me all at once fills me with the greatest confidence. What a sign it is, over and in front of he who walks. Everyone should Walk."

Jean-Jacques Rousseau: The Reveries of the Solitary Walker

THE TITLE SAYS everything of this posthumous book. *Les Rêveries du Promeneur Solitaire* is the last thing Rousseau wrote; he worked on it until a few weeks before he died, in 1778. The word "walk" is a specific activity in the book, but it also implies an essay, the word Montaigne used to mean a try, or an attempt.

"I am now alone on earth," Rousseau writes in the first line of the "First Walk", and announces that this sequence of walks will take the form of self-examination. Detached from everything and everyone for fifteen years (because of exile, condemnation, and harassment), utterly alone, he asks, "What am I?"

His serene condition, which he calls renunciation, is like that of the mendicant *saddhu* who wanders in India. "Everything is finished for me on earth. People can no longer do good or evil to me here. I have nothing more to hope for or to fear in this world; and here I am, tranquil at the bottom of the abyss, a poor unfortunate mortal, but unperturbed, like God himself."

Through walking, Rousseau remembers events, interprets his actions, and recalls embarrassments — a key one in the "Fourth Walk" when, asked about his children, he claims he doesn't have any. It is, as he writes, a lie. Rousseau had five children, who, for their own good (so he claimed in his *Confessions* and here too), he stuck in a foundling home. But this memory provokes a reverie about being untruthful.

His meditation on happiness in the "Fifth Walk" produces one of the many bittersweet reflections on the transitory nature of joy: "Happiness [is] a fleeting state which leaves our heart still worried and empty."

In later walks he speaks of how a country ramble can be spoiled or overpowered by certain conditions, how "memory of the company I had left followed me into solitude", and how particular itineraries had put him into contact with people he found upsetting. A tone of resignation permeates the *Reveries*. Rousseau was through trying to persuade anyone that he was worthy. Intensely autobiographical, it is a set of excursions that become reflections on life and death, for a man who is about to die.

Wordsworth: A Nature Poet with "Serviceable Legs"

WORDSWORTH'S PASSION FOR walking inspired his poems, which often praise the joyful activity of walking. At the age of seventy-three, reflecting on one of his earliest poems, "An Evening Walk", he wrote that he was an "eye-witness" to the features of the countryside that he put into the poem. Speaking of a particular couplet, he wrote, "I recollect distinctly the very spot where this first struck me. It was in the way between Hawkshead and Ambleside, and gave me extreme pleasure. The moment was important in my poetical history; for I date from it my consciousness of the infinite variety of natural appearances which had been unnoticed by the poets of any age or country, so far as I was acquainted with them; and I made a resolution to supply, in some degree, the deficiency."

His life was shaped by walking. Walking home after a party, while in his teens, overcome by a sunrise and a glimpse of mountains, he felt he was witnessing a revelation, and was so moved he decided that his role in life would be a "Dedicated Spirit."

Walking became part of his routine, living with his sister Dorothy at Dove Cottage in Grasmere. Dorothy remarked on how he walked for hours, even in the rain, and that "he generally composes his verses out of doors".

"He was, upon the whole, not a well-made man. His legs were pointedly condemned by all female connoisseurs in legs," Thomas De Quincey wrote waspishly, yet his legs were "serviceable", adding, "I calculate, upon good data, that with those identical legs Wordsworth must have travelled a distance of 175,000 to 180,000 English miles."

Wordsworth ambled around Ireland, Scotland, and Wales. In his fifties he toured the Continent, walking up and down France, Holland,

Switzerland, Italy, and elsewhere, writing the whole time. Even in his sixties he was able to walk twenty miles a day. Dorothy wrote, "And as to climbing of mountains, the hardiest & the youngest are yet hardly a match for him." At seventy he climbed Helvellyn, at over three thousand feet the third-highest peak in the Lake District.

He died at the age of eighty, a few weeks after being taken ill on a walk. One of the oddities of Wordsworth as a lover of flowers and fresh air is that (so everyone who knew him testified) he had no sense of smell.

Thoreau's "Walking"

HENRY DAVID THOREAU, who made a sacrament of walking, was a relentless analyser of his experience and a constant refiner of his prose style, as his voluminous journals attest. And Thoreau was never happier than when he was robustly explaining the crochets of his life. His essay "Walking", which appeared in his posthumous volume *Excursions*, is one of his happiest pieces. It is also one of the best essays on the subject of perambulation. Thoreau lived near enough to nature in Concord that he did not have to go far to feel he was surrounded by wilderness, even when he could hear train whistles.

He is specific about miles — he walked as much as twenty a day, he says — and about hours too: "I think that I cannot preserve my health and spirits, unless I spend four hours a day at least, and it is commonly more than that, sauntering through the woods and over the hills and fields, absolutely free from all worldly engagements."

This sacramental walking must not be confused with mere physical exercise, he says, but is more akin to yoga or a spiritual activity. "The walking of which I speak has nothing in it akin to taking exercise, as it is called, as the sick take medicine at stated hours, as the swinging of dumb-bells or chairs; but is itself the enterprise and adventure of the day. If you would get exercise, go in search of the springs of life. Think of a man's swinging dumb-bells for his health, when those springs are bubbling up in far-off pastures unsought by him!" Since walking cannot be separated from the process of thought, "you must walk like a camel, which is said to be the only beast which ruminates when walking. When a traveller asked Wordsworth's servant to show him her master's study, she answered, 'Here is his library, but his study is out of doors.'"

In "Walking" Thoreau writes, "Two or three hours' walking will carry me to as strange a country as I expect ever to see. A single farmhouse which I had not seen before is sometimes as good as the dominions of the King of Dahomey." This is a classic Thoreau conceit, the isolated farmhouse every bit as satisfying as distant Dahomey. In fact, Thoreau was a wide reader of travel books, and though Sir Richard Burton's *Mission to Gelele, King of Dahome* came out two years after Thoreau died, he was familiar with Burton's travels in the lake regions of central Africa and elsewhere — twelve of Burton's books of travel and discovery were published in Thoreau's lifetime, including *Wanderings in West Africa*.

He invokes Burton in this essay, saying, "Give me the ocean, the desert or the wilderness! In the desert, pure air and solitude compensate for want of moisture and fertility. The traveller Burton says of it, 'Your morale improves; you become frank and cordial, hospitable and single-minded . . . In the desert, spirituous liquors excite only disgust. There is a keen enjoyment in a mere animal existence.'"

But Thoreau, who avoided travelling on ocean, in desert, or through wilderness, belittled foreign travel, persuasively insisting it was not necessary to the serious walker. It is this persuasiveness — the triumph of his prose style — that made him far more influential than men and women who lived heroic lives of travel. Never mind counting the cats in Zanzibar, Thoreau says: "There is in fact a sort of harmony discoverable between the capabilities of the landscape within a circle of ten miles' radius, or the limits of an afternoon walk, and the threescore years and ten of human life. It will never become quite familiar to you."

John Muir: "Fond of Everything That Was Wild"

LATE IN HIS life, when he was seventy-five and had only a year more to live, John Muir, one of the greatest of walkers, wrote *The Story of My Boyhood and Youth* (1913), beginning it with this sentence: "When I was a boy in Scotland I was fond of everything that was wild, and all my life I've been growing fonder and fonder of wild places and wild creatures."

The large family (Muir was one of eight children) emigrated from Scotland to America, settling first in a shack, then on a farm in Wisconsin. Muir's father, Daniel, was a severe disciplinarian: "The old Scotch fashion of whipping for every act of disobedience or of simple playful forgetfulness was still kept up in the wilderness, and of course many of those whippings fell upon me."

A combination of his strict religious upbringing and a love for nature seems to have driven Muir from home and given him a mystical love for the natural world and a way of understanding wilderness. He lost his faith in organized religion but never failed to see something spiritual in nature.

A tinkerer and an inventor, he dreamed of exploring the Amazon jungles, like Alexander von Humboldt, one of his heroes. But apart from a short spell in Cuba he remained in the United States and became an early advocate for the preservation of wilderness areas, a co-founder of the Sierra Club, and the moving force behind the creation of America's national parks.

He was by nature a wanderer, and even as a fairly young man he was as bearded and bright-eyed as an Old Testament prophet. In 1867, at the age of twenty-nine, restless after a series of setbacks, he decided to walk from Indianapolis to Florida. His diary from this journey was published after his death as *A Thousand-Mile Walk to the Gulf.* "My plan," he wrote, "was simply to push on in a general southward direction by the wildest, leafiest, least-trodden way I could find, promising the greatest extent of virgin forest."

The forests of this great walk are lovely, but many of the people are distinctly menacing, for in the aftermath of the Civil War (unconscripted, Muir spent most of the war years sauntering in Canada), the South was in a state of derangement. He meets robbers, though he carries nothing worth stealing; he is confronted by "guerrillas" on horseback, ten of them at one point; and he encounters desperate former slaves. He stumbles upon a cotton plantation, three years after the war ended, still being run by a man known as "massa" whose field hands are "large bands of slaves".

What Muir had intended as a long walk through America was marked by hunger, danger, and uncertainty. Two years later he was in San Francisco, unhappy as always among crowds of people and eager to leave the city. He asks for the nearest way out.

"But where do you want to go?" a stranger responds.

"To any place that is wild," Muir says.

Directed to the Oakland ferry, he sets off for the wilderness on the first of April 1868, a walk that would change his life. He described his trek as slow, enchanted, easterly, toward the Yosemite Valley.

Muir was eloquent in his descriptions of landscape. He was also, like many other nature writers, something of a misanthrope, a trait noted in *Driving Home* by Jonathan Raban, who is a persuasive dissident on the subject of Muir's style. (Raban deconstructs Muir's sublime language as misleading, even subversive, the origin of today's "cult of 'pristine' wilderness".) Muir's charismatic personality aided his evangelism in the cause that wilderness must be preserved: Teddy Roosevelt became an important supporter after going on a journey with him. But it was Muir's prose, perhaps overegged, and his evocations of the Sierra that made his case and gave us the national parks as well as his shelf of distinguished books.

From his first glimpse of Yosemite, as he reminisced in *The Yosemite* (1912), his vision was apparent.

> Looking eastward from the summit of the Pacheco Pass one shining morning, a landscape was displayed that after all my wanderings still appears as the most beautiful I have ever beheld. At my feet lay the Great Central Valley of California, level and flowery, like a lake of pure sunshine, forty or fifty miles wide, five hundred miles long, one rich furred garden of yellow compositae. And from the eastern boundary of this vast golden flower-bed rose the mighty Sierra, miles in height and so gloriously coloured and so radiant, it seemed not clothed with light, but wholly composed of it, like the wall of some celestial city. Along the top and extending a good way down, was a rich pearl-grey belt of snow; below it a belt of blue and dark purple, marking the extension of the forests; and stretching along the base of the range a broad belt of rose-purple; all these colours, from the blue sky to the yellow valley smoothly blending as they do in a rainbow, making a wall of light ineffably fine. Then it seemed to me that

the Sierra should be called, not the Nevada, or Snowy Range, but the Range of Light. And after ten years of wandering and wondering in the heart of it, rejoicing in its glorious floods of light, the white beams of the morning streaming through the passes, the noonday radiance on the crystal rocks, the flush of the alpenglow, and the irised spray of countless waterfalls, it still seems above all others the Range of Light.

Peter Matthiessen: "All the Way to Heaven Is Heaven"

PETER MATTHIESSEN (BORN 1927) is a happy combination of fine writer, courageous traveller, scrupulous naturalist, and spiritual soul — he has his own Buddhist dojo at his home on Long Island. A committed walker, he has travelled and written about Asia, New Guinea, Africa, and Antarctica. His *The Snow Leopard* is one of the great accounts of someone "paying respects to a mountain". Toward the end of the book, suffused with the spirit of the trip, exhausted but uplifted, Matthiessen writes: "I lower my gaze from the snow peaks to the glistening thorns, the snow patches, the lichens. Though I am blind to it, the Truth is near, in the reality of what I sit on — rocks. These hard rocks instruct my bones in what my brain could never grasp in the Heart Sutra, that 'form is emptiness and emptiness is form' — the Void, the emptiness of blue-black space, contained in everything. Sometimes when I meditate, the big rocks dance."

This is also an example of someone solving philosophical problems by walking, a deeply felt, subtly written, and arduously tramped-out account of Matthiessen's search for the elusive snow leopard of the Himalayas — in essence a search for his own peace of mind.

"In late September of 1973," he explains at the beginning, "I set out with GS [George Schaller] on a journey to the Crystal Mountain, walking west under Annapurna and north along the Kali Gandaki River, then west and north again, around the Dhaulagiri peaks and across the Kanjiroba, two hundred and fifty miles or more to the Land of Dolpo, on the Tibetan Plateau."

The snow leopard, the "most beautiful of the great cats," had been sighted by only two Westerners in the previous twenty-five years. To get a glimpse of one of these "near-mythic" beasts was the formal reason for the trip, but in effect this is Matthiessen's pilgrimage: a search for healing after the death of his wife, a search for the sources of Buddhism, and a contemplation of a landscape regarded as holy by the Nepalese who live in the region. If there is a journey that is the opposite of the expensive, breathless guided climbs up Everest that Jon Krakauer writes about, it is this book, which has much more in common with Bashō, whom Matthiessen quotes with approval.

In ten- and eleven-hour treks, Matthiessen and Schaller rise higher and higher into the mountains, suffering from the cold and the altitude and the difficult trail, creeping on narrow traverses above deep and precipitous valleys. Such obstacles are inevitable, as Matthiessen writes: "Tibetans say that obstacles in a hard journey, such as hailstones, wind, and unrelenting rains, are the work of demons, anxious to test the sincerity of the pilgrims and eliminate the fainthearted among them."

One of the more terrifying obstacles — this, at eleven thousand feet — are the fierce guard dogs of the Tibetan refugees who inhabit their heights. "In Tibet, where wolves and brigands prosper, the nomad's camps and remote villages are guarded by big black or brindle mastiffs. Such dogs are also found in northern Nepal." Matthiessen successfully fights off an attack by a slavering mastiff and pushes on.

The book is a self-portrait of Matthiessen the pilgrim, but also a portrait of George Schaller, a scientist, sceptic, and part-time misanthrope whom Matthiessen takes pains to enlighten. He teaches him the tenets of Zen Buddhism, and then "I tell GS of the Christian mystics such as Meister Eckhardt and Saint Francis, Saint Augustine, and Saint Catherine of Siena, who spent three years in silent meditation: 'All the way to Heaven is Heaven,' Saint Catherine said, and that is the very breath of Zen, which does not elevate divinity above the common miracles of every day."

In a treacherous part of the mountains he reflects on the possibility of dying in this dangerous place — and he accepts the idea: "Between clinging and letting go, I feel a terrific struggle. This is a fine chance to let go, to 'win my life by losing it', which means not recklessness but acceptance, not passivity but non-attachment."

Toward the end of the journey, the snow leopard unglimpsed yet still inspiring his pilgrimage, missing his family and friends, Matthiessen receives a batch of mail from home. Wishing to be at one with the landscape and people around him, he deliberately does not open them; he puts them in his pack, to be opened when this journey is over. If the news is bad, he says, there is nothing he can do to leave any earlier from this remote place. "And good news, too, would be intrusive, spoiling this chance to live moment by moment in the present by stirring up the past, the future, and encouraging delusions of continuity and permanence just when I am trying to let go, to blow away, like that white down feather on the mountain."

In our present overconnected, hyperactive age, this is a salutary book and worthy of its predecessors: Bashō, Wordsworth, Thoreau.

ᔐᗯ 14 ᗯᔐ
Travel Feats

SPEAKING OF "THE WINTER JOURNEY" — SIX weeks of complete darkness and low temperatures (minus 79°F) and gale-force winds — an experience of which gave him the title for his book *The Worst Journey in the World,* Apsley Cherry-Garrard reflected on dangerous feats in travel. "Why do some human beings desire with such urgency to do such things regardless of the consequences, voluntarily, conscripted by no one but themselves? No one knows. There is a strong urge to conquer the dreadful forces of nature, and perhaps to get consciousness of ourselves, of life, and of the shadowy workings of our human minds. Physical capacity is the only limit. I have tried to tell how, and when, and where. But why? That is a mystery."

Maybe there is an answer. When I was preparing to write the introduction to the American edition of *Alone*, Gérard d'Aboville's account of
his single-handed journey rowing across the Pacific, I pressed d'Aboville
on his reasons for making this dangerous voyage. He became silent. After
a long while he said, "Only an animal does useful things. An animal gets
food, finds a place to sleep, tries to keep comfortable. But I wanted to
do something that was not useful — not like an animal at all. Something
only a human being would do."

What separates some feats from others is the way the tale is told. Sir
Richard Burton's book about how he, an infidel, travelled to Mecca in
disguise is a classic. After Joshua Slocum sailed around the world alone,
he wrote a good book about the experience; so did Tschiffely, in *Tschiffely's Ride*, the story of his trip on horseback from Argentina to New
York. Breaking out of a POW camp in Kenya and climbing Mount Kenya
would have been a hilarious anecdote, but Felice Benuzzi wrote a detailed account of the feat, and so did Gérard D'Aboville after he rowed
across the Pacific Ocean.

Now and then a great feat is forced upon the traveller, as with Captain Bligh's open-boat voyage of 4,000 miles with eighteen men after
the mutiny on the *Bounty*, or Shackleton's heroic rescue of his men,
which necessitated his travelling almost a thousand miles through the
Southern Ocean in a freezing lifeboat. But these epics of survival were
unintentional.

There are many other notable travel feats: a man windsurfed across
the Atlantic (M. Christian Marty, in February 1982); a woman windsurfed across the Indian Ocean (Raphaëla le Gouvello, sixty days in
2006, 3,900 miles, from Exmouth in Western Australia to the island
of Réunion); a man skied down Everest in 2000 (the Slovenian Davo
Karničar), and a woman did it in 2006 — Kit DesLauriers, who has
also skied down the highest peaks on every continent, including Antarctica. Kayakers have gone everywhere, across oceans, around Cape
Horn, and made ambitious circumnavigations (Japan, Australia, New
Zealand). Some of these are admirable, even heroic journeys, and some
are stunts; I am mainly interested in travel feats that have resulted in
memorable books.

A Disguised Infidel Penetrates Mecca

IN HIS *Personal Narrative of a Pilgrimage to Al-Madinah and Meccah* (1855–56), Sir Richard Burton claimed he was "the only living European who has found his way to the Head Quarters of the Moslem Faith".

He did it for a reason common to travellers setting off: he was, among other things, "thoroughly tired of 'progress' and of 'civilization'; curious to see with my eyes what others are content to 'hear with ears', namely Moslem inner life in a really Mohammedan country; and longing, if truth be told, to set foot on that mysterious spot which no vacation tourist has yet described, measured, sketched and photographed".

As with his long trips through Africa and the American West, Burton was happiest when he was in a remote place. "Believe me, when once your tastes have conformed to the tranquillity of [desert] travel, you will suffer real pain in returning to the turmoil of civilization. The air of the cities will suffocate you, and the care-worn and cadaverous countenances of citizens will haunt you like a vision of judgement."

The trip, Burton says, took nine months, but in reality it took much longer, because he needed to be fluent in Arabic, knowledgeable in all aspects of Islam, and well versed in the Koran. This had taken years, while he had been a soldier in India from 1842 to 1849. He also needed to be circumcised. This he accomplished, probably in India, before the trip, when he was about thirty. He said that "external" physical evidence that he was a Muslim was essential.

One of the pleasures of the book is that Burton delights in his disguise, as the Afghan dervish Mirza Abdullah. "Little did he suspect who his interrogator was," he remarks of a slave dealer. And he flirts with a pretty slave girl, telling her how beautiful she is. ("They were average specimens of the steatopygous Abyssinian breed, broad-shouldered, thin-flanked, fine-limbed, and with haunches of prodigious size.")

She says, "Then why don't you buy me?"

So as to make himself seem a humble haji (pilgrim), Burton travels in the lowest class on the ship, quietly mocking his fellow passengers. Though he speaks of the rigours of the trip, the discomforts and the heat, he seldom complains. He is on a mission. Three months after he sets out, in the month of July ("sickening heat"), he arrives in Medina and visits the Prophet's tomb.

He moves on to Mecca with the other pilgrims, and achieves the objective of the trip, pretending to pray while examining the enormous stone known as the Kaaba, the heart and soul of Islam, forbidden to the unbeliever.

> I may truly say that, of all the worshippers who clung weeping to the curtain, or who pressed their beating hearts to the stone, none felt for the moment a deeper emotion than did the Haji from the far-north. It was as if the poetical legends of the Arab spoke truth, and that the waving wings of angels, not the sweet breeze of morning, were agitating and swelling the black covering of the shrine. But, to confess humbling truth, theirs was the high feeling of religious enthusiasm, mine was the ecstasy of gratified pride.

Being Burton, though, another ecstatic experience is his glimpse of a flirtatious pilgrim, a girl he calls Flirtilla.

> Close to us sat a party of fair Meccans, apparently belonging to the higher classes, and one of these I had already several times remarked. She was a tall girl, about eighteen years old, with regular features, a skin somewhat citrine-coloured, but soft and clear, symmetrical eyebrows, the most beautiful eyes, and a figure all grace. There was no head thrown back, no straightened neck, no flat shoulders, nor toes turned out — in fact, no "elegant" barbarisms: the shape was what the Arabs love, soft, bending, and relaxed, as a woman's figure ought to be. Unhappily she wore, instead of the usual veil, a "Yashmak" of transparent muslin, bound round the face; and the chaperone, mother, or duenna, by whose side she stood, was apparently a very unsuspicious or complaisant old person. Flirtilla fixed a glance of admiration upon my cashmere. I directed a reply with interest at her eyes. She then by the usual coquettish gesture, threw back an inch or two of head-veil, disclosing broad bands of jetty hair, crowning a lovely oval. My palpable admiration of the new charm was rewarded by a partial removal of the Yashmak, when a dimpled mouth and a rounded chin stood out from the envious muslin. Seeing that my

companions were safely employed, I entered upon the dangerous ground of raising hand to forehead. She smiled almost imperceptibly, and turned away. The pilgrim was in ecstasy.

No non-Muslim since Burton has made the pilgrimage to Mecca and lived to tell the tale.

Sailing Alone Around the World

JOSHUA SLOCUM DECIDED to be the first man to sail single-handedly around the world. He was an experienced sailor — and restless from the time of his youth in Canada, where he had been an inveterate runaway. He found an old thirty-seven-foot sloop, rebuilt and refitted her, named her *Spray*, and left in 1895 on his voyage, without a chronometer but using dead reckoning. The trip, which took three years and covered forty-six thousand miles, was full of incident, and Slocum's account of the voyage, *Sailing Alone Around the World* (1899), is a well-told book — vivid, detailed, and very funny, right from the beginning, where he says, "I was born in a cold spot, on coldest North Mountain, on a cold February 20, though I am a citizen of the United States — a naturalized Yankee."

Slocum, self-educated, wrote that "my books were always my friends" — in his library he had Darwin, Twain's *Life on the Mississippi*, *Don Quixote*, R. L. Stevenson, and Shakespeare. His book made him famous, and he continued voyaging, as well as lecturing about his exploits. He also spent forty-two days in jail on a charge of molestation (see Chapter 8, "Fears, Neuroses, and Other Mental Conditions"). In the fall of 1909, he left Martha's Vineyard, intending to sail the *Spray* to the Amazon. Nothing was heard from him after that — he was lost at sea, presumed to have been sunk after having been hit by a steamer, though he (as always using his self-steering device) was snug in his cabin, reading a book, his normal practice when sailing.

In *The Cruise of the Snark* (1911), which was inspired by Slocum's voyage, Jack London wrote:

Joshua Slocum sailed around the world a few years ago in a thirty-seven-foot boat all by himself. I shall never forget, in his narrative of the voyage, where he heartily indorsed the idea of young men, in similar small boats, making similar voyage. I promptly indorsed his idea, and so heartily that I took my wife along. While it certainly makes a Cook's tour look like thirty cents, on top of that, and on top of the fun and pleasure, it is a splendid education for a young man — oh, not a mere education in the things of the world outside, of lands, and peoples, and climates, but an education in the world inside, an education in one's self, a chance to learn one's own self, to get on speaking terms with one's soul.

No Picnic on Mount Kenya

THE UNUSUAL ITINERARY in this book clearly illustrates one of the principal motives in travel: the wish to escape from boring, nagging, pestiferous people. That wish can inspire long journeys and ambitious travel feats.

In 1943, Felice Benuzzi (1910–1988) was bored and irritated with confinement and his annoying fellow Italians in a British prisoner of war camp outside the town of Nanyuki in Kenya. He was surrounded by "every kind of person . . . old and young, sick and healthy, crazy and sensible". He says that the lunacies and achievements of the other prisoners could fill a book, and he proves this with examples. But his mind was on other things. From behind the barbed wire of the camp Benuzzi had a view of majestic Mount Kenya: "An ethereal mountain emerging from a tossing sea of clouds framed between two dark barracks — a massive blue-black tooth of sheer rock inlaid with azure glaciers, austere, yet floating fairy-like on the near horizon. It was the first 17,000-foot peak I had ever seen."

A junior colonial officer in Italian-controlled Ethiopia, he had been captured by British soldiers along with thousands of other Italians and imprisoned in the British colony of Kenya. (Benuzzi does not mention that other Italian prisoners, as forced labourers, helped build the western road out of Nairobi that traverses the Great Rift Valley, as well as a lovely chapel in one of the bends in the road.)

More than a year of imprisonment passed before he was able to choose two fellow prisoners, Giuan and Enzo, for his team. With great ingenuity they made ice-climbing equipment (crampons, axes) out of scrap metal, and they stockpiled warm clothes and food. "Life [in prison] took on another rhythm because it had a purpose." With a copied key and an attitude, they bamboozled the camp guards and broke out, leaving a letter behind for the prison authorities stating their intention and apologizing for the bother they might be causing.

Their climb took them through the lairs of leopards and lions, through dense bamboo forests and fields of lobelia. Enzo was ill; rations were often short; the cold and the necessity to avoid detection were also problems. Yet given the circumstances, they were equipped for the assault on the summit. Without a map, they used their judgement and experience of other climbs. They struggled upward, at times in deep snow, blazing their own trail. On one of their climbs they were in the snow and cold for eighteen hours. Although they were defeated in their attempt to reach Batian, the highest peak, they summited Point Lenana, 16,300 feet, where they left an Italian flag that was later found.

After their arduous climb they descended the mountain, returned to the prison camp, and surrendered. The punishment for escaping was twenty-eight days in solitary confinement, but the British camp commandant, saying he "appreciated our sporting effort", gave them seven days.

Yes, a sporting effort. But it was something else — a disgust with confinement and a wish, as herded-together prisoners, to reclaim their humanity. "Forced to endure the milieu [of the camp]," Benuzzi says early in the book, "we seemed almost afraid of losing our individuality." Thus Benuzzi and his comrades saw a kind of salvation in the climb, as many people see liberation in travel and the triumph of the will in a singular travel feat.

After the war, Benuzzi wrote his book, *Fuga sul Kenya: 17 Giorni di Libertà*, which was translated under the less-than-gripping title *No Picnic on Mount Kenya* (1952).

Benuzzi's experience parallels that of the German Heinrich Harrer, who was captured in India in 1939 when he was on his way to climb Nanga Parbat. Harrer was interned near Dehra Dun, in sight of the Himalayan foothills, the heights of which (as in the case of Benuzzi's glimpse

of Mount Kenya) inspired him to escape. After repeated attempts he succeeded, in 1944, making his way to Tibet, a tale he recounted in *Seven Years in Tibet* (1953).

Rowing Across the Pacific

GÉRARD D'ABOVILLE ROWED a twenty-five-foot boat from Japan to Oregon in 1991 and wrote about it in *Alone.* He had previously rowed a boat
across the Atlantic ten years earlier, from Cape Cod to Brittany. This had
been done before, but no one had succeeded in rowing across the Pacific
alone. He set out late in the season and was pummelled by heavy weather,
tumultuous storms, and forty-six-foot waves. There are no islands in the
North Pacific. A Russian freighter offered to rescue him. "I was not even
tempted," d'Aboville says. But he repeatedly overturned in the high waves
and nearly drowned on his final approach to the coast of Oregon.

After he completed his journey he quietly returned to teaching survival skills in his Outward Bound school in Brittany.

Riding a Horse from Buenos Aires to New York City

AIMÉ TSCHIFFELY (1895–1954), a Swiss, rode ten thousand miles by
horseback to New York. He had two horses, Mancha and Gato, and it
took him three years, from 1925 to 1928. He crossed the Andes, the
Darien Gap, and the length of Mexico, but not until he got to the United
States did he have a serious problem: he barely survived being deliberately sideswiped by a lunatic motorist. The whole story is told in his
best-selling book, *Tschiffely's Ride* (1933).

Swimming the Panama Canal

RICHARD HALLIBURTON (1900–1939) described his swimming the Panama Canal in his second book of travel, *New Worlds to Conquer* (1929). He
had swum the Hellespont in his first book, *The Royal Road to Romance*
(1925). He specialized in travel feats — the first documented winter as-
cent of Mount Fuji, sneaking into the Taj Mahal at night and bathing in

the tank by moonlight, and other efforts — some actual feats, some silly stunts. In *Seven League Boots* (1935) he travelled through Arabia and Ethiopia, where he met and dined with Emperor Haile Selassie. He has been described as a tormented homosexual and an imaginative traveller and thinker. In his last effort, attempting to cross the Pacific in a Chinese junk, the *Sea Dragon*, he was lost at sea and declared dead some months later.

His exuberant books, his purple prose, inspired a generation of youngsters to become travellers. In *The Royal Road to Romance* he wrote, "Youth — nothing else worth having in the world . . . and I had youth, the transitory, the fugitive, now, completely and abundantly. Yet what was I going to do with it? Certainly not squander its gold on the commonplace quest for riches and respectability, and then secretly lament the price that had to be paid for these futile ideals. Let those who wish have their respectability — I wanted freedom, freedom to indulge in whatever caprice struck my fancy, freedom to search in the farthermost corners of the earth for the beautiful, the joyous and the romantic."

Circling the Poles

BETWEEN 1979 AND 1982, Sir Ranulph Twisleton-Wykeham-Fiennes (aka Ran Fiennes) travelled fifty-two thousand miles around the world on a polar axis, the Transglobe Expedition, with a partner, Charles Burton; the trip was mostly over land. Fiennes also attempted a solo expedition to the North Pole, but crashed through the ice and took his frostbitten self away, abandoning the Arctic. Other Fiennes feats: by hovercraft up the Nile, discovering the lost city of Ubar in Oman, and running seven marathons in seven days, after undergoing double bypass heart surgery. His memoir *Living Dangerously* (1987) is highly hubristic but a readable account of his exploits.

The Ultimate Everest Experience

GÖRAN KROPP (1966–2002) biked seven thousand miles from Stockholm to Nepal (via Turkey, Iran, and Afghanistan) and then climbed Everest, making an unsuccessful assault (without oxygen) and finally a

THE TAO OF TRAVEL

successful summiting (at the same time as the *Into Thin Air* disaster, described by Jon Krakauer; see Chapter 10, "Travel as an Ordeal"). Afterward Kropp biked back to Sweden, being assaulted on the way by xenophobes and stone-throwing people. All the details are in his account of the trip, *Ultimate High: My Everest Odyssey* (1997). Kropp died from a fall while rock climbing in Washington in 2002.

Walking from Cape Town to Cairo

EWART GROGAN TREKKED from Cape Town to Beira, Mozambique, in 1898, and continued from Beira north through Nyasaland, Tanganyika, Uganda, and Sudan, and reached Cairo in early 1900. His account of the journey is *From the Cape to Cairo: The First Traverse of Africa from South to North* (1900). He was said to have done this in order to impress the father of Gertrude Coleman-Watt with his manliness and determination. He later married her.

Walking Around the World

FFYONA CAMPBELL (BORN 1967), restless, despised by her father, needing approval, feeling rejected, walked the length of Britain from John o' Groats to Land's End at the age of sixteen. She followed this up by walking across the United States, coast to coast, becoming pregnant on the way by a member of her backup team; before getting an abortion in New Mexico, she accepted lifts and lied about that to the press. Later she came clean. She also walked across Australia, and through Africa, Cape Town to Tangiers. An amazing, contrary, opinionated, and admirable woman, Campbell recounted her experiences in three books: *The Whole Story*, *On Foot Through Africa*, and *Feet of Clay*. She recently described herself (in *Outside* magazine) as "a retired pedestrian".

Youngest to Sail Around the World Nonstop

PERHAPS THE FUTURE of the travel book is the travel blog, with all its elisions, colloquial tropes, and chatty stream of consciousness. It is obvious from the circumnavigation of the Australian Jessica Watson that the great advantage of the travel blog — especially one reporting a feat-in-progress — is the way in which anyone with a computer can be in touch. The highs and lows of such a trip can be experienced and shared by the world in real time. What this trip demonstrated was the exuberance, resilience, and modesty of this sixteen-year-old sailor and her successful voyage.

Jessica Watson (born 1993) is the youngest person to have sailed nonstop, alone, and unassisted around the world. She left Sydney, Australia, on October 18, 2009, on *Ella's Pink Lady*, a thirty-four-foot sailboat, and arrived back on May 15, 2010. Had her trip taken four more days, she would have turned seventeen.

The 24,000-mile trip was very difficult and eventful — six knockdowns (the mast underwater), towering seas (35-foot waves), 70-knot winds, engine failure, torn sails, and occasionally dampened spirits. But Jessica was never out of touch, posting messages most days, and after each of the blog entries she usually received well over a thousand replies from well-wishers. The followers of her blog grew dramatically as she neared her home port. She posted videos, updates, photos, and news; her website even sold merchandise (caps, posters, etc.) online to fund her trip. In the manner of blogging, her circumnavigation had an interactive element, as she chatted back and forth with the people monitoring her progress.

The tone of her blog is so sunny, it is obvious that such a difficult feat can best be achieved by someone with a positive frame of mind, reminding me that difficult travel is essentially a mental challenge.

Here is Jessica, halfway through her trip, in January 2010: "The picture below is of my very cool new t-shirt which was a present from Mum in my latest food bag. I had to share it with you guys as my crew aren't doing a very good job of sharing my excitement!" And the accompanying photo shows her wearing a T-shirt with the message "One Tough Cookie".

On her arrival home, she was greeted by tens of thousands of people, including the prime minister, who called her a hero. Likable to the last, she disagreed, saying she wasn't a hero, "just an ordinary girl who had a dream and worked hard at it and proved that anything is possible".

15

Staying Home

THE NON-TRAVELLER SEEMS TO ME TO EXIST in suspended animation, if not the living death of a homely routine or the vegetative stupor known to the couch potato. From an early age I longed to leave home and to keep going. I cannot imagine not travelling — stuck home all the time, in the confinement of a house or a community or a city. ¶ Yet some people never leave — distinguished writers and thinkers, chained to their desks, their towns, making a virtue of it. In his entire eighty-year life, Immanuel Kant never travelled more than a hundred miles from his birthplace, Königsberg (now Kaliningrad), where he died. Philip Larkin, who hardly stirred from his home in Hull on England's Humber estuary, said, "I wouldn't mind seeing China if I could come back home the same day." Needless to say, he lived for much of his life with his mother.

Thomas Merton, who travelled widely in his early life, entered a Trappist monastery at the age of twenty-six, and for the next twenty-seven years seldom uttered an audible word, having taken a vow of silence. He did not leave his monastery in Kentucky until 1968. Invited to a conference in Bangkok, on this first encounter with the wider world after all those years of seclusion, he accidentally electrocuted himself in his hotel room. Edgar Allan Poe spent a few youthful years in Britain. Thoreau never left the United States. Emily Dickinson was more or less housebound. Yet all these people wrote brilliantly of other lands. Something about staying home, staying inside, or going in circles can stimulate a mind in the manner of conventional travel.

In fiction, the character with the most convincing philosophical objection to travel is the decadent Duc Jean Floressas des Esseintes, in Huysmans's *Against Nature* (1884). He makes an elaborate plan for a trip to London, but overcome with sloth, satiated (and "somewhat stupefied") with the Dickensian atmosphere of the English-style pub in Paris, he reflects on the tedium of the Channel crossing and decides to stay put: "After all, what was the good of moving, when a fellow could travel so magnificently sitting in a chair? Wasn't he already in London, whose smells, weather, citizenry, and even cutlery, were all about him? What could he expect to find over there, save fresh disappointments?"

Henry Fielding's Voyage to Lisbon

FIELDING, LOOKING FOR a rest cure and a mild climate, sets out from London for Lisbon toward the end of June 1754; and after hundreds of pages, toward the end of July, he is still off the coast of England, becalmed. In the delay and idleness he grows irritable and confides his irritation to his journal. He called himself a "great, tattered bard", and was highly sceptical of "voyage-writers", as he explains in his long preface to the published *Journal*.

This seems a superb Fielding farce, the absurdity of setting out and going nowhere — he'll never make it! Much of the book is satirical, ironic, blustering, and his ailments so numerous and debilitating, it is like self-satire, or at least comic exaggeration. Only forty-seven, he is plagued by "lingering imperfect gout . . . [and] besides being lame, I was very ill with the great fatigues I had lately undergone, added to my distemper . . . my health was now reduced to the last extremity . . . I went into the country [Bath] in a very weak and deplorable condition, with no fewer or less diseases than a jaundice, a dropsy [oedema], and an asthma, altogether uniting their forces in the destruction of a body so entirely emaciated, that it had lost all muscular flesh . . . I was now, in the opinion of all men, dying of a complication of disorders."

Still in England, he recovers with a regimen of tar-water treatments and then, with "the first dawnings of my recovery I had conceived of removing to a warmer climate". He rejects Avignon and decides on Lisbon for convalescence, leaving home in a lugubrious frame of mind. "On this day, the most melancholy sun I had ever beheld arose, and found me awake at my house at Fordhook. By the light of this sun, I was, in my own opinion, last to behold and take leave of some of those creatures on whom I doated with a mother-like fondness."

His book is a chronicle of delay and frustration. It's true that Fielding ultimately arrives in Lisbon, but the greater part of the voyage is spent at various anchorages and moorings on the English coast, the winds too light to bear the ship away, so Fielding and his party go ashore and stay in public houses and inns to pass the time. The contentious and tyrannical captain cruises back and forth from Ryde to Portland to Spithead, awaiting a favourable wind and complaining.

"The captain now grew outrageous, and declaring open war with the wind, took a resolution, rather more bold than wise, of sailing in defiance of it, and in its teeth." This tactic fails; they are soon back on the English coast. Fielding fills his journal with reflections on eating, on the difference between seamen and landlubbers, on tyranny and officialdom, on his quarrels with the captain and the customs officers, on mythology. He writes that if his disquisitions can serve as a remedy for "the most inveterate evils at least, I have obtained my whole desire, and shall have lain so long wind-bound in the ports of this kingdom to some purpose".

Never less than adversarial, the captain believes that he is "under the spell of witchcraft" and spends less and less time on his ship, going ashore or to other ships to socialize, as Fielding — fading again — is attended by doctors.

Toward the end of July, the wind picks up and proves helpful, and a full month after setting off, Fielding is at last on his way, at sea. The rest of the voyage is brisk. Next day they are "thirty miles to the westward of Plymouth", and the day after in the Bay of Biscay, and becalmed, then in a gale: "Our voyage was retarded." Several days after the gale they are off the Portuguese coast and soon at Lisbon. The actual voyage is so abbreviated as to seem an anti-climax: "About seven in the evening I got into a chaise on shore, and was driven through the nastiest city in the world, tho' at the same time one of the most populous, to a kind of coffee-house, which is very pleasantly situated on the brow of a hill, about a mile from the city, and hath a very fine prospect of the river Tajo from Lisbon to the sea."

He hoped to regain his health in Lisbon, but the last lines of the *Journal* are ominous, and seem like a premonition of his own death. Horace: "This is the end of the story, and the journey" (*hic Finis chartaeque, viaeque*).

Fielding died in Lisbon a little over two months after arriving, in October 1754. The book was published posthumously in 1755.

Xavier de Maistre: Travelling Around His Room

A JOURNEY ROUND My Room is one of the curiosities of travel literature. De Maistre (1763–1852), born in Savoy, peripatetic as a soldier and landscape painter, ended his life as a naturalized Russian subject. Arrested in Italy while serving in the Austro-Russian army, he was put under house arrest in Turin for forty-two days, where he wrote this book of forty-two chapters. He hadn't planned to publish it, but when his brother Joseph, a political philosopher, read it, he persuaded Xavier to do so, and the book appeared in 1794. It has been described as "a delightful chat with the reader, filled with delicate observations, in which an artless grace, humour, and spontaneous wit are wedded to a gentle and somewhat dreamy philosophy". In fact, it is parody, self-mockery, and willfully eccentric, a deliberate attempt to stave off the boredom of confinement, calling this a "new mode of travelling I introduce into the world". Hyperbolic (one chapter describes "Latitude and Topography"), it is also a disquisition on the meaning of ordinary things.

"The voyages of Cook and the observations of his fellow-travellers . . . are nothing compared with my adventures in this one district." He anatomizes the pictures on the walls, his furniture, his bed: "A bed sees us born and sees us die. It is the ever changing scene upon which the human race play by turns interesting dramas, laughable farces, and fearful tragedies. It is a cradle decked with flowers. A throne of love. A sepulchre".

Kamo-no-Chōmei: Recluse in a Remote and Tiny Hut

THE TEN FOOT Square Hut, a brief account of the withdrawal of a man from public life to a tiny hut, where he ended his days, is often compared with Thoreau's *Walden*. The work is attributed to Kamo-no-Chōmei, a twelfth-century Japanese aristocrat who, disappointed at being passed over for the post of warden of the shrine of Kamo in Kyoto, simply retreated, rusticating himself to the mountains, living alone, "a friend of the moon and the wind".

He was in his fifties when he forsook the world, first for a hut near Mount Hiei, and after five years he moved into greater seclusion in Hino, near Tokyo, for a hut that was hardly ten feet square and seven feet high. Like Thoreau, he describes his simple furnishings (baskets, a brazier, his straw mat, his desk). It is the ultimate in simplicity. Altogether he was a recluse for eight years, and his writing shows the effects of his retreat and renunciation and his non-attachment, achieving a Buddhist ideal. Calmly, he lists the catastrophes of all sorts — acts of God, acts of man — that have befallen Japan. And he sums up his existence in the tiny hut: "Since I forsook the world and broke off all its ties, I have felt neither fear nor resentment. I commit my life to fate without special wish to live or desire to die. Like a drifting cloud I rely on none and have no attachments. My only luxury is a sound sleep and all I look forward to is the beauty of the changing seasons."

Thoreau: Home Is the Heavenly Way

HENRY DAVID THOREAU was so emotionally attached to his home in Concord that he found it almost impossible to leave. In fact, after 1837 he did so only for short periods — thirteen days on the Concord and Merrimack rivers, some visits to Cape Cod, three trips to the Maine woods, brief spells in Staten Island and Minnesota. He was never alone on these excursions; he always went with a friend or relative. Although he philosophized constantly about travel (he was widely read in the travel books of his time), he is a much better example of someone who really didn't go anywhere. The Maine trip was a team effort, and Thoreau was a follower. *A Yankee in Canada* is about a one-week train trip with several hundred tourists, what we would call a package tour today. He made no bones about not being a traveller. He boasted of staying home; indeed, he made a virtue of it: "Live at home like a traveller." Homesick on Staten Island, he wrote, "My thoughts revert to those dear hills . . . Others may say, 'Are there not the cities of Asia?' But what are they? Staying at home is the heavenly way" (letter to Ralph Waldo Emerson).

Travel in your head, Thoreau preached in *Walden*: "Be a Columbus to whole new continents and worlds within you, opening new channels, not of trade but of thought." He went on to say that it is "easier to sail many thousand miles through cold and storm and cannibals . . . than it is to explore the private sea, the Atlantic and Pacific Ocean of one's being alone."

A frequent hyperbolic flourish in a Thoreau book or essay is his comparing an aspect of his neighbourhood with an exotic place. And these deflations are often paradoxes. Why leave Concord when, as he wrote in a poem,

> Our village shows a rural Venice,
> Its broad lagoons where yonder fen is;
> As lovely as the Bay of Naples
> Yon placid cove amid the maples;
> And in my neighbour's field of corn
> I recognize the Golden Horn.

In 1853, as the explorer Paul Du Chaillu (whom Thoreau would later read) is preparing to return to Equatorial Africa, Thoreau is confiding to his journal, "I cannot but regard it as a kindness in those who have the steering of me — that by the want of pecuniary wealth I have been nailed down to this my native region so long & steadily — and made to love and study this spot of earth more and more — What would signify in comparison a thin and diffused love and knowledge of the whole earth instead, got by wandering? — The traveller's is but a barren and comfortless condition."

Though his friend and literary mentor Emerson went to England in search of inspiration, and other contemporaries travelled around the globe — Hawthorne to England, Washington Irving to Spain, Melville to the Pacific — Thoreau was not impressed. The reports of such peregrinations roused him to be defiant and sometimes condescending. He was self-consciously a contrarian. He cultivated his eccentricity and talked it up in his writing, but his personality was a great deal stranger than he knew, and perhaps beyond cultivation.

Thoreau's three Maine trips from 1846 to 1857 overlap the publication of Melville's greatest works. There is no proof that Thoreau read *Moby-Dick*, but there is ample evidence that he read *Typee*, which appeared at the time of his first visit to Maine, and which he discussed in a discarded early version of "Ktaadn". Somewhat combative in comparing wildernesses, Thoreau argued that he experienced deeper wilderness in Maine than Melville had as a castaway in the high volcanic archipelago of the remote Marquesas, among the lovely maiden Fayaway and the anthropophagous islanders. It seems a stretch, but there it is.

Emily Dickinson: The Argument for Staying Home

"To SHUT OUR eyes is Travel," Emily Dickinson wrote to a Mrs. Holland in 1870. By then, at age forty, she had been housebound for almost ten years, and she had another fifteen reclusive years to live. She had begun her studies at Mount Holyoke College, in South Hadley, about ten miles from Amherst, but lasted only a year and, homesick, returned to the family house.

Agoraphobic? Probably not. She made a trip to Boston in 1865, without the fantods, but after that she did not set foot out of the house. Was she lovesick? "Neurasthenic"? One of her recent biographers suggests that Emily might have been epileptic: some of her family suffered from seizures, and she apparently took a drug that was then regarded as efficacious for epilepsy. But Edward Lear, an exact contemporary, was epileptic and a wide traveller — Corsica, Egypt, the Middle East, and India. Like Dickinson, Lear was a loner, craving solitude, because the affliction was regarded as shameful; perhaps that is the key.

Like many other shut-ins, Dickinson made a virtue of her confinement, and denigrated travel in both her poetry and her letters, extolled the joy of being home, and was prolific as a letter writer and a poet — almost two thousand poems. A mere dozen were published in her lifetime, but anonymously.

Like Thoreau, she placed a high value on simplicity and austerity, even deprivation. Also like Thoreau, she was a passionate reader — of novels, poems, essays: Dickens, Emerson, De Quincey, George Eliot, Thoreau's *Walden*. Her library survives, with all her scratchings on the pages. The English critic Michael Meyer shrewdly wrote, in *Thinking and Writing About Literature*, "She simplified her life so that doing without was a means of being within. In a sense, she redefined the meaning of deprivation, because being denied something — whether it was faith, love, literary recognition, or some other desire — provided a sharper, more intense understanding than she would have experienced had she achieved what she wanted."

Consider this poem:

> Water is taught by thirst.
> Land — by the Oceans passed.
> Transport — by throe —
> Peace — by its battles told —
> Love — by Memorial Mold —
> Birds, by the snow.

The intensity of vision comes from meditation and expectation, by "throe" — a pang. This view of existence borders on the mystical. Denial, fantasy, imagination, eager anticipation, expectation, all these mattered more to her than the thing itself. Another of her denial poems contains the line "sumptuous Destitution".

She does not say: Stay home and the world seems wonderful. "Home is a holy thing — nothing of doubt or distrust can enter its blessed portals," she wrote in an 1851 letter to her brother. And "Duty is black and brown — home is bright and shining." And again, home "is brighter than all the world beside".

❧ Travel Wisdom of ❧
FREYA STARK

English by nationality but born in Italy (in 1893), where she died a hundred years later, Freya Stark was conflicted by nature, though good-humoured and appreciative in her travel. An accomplished linguist and a wonderful descriptive writer, she travelled throughout the Middle East, Turkey, and Arabia. Her books include *The Valleys of the Assassins* (1934), *The Southern Gates of Arabia* (1936), and *A Winter in Arabia* (1940). She wrote, "I have met charming people, lots who would be charming if they hadn't got a complex about the British and everyone has pleasant and cheerful manners and I like most of the American voices. On the other hand I don't believe they have any God and their hats are frightful. On balance I prefer the Arabs." Stark herself was famous for her hats, which she wore to cover a disfigurement of scalp and ear, resulting from a painful accident in childhood. ¶ She was one of the singular discoverers (and photographers) of traditional cultures and old ways. In her first book, *The Valleys of the Assassins*, she speaks of "the old days how bad and how pleasant, the new how good and how dull."

———————•———————

Travel does what good novelists also do to the life of everyday, placing it like a picture in a frame or a gem in its setting, so that the intrinsic qualities are made more clear. Travel does this with the very stuff that everyday life is made of, giving to it the sharp contour and meaning of art.

— *Riding to the Tigris* (1959)

———————•———————

One can only really travel if one lets oneself go and takes what every place brings without trying to turn it into a healthy private pattern of one's own and I suppose that is the difference between travel and tourism.

— *Riding to the Tigris*

———————•———————

The Turks, with the most splendid, varied and interesting country in the world, are naturally anxious to obtain tourists, and their difficulties in this respect are caused chiefly by the quite phenomenal badness of their hotels.

— *Riding to the Tigris*

———————•———————

We English rely for success almost desperately on the breaking of rules, and it will be a poor day when we forget to do so, for this idiosyncrasy may rescue us in a deluge of the second-rate. It incidentally gives us an advantage in the understanding of traditions other than our own which more logical nations find difficult to master.

— *Riding to the Tigris*

———————•———————

"How can I know what I think till I hear what I say?" The quotation came into my mind, and another one from Mr. Gladstone, who is supposed to have remarked that he never met anyone from whom he couldn't learn something, but it was not always worth while to find out what it was. Perhaps to find out what one thinks is one of the reasons for travel and for writing, too.

— Riding to the Tigris

———·———

Solitude, I reflected, is the one deep necessity of the human spirit to which adequate recognition is never given in our codes. It is looked upon as a discipline or a penance, but hardly ever as the indispensable, pleasant ingredient it is to ordinary life, and from this want of recognition come half our domestic troubles. The fear of an unbroken tête-à-tête for the rest of his life should, you would think, prevent any man from getting married . . . Modern education ignores the need for solitude: hence a decline in religion, in poetry, in all the deeper affections of the spirit: a disease to be *doing* something always, as if one could never sit quietly and let the puppet show unroll itself before one: an inability to lose one-self in mystery and wonder while, like a wave lifting us into new seas, the history of the world develops around us. I was thinking these thoughts when Husein, out of breath and beating the grey mare for all he was worth with the plaited rein, came up behind me, and asked how I could bear to go on alone for over an hour, with everyone anxious behind me.

— The Valleys of the Assassins

———·———

The great and almost only comfort about being a woman [traveller] is that one can always pretend to be more stupid than one is and no one is surprised. When the police stopped our car at Bedrah and enquired where we were staying, the chauffeur, who did not know, told him to ask the lady.

"That is no good," said the policeman. "She's a woman."

. . . To be treated with consideration is, in the case of female travellers, too often synonymous with being prevented from doing what one wants.

— *The Valleys of the Assassins*

⤚ 16 ⤙

Imaginary Journeys

WHAT IS STRIKING ABOUT MANY NARRATIVES
of imaginary journeys is the great number
written by actual travellers who know the
world. In most cases such elaborate fictions are created
by writers who have ranged widely. Samuel Butler sailed
from Britain to New Zealand and back, Henri Michaux
travelled through South America and extensively in Asia,
Jan Morris has been practically everywhere on earth.
Italo Calvino, born in Cuba, raised in Italy, travelled
to the United States and returned to Cuba for a while,
lived in Paris, and ended up in Italy. As travellers they
were better able to invent journeys and create imaginary countries that were wholly credible, and their fictional travel is clearly based on their own travel.

"A Christian culture could more easily believe in the existence of the monstrous than of the perfect or near perfect," Susan Sontag wrote in "Questions of Travel", in the collection *Where the Stress Falls.* "Thus, while the kingdoms of freaks appear century after century on maps, exemplary races figure mostly in books of travel to utopia; that is, nowhere."

Robinson Crusoe and *Gulliver's Travels* are obvious choices for this chapter, since Crusoe's desert island was imagined by the widely read Daniel Defoe, who had travelled throughout Europe but never to the landscapes of his masterpiece — Brazil or the Caribbean. Jonathan Swift sailed back and forth from Ireland to England, and created Brobdignagian giants as well as tiny Lilliputians and Yahoos for Gulliver's various voyages. But these books are so well known I decided to omit them.

None of the fictions I've chosen are utopias. I find there is always something bloodless and unbelievable about a utopia. Its contrary, dystopian fiction, with its messy lives and its decaying buildings, more often has the ring of truth. What these books of imaginary places have in common is an element of satire — often a characteristic, or even the whole point, when the subject is an imaginary journey.

Samuel Butler: Erewhon: or, Over the Range

SAMUEL BUTLER, WELL educated, clear-thinking, oppressed by his father, had been heading for a career as a clergyman, but between his life at home and his work in a London parish after university, he lost his faith. Later, he was to write in his *Notebooks*, "As an instrument of warfare against vice, or as a tool for making virtue, Christianity is a mere flint implement."

And something of his attitude toward family life can be deduced from a notebook entry on the family: "I believe that more unhappiness comes from this source than from any other — I mean from the attempt to prolong family connection unduly and to make people hang together artificially who would never naturally do so."

Not surprisingly, Butler fled from his family to New Zealand in 1859. His four-year spell running a sheep ranch there gave him time to read (Darwin among others) and think about the world he had left. When he returned to England in 1864 and wrote about his imagined world of Ere-whon, he included details from the New Zealand he had seen: landscape, manners, aspects of the native population — the people of Erewhon are superficially reminiscent of the Maori.

One of the virtues of *Erewhon* is its evocation of landscape, its powerful and persuasive sense of place. It opens, and proceeds, like a classic Victorian travel book, describing a once empty land that although colonized still has a great unknown and mountainous hinterland, which exists as a temptation: "I could not help speculating upon what might be farther up the river and behind the second range." With the help of a native, Chowbok, the narrator, Higgs, sets off for the ranges, discovering a material culture and a dark-skinned population who he speculates might be part of the lost tribes of Israel. Before he can decide on anything concrete, he is brought before a magistrate and some others who are disturbed by the appearance of his pocket watch. Some broken machinery in the town's museum indicates that the people have a horror of anything mechanical. Higgs is put in prison.

The inhabitants seem to him no further advanced than "Europeans of the twelfth or thirteenth century." He learns the language. He makes friends. Later he mentions that he has a cold — a mistake: "illness of any sort was considered in Erewhon to be highly criminal and immoral", and he is punished.

After three months in prison Higgs is released, to visit the metropolis and its College of Unreason, where he learns that one of the professors has written a book warning of the possibility that "machines were ultimately destined to supplant the race of man". There also exists a class of men "trained in soul-craft". They are called "straighteners". But what Butler goes on to describe is a society much like that of the Victorian England he knew, yet without a tyrannizing religious sense.

"The Book of the Machines", which Higgs quotes extensively, warns against "the ultimate development of animal consciousness" — what we would call artificial intelligence. The rights of animals are also described: animal rights are protected.

At last Higgs escapes in a hot-air balloon, and we are left to reflect on the fact that his descriptions of machines, banks, criminality, and animals have echoes in Darwinism, the church, and Victorian law; that the "straighteners" have their counterparts in doctors and priests; that the seemingly distant place he has described is not so distant.

Henri Michaux: Voyage to Great Garaban

HENRI MICHAUX, WHO was born in Belgium in 1899 and lived most of his life in France, where he died in 1984, is an obscure figure at the fringes of surrealism, known for his poems, his odd short stories, his hectic journeys, his strange paintings and drawings, and most of all for his experiments with practically every drug known to man. He probably had more acid in his body than the average car battery. Hallucinatory experiences and drug dreams were his chosen recreation as well as his access to a higher consciousness and a heightening of his imagination.

Because of the intensity of his vision, and his humour, it is hard to sort out his actual travels from his drug trips. He spent a decade on the move, from 1927 to 1937. His travels in China, Japan, and Malaysia in the thirties resulted in *A Barbarian in Asia*, little more than a travel diary. *Ecuador*, which appeared in France in 1968, is also diaristic but more personal and relentless — angry, impatient, cranky, highly readable, and still relevant. Michaux's books are hard to find; he is obscure now as he was in his lifetime; in spite of his achievement, he never enjoyed any fame or material success, but he said he didn't care.

"There exists a banality of the visionary world," he wrote in *The Major Ordeals of the Mind, and the Countless Minor Ones*, first published in French in 1966. (Michaux's titles are superb.) This suggests to me that his imaginary travels are based more on his actual travels than on his drug trips. Even so, it is impossible to tell from some of his works whether he is describing a lived experience or a dream state.

In three books, gathered under the one title *Ailleurs* (*Elsewhere*), he wrote about three imaginary countries. The works are *Voyage to Great Garaban, In the Land of Magic*, and *Here Is Poddema*. One of the pieces in his book *Spaced, Displaced* is called "Journey That Keeps at a Distance", the sort of trip that is so full of frustrations, incomplete encounters, and half-baked impressions that it resembles that of the travel writer who arrives in a place and finds nothing to write about except frustration — one of the less readable sorts of travel books.

Voyage to Great Garaban, first published in 1936, illustrates another feature of imaginary travels: the detailed sociology and anthropology of such places; the politics, the history. When a traveller invents a place, he or she usually describes more of the place and its people than if it were real. So the land of the Hacs, in Garaban, is described as a set of brutal spectacles, each with a number, and growing in violence. There is hand-to-hand combat (vicious street fighting, families battling in muddy swamps), animals attacking humans (an entertainment), and animal fights ("caterpillars that were ferocious, and demon canaries"). Some Hacs make an attempt to kill their king for the sole purpose of being arrested and condemned to death, and for the splendour of being executed in style — "Spectacle Number 30 which is called 'Receiving one's death in the Palace courtyard.'"

Though the anonymous traveller doesn't condemn these outrages, he flees the Hacs and moves on to the Emanglons. He describes the Emanglons as an anthropologist would, even using the heading "Manners and Customs". We learn of their death rituals, the implications of sickness, their contempt for work and its danger ("After a few days of sustained labour an Emanglon will be unable to sleep"), their odour ("a complex perfume"), their tendency to weep for no reason, their aversion to flies: "Emanglons cannot endure living in the same room with a fly. In their eyes the cohabitation has something monstrous about it."

The Hivinizikis, the last group in Great Garaban, are manic, furiously rushing about, praying madly and prostrating themselves. Unbalanced, in a froth, they are "always outdoors. If you see someone inside, he doesn't live there. No doubt about it, he's visiting a friend." Everything about the Hivinizikis is hectic — religion, politics, the theatre, all is rough-and-tumble.

Michaux had travelled fairly widely in the world before he wrote his imaginary travels, so these tales are both satires of actual travel and comic fantasies. As a surrealist Michaux is keenly aware of the necessity for satire to be absurd; even when a narrative is not understood, it must bring a smile to the reader's lips. In a scholarly introduction to

Michaux's *Selected Writings* (1944), Richard Ellmann quotes André Gide, a supporter of Michaux, saying that Michaux "excels in making us feel intuitively both the strangeness of natural things and the naturalness of strange things".

Miguel de Unamuno: *"Mecanópolis"*

YOU COULD PUT this short story, written in 1913, down to science fiction or speculative fiction were it not for the fact that the author says he was directly inspired by the satire of Samuel Butler's *Erewhon*. Unamuno (1864–1936), who depicts the same horror of technology in this intense and compressed tale, was a distinguished philosopher and the author of a work on man's ambiguous relationship with God, *The Tragic Sense of Life*.

"There sprang to mind the memory of a traveller's tale told me by an explorer friend who had been to Mechanopolis, the city of machines," begins Unamuno's story (translated by Patricia Hart).

Lost in the desert, dying from thirst and weakness, the traveller "began sucking at the nearly black blood that was oozing from his fingers raw from clawing about in the arid soil". He sees something in the distance. A mirage? No, an oasis. He recovers, sleeps, and when he wakes discovers a railway station with an empty train at the platform — no engineer, no other passengers. He gets in, the train departs, and later deposits him at a fabulous city. No people can been seen in the city, nor any life. "Not one dog crossed the street, nor one swallow the sky." But there are streetcars and automobiles, which stop at a given signal. He goes to a museum, which is full of paintings but sterile in mood, and then to a concert hall "where the instruments played themselves."

That he is the only person in the city is a news item in the *Mechanopolis Echo*: "Yesterday afternoon — and we do not know how it came about — a man arrived at our city, a man of the sort there used to be out there. We predict unhappy days for him."

Among the machines, without any human company, the traveller begins to go mad. This too is an item in the daily paper. "But all of a sudden a terrible idea struck me: what if those machines had souls, mechanical souls, and it were the machines themselves that felt sorry for me?"

In a panic, he attempts suicide by leaping in front of a streetcar, and he awakes at the oasis where he started out. He finds some Bedouins and celebrates his deliverance. "There was not one machine anywhere around us.

"And since then I have conceived a veritable hatred toward what we call progress, and even toward culture, and I am looking for a corner where I shall find a peer, a man like myself, who cries and laughs, as I cry and laugh, and where there is not a single machine and the days flow with the sweet, crystalline tameness of a street lost in a forest primeval."

This remarkable piece of fiction about an imaginary journey combines the rejection of technology that Samuel Butler satirized, the over-civilized life that Richard Burton deplored, the horror of a dehumanized urban world that Thoreau condemned, and the wish to find an unspoiled people in a remote place — an Edenic place of happy humans.

Italo Calvino: Invisible Cities

MOST OF CALVINO'S fictions could be included under the heading "Imaginary Journeys". But *Invisible Cities* is the most appropriate for an anthology of travel, since the narrator is Marco Polo — a variant Marco Polo, in an extended audience with a variant Kublai Khan — Khan in old age, impatient, combative, at the end of his rule. Marco Polo seems to be spinning out his description of the cities in the manner of Scheherazade, filling the time and diverting the fading emperor.

Dense, playful, paradoxical, and whimsical, the book has inspired a great deal of analysis and some pompous criticism. In general, Calvino's reputation suffers at the hands of his many well-wishers' special pleading. Much of his work is based on elaborate jokes, and the label of magical realism — which is often no more than whimsy writ large — is unhelpful. The structural flaw in the book is that it is a rather formless disquisition and a dialogue, not a narrative of discovery.

But as a set of imaginary journeys to strange cities, it is vastly enjoyable — and it must be enjoyed rather than analysed or probed, or it will fall apart. The cities have themes — the cities representing memory, desire, signs, eyes; thin cities, trading cities, hidden cities; cities and the dead;

continuous cities. Though the book is short, the 164 chapters keep repeating the cities' themes, with variations. Much could be made of the fact that all the cities, more than fifty of them, have women's names — Dorothea, Zenobia, Sophronia, Trude, and so forth. And perhaps these names stand for the siren song that the traveller hears, the romance of far-off places.

The wise observations, travellers' truths, relieve the repetitious narrative: "The more one was lost in unfamiliar quarters of distant cities, the more one understood the other cities he had crossed to arrive there; and he retraced the stages of his journeys, and he came to know the port from which he had set sail, and the familiar places of his youth." Another: "Arriving at each new city, the traveller finds again a past of his that he did not know he had: the foreignness of what you no longer are or no longer possess lies in wait for you in foreign, unpossessed places." This is ingenious and strikes me as true.

In another city, Adelma, Marco sees a vegetable vendor and recognizes his grandmother, and thinks: "You reach a moment in life when, among the people you have known, the dead outnumber the living. And the mind refuses to accept more faces, more expressions: on every new face you encounter, it prints the old forms, for each one it finds the most suitable mask." That is an accurate expression of the traveller's imagination, and a polite way of illustrating Sir Richard Burton in Arabia seeing Maula Ali, "a burly savage, in whom I detected a ridiculous resemblance to the Rev. Charles Delafosse, an old and well-remembered schoolmaster".

It is misleading, I think, to look for echoes of Borges in Calvino's work. Borges creates new worlds, yet many of Calvino's cities, for all their exoticism, seem quite familiar. Here is the city of Chloe: "In Chloe, a great city, the people who move through the streets are all strangers. At each encounter, they imagine a thousand things about one another; meetings which could take place between them, conversation, surprises, caresses, bites. But no one greets anyone; eyes lock for a second, then dart away, seeking other eyes, never stopping." How is this city different from Chicago or Paris?

Other cities are purely satirical — cities where fashion is an obsession; cities that do not begin or end ("Only the name of the airport changes"); cities where memories are traded.

What does it add up to? Certainly it is a critique of travellers' tales and reminiscences about cities, litanies that are no more than variations on a theme. And perhaps these cities, apparently hermetic and separate and far-flung, are the same city, observed or remembered according to a particular mood.

The book — seeming more of a puzzle than it actually is — also tells us a great deal about how we live in cities, how we adapt to new cities, how even the most terrifying cities can be habitable. My own feeling (and it seems to be Calvino's too) is that city dwellers invent the cities they live in. The great cities are just too big to be comprehended as a whole, so they are invisible, or imaginary, existing mainly in the mind. A New Yorker lives in his or her version of New York, creating a city that is familiar and unthreatening, not the enormous, multilayered, and towering place but a particular set of friends, houses, shops, restaurants, theatres, and, crucially, a complex network of routes — streets, trains, and neighbourhoods that are safe and supportive. In his book of apparently extravagant fables, Calvino shows us how we accommodate ourselves to the real world.

Jan Morris: Last Letters from Hav

HAVING TAKEN NUMEROUS journeys across the world — one of the most widely travelled of living writers — Jan Morris invented a country, gave it a history, art, religion, and literature, and was so scrupulous in her details that people earnestly asked her afterward where exactly it was and how they might visit.

The imaginary country of Hav seems to be in the eastern Mediterranean, and has not only a highly diverse population of Muslims and Christians, but also an ancient indigenous population, of troglodytes possibly of Celtic origin, who named Hav, their word (and the Welsh word) for summer. The troglodytes are called the Kretev, "thought to be etymologically related to the Welsh *crwydwyr,* wanderers."

One of the annual festivals is the Roof Race, where contestants leap from roof to roof across Hav.

Many distinguished visitors to Hav recorded their impressions: Chekhov, Lady Hester Stanhope, Ibn Battuta, and Marco Polo — the greatest and most literate of travellers. But also we learn that later visitors included Noël Coward, Coco Chanel, Thomas Mann, Winston Churchill, James Joyce, and Sir Richard Burton. Marco Polo remarked on Hav as "a place of strange buildings and rites, not like other places". The elaborate architecture is described, with quotations from Alexander Kinglake, Mark Twain, D. H. Lawrence, and others.

The narrator says, midway through the book, "The meaning of Hav is easy."

In terms of politics, art, war, and climate, Hav is the essence of the Mediterranean, a cultural confusion, layer upon layer, Greek, Turk, Italian, the great glittering talkative mass of conquerors and imperialists and evangelists — and writers: Edward Lear, James Joyce, Richard Burton, T. E. Lawrence.

"But then the advantage of going native in Hav is that nobody knows what native is . . . you can take your choice!"

In this believable book, Jan Morris, the writer who has been everywhere, has created out of her travels and her reading a sunny, polyglot nation that is claimed by many nationalities, but in its very complexity is a fragility. It is, incidentally, also a way of showing how the somewhat despised Kretevs — those ancestors of the Welsh, of whose nation Jan Morris is a proud member — have been overwhelmed. Though the book is partly a satire on the multicultural Mediterranean, it is also a capriccio — one of the few successful ones I know in fiction — good-hearted, learned, and enlightening.

I asked Jan once what was going through her head as she was writing it. She said, "I wrote *Last Letters from Hav* because I had come to realize that I had never scratched more than the surface of any place or period I'd ever written about, and it was intended to be an allegory of civic and historical complexity — though nobody ever read it that way."

∽ 17 ∽
Everything Is Edible Somewhere

"**Y**OU MUST HAVE EATEN SOME WEIRD STUFF,"
I am frequently told. I quite liked *fufu* (mashed
yams) in Nigeria, and snake and turtle in China;
I drew the line at owlet, because I felt sorry for those
vexed-looking birds roosting in a cage, waiting to be chosen for a meal. One night I bought one at a restaurant, at
the chef's suggestion. And I set it free, much to his con-
sternation. Cow's tendon in soup, looking like shreds of
Tupperware, was not tasty. ("If it has four legs and is not
a chair, has wings and is not an airplane, or swims and is
not a submarine, the Cantonese will eat it," Prince Philip
once said, and was booed.) I ate some sparrows in Burma

and reported on them in *The Great Railway Bazaar*. Alligator tail on the Zambezi was fairly common, served in stew or as steaks. "Carrion and garbage of every kind can be eaten without the stomach rejecting it," Francis Galton wrote in the chapter "Revolting Food That May Save the Lives of Starving Men" in *The Art of Travel*. "Life can certainly be maintained on a revolting diet."

I was prepared for a life of travel food by the cold lumpy oatmeal my mother served me on winter mornings. "You can't go to school until you finish it!" Tears of disgust sprang to my eyes as I sat, repelled by the sight, and I retched when I tried to swallow even a little bit. My Italian grandmother, who immigrated to America when she was a small girl, served us familiar-looking greens in salad, and when we asked about these slightly bitter leaves, she admitted that they were dandelions (*soffione*) she had dug up that morning. Many hard-up Italians in America foraged for dandelions.

"Objectively, nothing's more disgusting than eating milk or cheese," my son Marcel said to me one day when we were discussing this subject. Most Chinese agree, but nearly all are physically unable to digest the stuff, being lactose intolerant. (Many Chinese believe that the so-called white race has an odd cheesy smell.) The writer and traveller Ted Hoagland told me, "My exotic foods include bobcat, porcupine liver, and squirrel, but muskrat was the best." And my travelling friend Larry Millman has eaten dogs from Greenland to Micronesia, and remarked on the varieties of canine cuisine.

Sir John Mandeville's *Travels* is full of strange meals; the book was hugely popular for the culinary oddities it described. Given that Mandeville probably did not exist, and that his book was probably plagiarized, embellished with mostly outrageous lies and self-serving distortions, hardly mattered to a reading public eager for details of weird meals. Herman Melville must have been keenly aware of this fascination for exotic food when he included "The Whale as a Dish" as a chapter in *Moby-Dick*. In it, Ishmael discusses the cooking and eating of whale meat, as well as strips of fried blubber ("fritters") and the sperm whale's brains. As an aside, he adds that the whale is "a noble dish, were there not so much of him; but when you come to sit down before a meat-pie nearly one hundred feet long, it takes away your appetite".

The Japanese have gone to enormous lengths to continue killing whales so that they can dine on whale sashimi. *Kujira* (whale) is thinly sliced and served raw. The meat is marbled, looks like beef, has a briny, somewhat fishy taste, and can be tough. In order to go on hunting whales the Japanese have bribed Third World countries with development aid, to get them on their side, and have hidden behind their own indigenous people, the Ainu, who are otherwise despised for being primitive. The slaughter and eating of bottle-nosed dolphins is another Japanese pleasure. When this was revealed in a prize-winning documentary, *The Cove*, released in 2009, the mayor of the fishing village of Taiji, offended by the way his village was portrayed in the dolphin massacre, issued a statement saying that it was "important to respect and understand regional food cultures, which are based on traditions with long histories".

Other travellers sing the praises of *balut*, duck embryo, eaten in the Philippines; Thai duck-tongue soup; and *finanziera*, cockscomb stew, of the Italian Piedmont. *Lutefisk*, mocked by W. H. Auden in his travels in Iceland, is beloved there, along with *hakuri*, the putrefied shark. In Sicily and Sardinia you might be offered "maggot cheese", known as *casu marzu*, which you could mistake for squirmy rice. The dusky big-assed ant of the Colombian Amazon (*hormigas culonas de Santander*) is harvested by the indigenous Guane people and toasted and served as a "nutty snack". Korea is full of culinary specialties, besides dog: *dalk bal* is deep-fried chicken anus, and at the raw bar *saeng nakji* are octopus tentacles, simply prepared: a small, live octopus is knifed apart, each tentacle chopped off and, still wiggling, eaten raw, with a special sauce. Bull's testicles (*criadillas*) are standard fare in Spain, and lark pâté (*pâté d'alouettes*) is a popular spread in France. Caterpillar fungus (*yartsa gunbu*), an inch-long larva with a two-inch fungoid growth on its head, is a gustatory marvel, with medicinal properties, found in Bhutan, Tibet, and Nepal. Black-ant larvae (*escamoles*) are a part of the combination plate in parts of Mexico. And last, bear paw, which I was offered in Harbin, in Heilungjiang province. From the Ming Dynasty onward, cooked bear paw has been on the menu all over China. A widely advertised specialty, it is an "imperial tonic food" that supposedly enhances virility, like rhino horn and tiger's penis, also eaten when poachers are successful.

None of these, and nothing I have eaten in travel, can compare in revolting looks or taste with a meal I attempted one day in Glasgow. I ordered a hamburger and was treated to the sight of a man forming a mass of raw meat and gristle into a billiard-size ball, which he tossed into a wire basket and lowered into a frothy container of boiling yellow fat. After he deep-fried this now smaller and black-crusted ball, he clamped it between two pieces of bread and handed it over. He smiled when I said I couldn't eat it: "You Yanks."

The Eating Habits of the Tartars

> And they eat hounds, lions, leopards, mares and foals, asses, rats and mice and all manner of beasts, great and small, save only swine and beasts that were defended by the old law. And they eat all the beasts without and within, without casting away of anything, save only the filth. And they eat but little bread, but if it be in courts of great lords. And they have not in many places, neither pease ne beans ne none other pottages but the broth of the flesh. For little eat they anything but flesh and the broth. And when they have eaten, they wipe their hands upon their skirts; for they use no napery ne towels.
>
> — *The Travels of Sir John Mandeville*,
> first English translation, early fifteenth century

Strange Fruit of the Asian Kingdom of Caldilhe

> And there groweth a manner of fruit, as though it were gourds. And when they be ripe, men cut them a-two, and men find within a little beast, in flesh, in bone, and blood, as though it were a little lamb without wool. And men eat both the fruit and the beast. And that is a great marvel. Of that fruit I have eaten, although it were wonderful, but that I know well that God is marvellous in his works.
>
> — *The Travels of Sir John Mandeville*

Tartar Travelling Cuisine

When going on a long expedition, [the Tartars] carry no baggage with them. They each carry two leather flasks to hold the milk they drink and a small pot for cooking meat . . . In case of need, they will ride a good ten days' journey without provisions and without making a fire, living only on the blood of their horses; for every rider pierces a vein of his horse and drinks the blood. They also have their dried milk, which is solid like paste; and this is how they dry it. First they bring the milk to the boil. At the appropriate moment they skim off the cream that floats on the surface and put it into another vessel to be made into butter, because so long as it remained the milk could not be dried. Then they stand the milk in the sun and leave it to dry. When they are going on an expedition, they take about ten pounds of this milk; and every morning they take out about half a pound of it and put it in a small leather flask, shaped like a gourd, with as much water as they please. Then, while they ride, the milk in the flask dissolves into a fluid, which they drink. And this is their breakfast.

— *The Travels of Marco Polo*, translated by Ronald Latham (1958)

A Morning Skalk in the Hebrides

Their fowls are not like those plumped for sale by the poulterers of London, but they are as good as other places commonly afford, except that the geese, by feeding in the sea, have universally a fishy rankness.

Their geese seem to be of a middle race, between the wild and domestick kinds. They are so tame as to own a home, and so wild as sometimes to fly away.

Their native bread is made of oats, or barley. Of oatmeal they spread very thin cakes, coarse and hard, to which unaccustomed palates are not easily reconciled. The barley cakes are thicker and softer; I began to eat them without unwillingness; the blackness of their colour raises some dislike, but the taste is not disagreeable. In most houses there is wheat flower, with which we were sure to be treated, if we staid long enough to have it kneaded and baked. As neither yeast nor leaven are used among them, their bread of every kind is unfermented. They make only cakes, and never mould a loaf.

A man of the Hebrides, for of the women's diet I can give no account, as soon as he appears in the morning, swallows a glass of whisky; yet they are not a drunken race, at least I never was present at much intemperance; but no man is so abstemious as to refuse the morning dram, which they call a *skalk*.

The word *whisky* signifies water, and is applied by way of eminence to "strong water", or distilled liquor. The spirit drunk in the North is drawn from barley. I never tasted it, except once for experiment at the inn in Inverary, when I thought it preferable to any English malt brandy. It was strong, but not pungent, and was free from the empyreumatick [burnt] taste or smell. What was the process I had no opportunity of inquiring, nor do I wish to improve the art of making poison pleasant.

Not long after the dram, may be expected the breakfast, a meal in which the Scots, whether of the Lowlands or mountains, must be confessed to excel us. The tea and coffee are accompanied not only with butter, but with honey, conserves, and marmalades. If an epicure could remove by a wish, in quest of sensual gratifications, wherever he had supped he would breakfast in Scotland.

In the islands however, they do what I found it not very easy to endure. They pollute the tea-table by plates piled with large slices of cheshire cheese, which mingles its less grateful odours with the fragrance of the tea.

— Samuel Johnson, *A Journey to the Western Islands of Scotland* (1775)

The Raw Meat of the Druze

The Druze custom of eating raw meat fascinated [Lady Hester Stanhope, in 1812]. She recounted later, "I purchased of a Druze an immense sheep, the tail weighing eleven pounds, and desired it to be taken to a village, where I ordered the people assembled to eat. When I arrived, the sheep was alive; the moment it was killed it was skinned, and brought in raw upon a sort of dish made of matting, and in less than half an hour it was all devoured. The women ate of it as well as the men: the pieces of raw fat they swallowed were really frightful."

— James C. Simmons, *Passionate Pilgrims: English Travelers to the World of the Desert Arabs* (1987)

Garlic, Food of the Fellah

Those skilled in simples [medicinal plants], Eastern as well as Western, praise garlic highly, declaring that it "strengthens the body, prepares the constitution for fatigue, brightens the sight, and, by increasing the digestive power, obviates the ill-effects arising from sudden change of air and water". The traveller inserts it into his dietary in some pleasant form, as "Provence butter", because he observes that, wherever fever and ague abound, the people ignorant of cause but observant of effect, make it a common article of food. The old Egyptians highly esteemed this vegetable, which, with onions and leeks, enters into the list of articles so much regretted by the Hebrews ... In Arabia, however, the stranger must use this vegetable sparingly. The city people despise it as the food of a Fellah — a boor. The Wahhabis have a prejudice against onions, leeks and garlic, because the Prophet disliked their strong smell.

— Sir Richard Burton, *Personal Narrative of a Pilgrimage to Al-Madinah and Meccah* (1855–56)

A Slave in Gabon for His Evening Meal

Then [Remandji, king of the Apingi] said, "Be glad, oh spirit! And eat of the things we give thee."

Whereupon, to my astonishment, a slave was handed over to me bound, and Remandji said, "Kill him for your evening meal; he is tender and fat, and you must be hungry." It took me a moment to recover from my astonishment. Then I shook my head, spat violently on the ground, and made Minsho tell them that I abhorred the people who ate human flesh, and that I and my people never did so.

To which Remandji replied, "We always heard that you white people eat men. Why do you buy our people [as slaves]? Why do you come from nobody knows where, and carry off our men, and women, and children? Do you not fatten them in your far country and eat them? Therefore I give you this slave, that you might kill him and make your heart glad."

It was a difficult matter to explain to the king that he was much mistaken.

— Paul Du Chaillu, *Explorations and Adventures in Equatorial Africa* (1861)

"Many Eat the Hedgehog"

SCOLDED BY BEDOUINS at the Teyma oasis for eating "swine's flesh", C. M. Doughty lost his temper, and raged:

> If God have commanded you anything, keep it; I see you eat crows and kites, and the lesser carrion eagle. Some of you eat owls, some eat serpents. The great lizard you all eat, and locusts, and the spring-rat; Many eat the hedgehog; in certain (Hejaz) villages they eat rats, you cannot deny it! You eat the wolf, too, and the fox and the foul hyena. In a word, there is nothing so vile that some of you will not eat it.
> — *Travels in Arabia Deserta* (1888)

Cats, Camels, Foxes, Owls, and Others

Andalusians do not eat cats and dogs even when they are very hungry, but in Estremadura they're regarded as delicacies. A woman from Alcantara who is fond of cats and would never kill one herself, tells me that she has eaten cat stew and that it is tastier than either rabbit or hare. The Estremadurans also eat martens and weasels and foxes, and declare, though I do not believe it, that a fried leg of fox is the best thing imaginable. But then they are a race of cattlemen and hunters, ancestors of the Argentine gauchos, and put in a pot whatever the gun brings down. The only animal they bar is the wolf. Gypsies eat frogs, snakes and lizards as well as farmyard animals that have died a natural death, while there is a whole village near

Jerez which till a few years ago spent its night hunting the camels that ran wild in the marshes at the mouth of the Guadalquivir. As for birds, they are all eaten in the south of Spain and the list includes eagles, owls and hawks. The only ones rejected are seagulls, crows and vultures, and the sacred swallow and stork.

— Gerald Brenan, *South from Granada* (1957)

Mr. Black, the Blood Drinker in Tangier

There was the somewhat sinister Mr. Black, whom I never met, but who, I am told, kept an outsize electric refrigerator in his sitting room, in which there was a collection of half-pint glass jars. Occasionally he would open the refrigerator door, inspect the labels on the bottles and select one. Then in front of his guests he would pour its contents into a glass and drink. A lady I know, who was present one day when he did this, innocently inquired if what he had in the glass were a combination of beet and tomato juice. "This is blood," he said. "Will you have some? It's delicious chilled, you know." The lady, who had lived in Tangier for many years, was thus determined to show no astonishment at anything, replied, "I don't think I will right now, thank you. But may I see the jar?" Mr. Black handed it to her. The label read *Mohammed*. "He's a Riffian boy," explained Mr. Black. "I see," she said, "and the other jars?" "Each one is from a different boy," her host explained. "I never take more than a half pint at a time from any one of them. That wouldn't do. Too debilitating for them."

— Paul Bowles, "Tangier", *Gentleman's Quarterly* (1963) (Note: Bowles based his 1985 short story "Hugh Harper" on this man's tastes.)

Evelyn Waugh on Tasso *in British Guiana*

Tasso is prepared in this way. The killing of a beast [pig in this case] is an event of some importance in the immediate neighbourhood. Indians get news of it and appear mysteriously like gulls round a trawler when the catch is cleaned. A few choice morsels are cut away and cooked and eaten fresh. The Indians carry off the head and the entrails. The rest is sliced into thin slabs, rolled in salt and hung up to dry. A few days of sun and savannah wind reduce it to a black, leathery condition in which it will remain uncorrupt indefinitely. Even the normally omnivorous ants will not touch it. It is carried under the saddle above the blanket to keep it tender and protect the horse from galling. When the time comes to eat it, it is scrubbed fairly clean of dust and salt and boiled in water. It emerges softened but fibrous and tasteless.

I can conceive it might be possible for a newcomer to stomach a little *farine* with a rich and aromatic stew; or a little *tasso* with plenty of fresh vegetables and bread. The food of the savannah is *farine* and *tasso* and nothing else.

> — *Ninety-two Days* (1934) (In *A Handful of Dust*, Waugh's
> captive hero Tony is given "*tasso* at noon . . . *farine* and
> *tasso* and sometimes some fruit for supper.")

For a Sharecropper in Alabama, Hardly a Crumb

"Sometimes it don't seem possible that we're living at all, especially when I wake up in the morning and see the children getting up and dressing and walking around in the kitchen where there's hardly a crumb of food. They make a fire in the cook-stove and I scrape together a little corn meal, when there's any to scrape, and I cook it with salt and water. Once in a while we have some molasses, or maybe just some sugar-water to eat with it. When noontime comes, they start another fire, and I cook some more cornbread. A lot of times lately I've just sat and wondered if there's anything else in the world to eat. I know there must be other things in the world to eat, because the rich wouldn't eat cornbread, and I wouldn't if I could help it. Not just cornbread and nothing else. Once in a while we have some store-bought canned beans, just one or two cans among us, and that don't go far when there's nine hungry children besides me. The two oldest boys manage to earn a little money somehow, and they bring home all they make. Altogether, what money there is comes to two or three dollars a week. We eat on that, except for the twenty-five cents a week house rent I pay the landlord. We've been getting along somehow for three years since my husband died. Every time it rains hard all of us have to crawl under the house to keep from getting wet, because I don't reckon there's a landlord in the country who would patch a roof for only twenty-five cents a week rent."

— quoted in Erskine Caldwell and Margaret Bourke-White,
You Have Seen Their Faces (1937)

In Tibetan Cuisine, Meat Is a Rarity

The staple food in this region is tsampa. This is how they prepare it. You heat sand to a high temperature in an iron pan and then pour barley corns onto it. They burst with a slight pop, whereupon you put the corns and the sand in a fine meshed sieve through which the sand runs: after this you grind the corn very small. The resulting meal is stirred up into a paste with butter tea or milk or beer and then eaten. The Tibetans make a special cult of tsampa and have many ways of preparing it. We soon got accustomed to it, but never cared much for butter tea, which is usually made with rancid butter and is generally repugnant to Europeans. It is, however, universally drunk and appreciated by the Tibetans, who often drink as many as sixty cups in a day. The Tibetans of Kyirong, besides butter tea and tsampa, eat rice, buckwheat, maize, potatoes, turnips, onions, beans, and radishes. Meat is a rarity, for as Kyirong is a particularly holy place no animal is ever slaughtered there. Meat appeared on the table only when it had been brought in from another district or, more often, when bears or panthers left part of their prey uneaten.

— Heinrich Harrer, *Seven Years in Tibet* (1953)

Redmond O'Hanlon's Jungle Tuck

TURTLE BRAIN

Chimo and Culimacare joined us from Chimo's house for break-fast and Simon returned, silent, from his walk. We ate turtle (rich, chewy) and manioc (like sawdust). Simon, declining both, opened a tin of Spam and sat apart on a rock of his own. Galvis, intending to cheer up his new friend, went to sit beside him . . .

Galvis took a severed turtle head out of his mess tin, picked its brains out from the neck with a fork, ate them, and turned to Simon. He held the blackened head in his fingers in front of Simon's face and moved the jaws open and shut.

"Quack!" said Galvis. "Quack! Quack! Quack!"

— *In Trouble Again* (1988)

ARMADILLO RISOTTO

As night fell we unloaded our ordinary stores from Chimo's dug-out and, leaving Valentine on guard, we set off downstream with the presents, with bowls of manioc, ready-cooked spaghetti, and — the centrepiece — our giant pot full to the brim with agouti and arma-dillo risotto.   — *In Trouble Again*

MONKEY EYES

We cut steps up the high muddy bank and made camp. Chimo and Pablo spread palm fronds on the ground and began to prepare the Howler monkey, scalding it with boiling water and scraping off the fur. Its skin turned white, like a baby's.

That night, when Pablo had jointed the body and Galvis boiled it, Chimo handed me a suspiciously full mess tin. As I spooned out the soup the monkey's skull came into view, thinly covered in its red meat, the eyes still in their sockets.

"We gave it to you specially," said Chimo with great seriousness . . . "If you eat the eyes we will have good luck."

The skull bared its broken teeth at me. I picked it up, put my lips to the rim of each socket in turn, and sucked. The eyes came away from their soft stalks and slid down my throat.

— *In Trouble Again*

ELEPHANT NOSE

"I give up," said Lary, scrutinizing the very tough, gristly, grey lumps of meat hiding among the fresh green manioc-leaf saka-saka in his mess-tin . . . "Marcellin," said Lary, chewing hard, "what is this stuff?"

"Elephant nose!"

Lary set down his mess-tin. He stood up, lurched slightly, held on to the corner of the hut, retched twice, and was sick onto the ground.

— *Congo Journey* (1996)

Bread Famine in the Sierra

July 6 [1869] — Mr. Delaney has not arrived, and the bread famine is sore. We must eat mutton a while longer, though it seems hard to get accustomed to it. I have heard of Texas pioneers living without bread or anything made from the cereals for months without suffering, using the breast-meat of wild turkeys for bread. Of this kind they had plenty in the good old days when life, though considered less safe, was fussed over the less. The trappers and fur traders in the Rocky Mountain regions lived on bison and beaver meat for months. Salmon-eaters, too, there are among both Indians and whites who seem to suffer little or not at all from want of bread. Just at this moment mutton seems the least desirable of food, though of good quality. We pick out the leanest bits, and down they go, against heavy disgust, causing nausea and an effort to reject the offensive stuff. Tea makes matters worse, if possible. The stomach begins to assert itself as an independent creature with a will of its own. We should boil lupine leaves, clover, starchy petioles, and saxifrage rootstocks like the Indians . . . We chew a few leaves of ceanothus by way of luncheon, and smell or chew the spicy monardella for the dull headache and stomach-ache that now lightens, now comes muffling down upon us and into us like fog. At night more mutton, flesh to flesh, down with it, not too much, and there are the stars shining through the Cedar plumes and branches above our beds.

July 7 — Rather weak and sickish this morning, and all about a piece of bread.

— John Muir, *My First Summer in the Sierra* (1916)

Congolese Monkey Stew, Batetela Style

MY FRIEND DOUG Kelly, a widely travelled Foreign Service officer, served in the Peace Corps in Tshumbe, central Congo, in the 1980s. Over the course of two years there, he frequently observed the Batetela people prepare and eat monkey. Most of the Batetela inhabit an area in the Sankuru district of Kasai Oriental province. Their language, Otetela, is considered very difficult to learn by other Congolese. In fact, it is often referred to as "*le Chinois du Congo*".

The Batetela are fortunate in that their homeland is still relatively rich in wildlife. The most common wild game, and thus the cheapest, is monkey. Following is the recipe for a repast of monkey cooked à la Batetela, as Doug Kelly describes it in a letter to me:

Take a dead monkey and hack it up. Keep the hands intact, but you can slice the rest of the carcass any way you want. Don't leave the pieces too big, because they will take longer to cook and you want to eat it soon because you are hungry.

Place the hacked-up pieces, including the intact hands, in a pot of boiling water and boil away. Don't add any spices, because you don't have any, and don't use too much water, because you're going to want to drink the watery "gravy" and you want it to have a lot of undiluted monkey taste.

After the monkey has been boiled for quite a while, take it out of the water and serve it on a bed of rice or millet. (Note: The Batetela are the only people who grow rice in Congo. The Arabs taught them how in the nineteenth century, when the Batetela were raiding tribes to the south and selling the captives into slavery to the Arabs. Millet is the traditional Batetela grain and is still raised in the dry season. Other Congolese tribes prefer manioc, or "fu fu".) Pour some of the monkey-water gravy on the rice or millet. Eat the whole concoction with your hands, or a spoon if you feel formality is necessary.

Now comes the good part. Serve the intact hands to your guests. A monkey hand resting on a plate looks like pretty upscale dining, at least if you are sitting in a mud hut in Sankuru. If you are the favoured guest, eat the whole hand — the Batetela never leave any bones when they are eating meat, unless it's a particularly big pig femur or something equivalent. For monkeys, ducks, and chickens, it's everything down the hatch. You are encouraged to gnaw the monkey knuckles, removing the meat before cracking them open with your teeth and sucking out the marrow. Yum.

Sampling Fried Sago Beetle in New Guinea

Stef cooked a dinner of fried catfish, along with a healthy portion of sago beetle. The larvae were fried brown in the pan. They were crisp and sort of fishy tasting on the outside, probably because they had been sautéed in fish oil. Inside, the larvae were the colour and consistency of custard. They were unlike anything I had ever eaten before, and the closest I can come to describing the taste is to say creamy snail.   — Tim Cahill, *Pass the Butterworms* (1997)

Dog Meat in Asia

THE SMELL OF a skinned, sinewy dog, hung by its hind legs in a Chinese butcher shop, can been detected from many feet away. So their term "fragrant meat" is related to the sort of euphemism that identifies a garbage truck as a honey wagon. In the literal-minded Philippines the dish is unambiguously called dog stew (*aso adobo*), and the key ingredient in the Korean soup *boshintang* is always understood to be dog meat. Dogs are eaten in many parts of Asia and the high Arctic, and have been a staple in much of the Pacific: Captain James Cook mentioned that a dish of Tahitian dog was almost as tasty as lamb. It is only the Western prohibition against pet-eating that horrifies us, but the edible dog is never a pet.

While it is generally known by educated travellers that the Cantonese (and, for that matter, *Dongbei Ren;* that is, north-Eastern Chinese) love dog meat, it is not as well known that (1) it is seasonal — dog meat is considered warming for the blood, so is overwhelmingly eaten in the winter; and (2) a dog is considered good to eat only if its fur is black or, in a pinch, dark brown. I've never been given a good explanation for the second requirement, although it seems to be linked to the first, seasonal reason for eating dog meat — dogs with dark fur have the highest warming quality. I don't know what this theory is based on, but it's real — a Cantonese would be shocked if you suggested he eat a white poodle, and it would confirm his belief that you are, after all, a barbarian.

In Shenyang, in eastern China, the walls of the U.S. consulate are occasionally scaled by asylum seekers from North Korea, which is not far away. These refugees, weakened by their escape ordeal, often ask to be restored to health by the Chinese equivalent of fortifying chicken soup, which is dog-meat soup (*xiang rou tang*). Since the canteen in the consulate did not offer dog-meat soup, a consular official would send for takeout: "There are innumerable restaurants in Shenyang, as throughout the north-East of China, that do fine dog-meat soup," I was told by my informant. And he added, "To make dog-meat soup, simply chop up a dog with dark fur and boil the hunks of meat, with the bone in, in water flavoured with green onions, red chillies, and soybean paste. You can also throw in noodles to make a heartier soup."

From the Eskimo Cookbook of Shishmaref, Alaska

IN 1952, IN order to raise money for the Alaska Crippled Children's Association, the students of Shishmaref Day School compiled a small cookbook. Shishmaref is on Sarichef Island in the Chukchi Sea — Russia is ninety-five miles to the west. Lately the island has been seriously threatened and impoverished by the effects of climate change. The students, living the traditional Inupiaq life, from foraging and fishing households, contributed recipes that were favourites at home, and sold the small booklet for fifty cents. Here are a few dishes.

WILLOW MEATS

Inside of barkbirch [birchbark] there is something that is yellowish. That is called the meat of the willows. They are very good to eat. People eat it with sugar and seal oil. First clean off the barkbirch from the meat of the willow. There is also soft green barkbirch inside of outside barkbirch. Never eat green stuff on willows. (Augustine Tocktoo)

PTARMIGAN

Take the feathers off the ptarmigan. Cut the meat and wash so they wont have dirt or feathers on. Put in a pot with water and salt. Sometimes some people make soup on it, I think they like them best without soup. (Pauline Tocktoo)

PTARMIGAN SMALL INTESTINE

Cook the small intestines about five seconds in boiling water. Old men and women always want to eat them. (Alma Nayokpuk)

SEALS' BARE FEET (SEAL FLIPPERS)

Put the seal's bare feet into a cooking pan. Cover them with blubber and keep in a hot place until the fur comes off. Then it is time to eat the seal's bare feet. You can cook them or eat them without cooking. (Pauline Tocktoo)

BEAR FEET (EE-TEE-YAIT')

Most of the people like the bear feet better than the meat. We cook them well, add salt. Four feet would take about one teaspoon salt. Take them out of the pot and let them get cool. Eat them with seal oil. (Nellie Okpowruk)

❧ 18 ❧
Rosenblum's Rules of Reporting

I N THE LOBBY OF THE SPEKE HOTEL IN KAMPALA, Uganda, in 1967, I saw a bushy-haired man holding a stenographic notebook and smiling wolfishly at a diplomat, demanding to know why he was killing people in Biafra. That was my first encounter with the foreign correspondent Mort Rosenblum. We were both covering the Nigeria–Biafra peace talks. I was a teacher at Makerere University but also moonlighting as the Time-Life stringer in Uganda. Mort was then the Associated Press bureau chief in Leopoldville (later Kinshasa), Congo. We have remained close friends ever since. I have marvelled at his life as a traveller, writing home from the field.

A self-described "old guy from the road", he has had the longest, hardest, most successful career as a foreign correspondent of any I know. Fluent in Spanish, he was head of the AP bureau in Buenos Aires during a turbulent time there. He covered the Bangladesh war, and South-East Asia, while he was based in Singapore. He was for a time editor in chief of the *International Herald Tribune*, and for many years was a special correspondent based in Paris. On his first day in Paris he interviewed President Valéry Giscard d'Estaing, speaking in fluent French. He has been to virtually every country I can name, and many I have only trailed my fingers upon in atlases.

In addition, Mort has done what many journalists promise they will do but seldom succeed at — write books. His *Olives: History of a Noble Fruit* won the James Beard Award, and his *Chocolate: A Bittersweet Saga of Dark and Light* was a bestseller. He has also written books on journalism, ecology, and Africa, as well as (when he was living on a houseboat in Paris) a travel book, *The Secret Life of the Seine*. I asked him to provide me with some rules of the road that have served him well in over forty years of writing in distant places.

1. Always arrive at roadblocks before noon, because in the afternoon the soldiers manning them are invariably drunk and abusive.

2. Learn French and Spanish, and then some other foreign languages. And learn to say, "Don't shoot, I'm a reporter," in at least a dozen. This might help but is no guarantee of your safety.

3. Take lots of notes and reread them as soon as possible, before they're lost beyond any deciphering. Or maybe that's just me. Recorders are tiny and reliable now; carry one, and you'll be amazed at what you thought you didn't miss.

4. If you are left-handed, learn to eat with your right in Islamic and Hindu countries, especially when gathered around a common platter. The left hand is for postprandial hygiene, and you may lose it if you thrust it into someone's lunch.

5. Carry lots of cash, dollars and euros, but keep it somewhere sneak thieves, bandits, and customs officials are not likely to look. They know about socks and money belts. Get a tailor to sew secret pockets in pant legs or jackets.

6. It is often insulting to refuse someone's food or water. It can also be seriously painful to accept. If the proffered comestible is merely disgusting, suck it up; if not, find some tactful excuse not to partake. Do not make a face or say, "Eeeyeuw."

7. Despite certain novelists' do-it-the-hard-way approach, try to get a visa and cross at border posts. If you are a reporter or a spy or have overriding reasons to skip formalities, use your judgement. Just remember that some countries hang people.

8. Put together a medical kit, including a range of antibiotics, field dressings, and antiseptics. Take lots of Lomotil or Imodium; few miseries compete with a long plane or bus ride, rebellious bowels, and no WC.

9. Think carefully about your kit. Binoculars can be handy, but they suggest to authorities that you might be up to no good. Don't wear military khaki, designer camo, or anything bright that prevents your blending in. And forget weapons. You are unlikely to shoot your way out of trouble, especially the trouble you face when armed dudes find you are packing.

10. On arriving in any distant place, the first thing you should do is learn the quickest way out — times and frequency of buses, trains, or planes. You have to know in advance how to leave.

❧ Travel Wisdom of ❧
CLAUDE LÉVI-STRAUSS

Lévi-Strauss memorably opened his travel book, *Tristes Tropiques*, with the line "I hate travelling and explorers. Yet here I am proposing to tell the story of my expeditions." (An early translation of the book, with a variation of this opening, is *A World on the Wane*.) He was trained as a philosopher but was one of the great theorists of anthropology and linguistics, an explainer of mythologies, and a describer of structuralism. He began his travels in Brazil, made journeys in India and Pakistan, and taught in the United States. He was a member of the Académie Française and lived to over a hundred (he died in 2009). The following are excerpts from *Tristes Tropiques*.

———————◆———————

Travel is usually thought of as a displacement in space. This is an inadequate conception. A journey occurs simultaneously in space, in time, and in the social hierarchy. Each impression can be defined only by being jointly related to these three axes, and since space is in itself three-dimensional, five axes are necessary if we are to have an adequate representation of any journey.

———•———

There was a time when travelling brought the traveller into contact with civilizations which were radically different from his own and impressed him in the first place by their strangeness. During the last few centuries such instances have become increasingly rare. Whether he is visiting India or America, the modern traveller is less surprised than he cares to admit.

———•———

Perhaps, then, this was what travelling was, an exploration of the deserts of my mind rather than those surrounding me.

ᴄᴏ 19 ᴀᴏ
Perverse Pleasures of the Inhospitable

U NWELCOMING PLACES ARE A GIFT TO THE
travelling writer. They have always been so,
an early example being Ibn Battuta's arrival in
Tunis in 1325, at the beginning of his global wandering. He "wept bitterly" because he met with utter indifference: "not a soul greeted me and no one there was
known to me." The winter darkness and killing cold of
Cherry-Garrard's Antarctica; the cannibals, disease,
and general hostility in Stanley's Congo; the devout
Muslims tormenting Charles Doughty with howls of
"Nasrani!" ("Christian!") in Arabia Deserta — these inhospitable situations gave us great books. Heartwarming

interludes, lovable locals, and delicious meals have informed the most tedious travel accounts — the blissful vacation is desirable but not a fit subject for a book.

The early travellers in Africa always kept in mind that the cannibal was a better subject than the missionary. Even the high-minded Mary Kingsley knew that, and spent much more time writing about (and exaggerating) the anthropophagous Fon people in Gabon than the pleasures of her botanizing of the jungle, which (so she said) was the whole point of her West African trip. You don't want to hear about the traveller's fun; what keeps you reading is the traveller's misery, outrage, and near-death experience. Either that or a well-phrased dismissal, as when the English traveller Peter Fleming took a close look at São Paulo and wrote, "São Paulo is like Reading, only much farther away."

"Looking for Trouble" might be the subtitle of the most readable, most memorable travel books. When Redmond O'Hanlon published *In Trouble Again,* my hand leaped to the shelf. *Congo Journey* promised more horror, and another delightful read. So I begin with him.

Making a Deal with the Chief of Boha

In his right hand [the Chief] gripped a spear against the inside of his right thigh, its end on the ground and its winged blade high above his head. His left hand lay on his left thigh, and from his right shoulder there hung a large liana-twine bag full, I presumed, of the royal fetishes . . .

Twelve spearmen stood at intervals in a circle before him, enclosing a line of three chairs; an old man in a brown shirt, torn grey trousers and red plastic sandals, standing on the Chief's left, tilted his spear towards us and then at the waiting seats . . .

The Chief inclined his head to his left: the old man, his *porteparole*, his word carrier, bent down until his right ear was close to the royal lips; the Chief spoke softly. The audience over, the old man straightened his back, held his spear upright, strode into the centre of the circle, filled his lungs, and sang out a speech in Bomitaba . . .

At the end of the pronouncement there were shouts from some of the spearmen and from other warriors around the square . . .

"The white man will pay 75,000 francs to the Chief of Boha," [the old man] shouted in French, "and 20,000 francs to the Vice-President of the People's Committee. Then if the Government come with soldiers to take our Chief to prison in Epéna they must take their Vice-President away too. The white man will keep faith with our Customary Rights."

"It's far too much!" I said.

The old man nodded. The warrior to the right and behind me lowered his spear and pricked me gently between the shoulder-blades.

"It's a bargain!" I said.

— Redmond O'Hanlon, *Congo Journey* (1996)

Fanny Trollope on American Hypocrisy

Had I, during my residence in the United States, observed any single feature in their national character that could justify their eternal boasts of liberality and the love of freedom, I might have respected them, however much my taste might have been offended by what was peculiar in their manners or customs. But it is impossible for any mind of common honesty not to be revolted by the contradictions in their principles and practice . . . You will see them with one hand hoisting the cap of liberty, and with the other flogging their slaves. You will see them one hour lecturing their mob on the indefeasible rights of man, and the next driving from their homes the children of the soil, whom they have bound to protect by the most solemn treaties. — *The Domestic Manners of Americans* (1832)

Elias Canetti: Unfathomable Prices in Marrakesh

In the souks, however, the price that is named first is an unfathomable riddle. No one knows in advance what it will be, not even the merchant, because in any case there are many prices. Each one relates to a different situation, a different customer, a different time of day, a different day of the week. There are prices for single objects and prices for two or more together. There are prices for foreigners visiting the city for a day and prices for foreigners who have been here for three weeks. There are prices for the poor and prices for the rich, those for the poor of course being the highest. One is tempted to think that there are more kinds of prices than there are kinds of people in the world.

— *The Voices of Marrakesh*, translated by J. A. Underwood (1978)

Edward Lear Being Pestered in Albania

No sooner had I settled to draw . . . than forth came the populace of Elbassan; one by one and two by two to a mighty host they grew, and there were soon from eighty to a hundred spectators collected, with earnest curiosity in every look; and when I had sketched such of the principal buildings as they could recognize a universal shout of "Shaitan!" [Satan] burst from the crowd; and strange to relate, the greater part of the mob put their fingers into their mouths and whistled furiously, after the manner of butcher boys in England. Whether this was a sort of spell against my magic I do not know . . . One of those tiresome Dervishes — in whom, with their green turbans, Elbassan is rich — soon came up, and yelled, "Shaitan scroo! — Shaitan!" [The Devil draws! The Devil!] in my ears with all his force; seizing my book also, with an awful frown shutting it, and pointing to the sky, as intimating that Heaven would not allow such impiety.

— *Journal of a Landscape Painter in Albania* (1851)

André Gide: Thoroughly Bored in Bosoum

The absence of individuality, of individualization — the impossibility of differentiating — which depressed me so much at the beginning of my journey, is what I suffer from too much of the landscape. (I experienced this sensation as early as Matadi on seeing the population of children all alike, all equally agreeable, etc. . . . and again on seeing the huts of the first villages, all alike, all containing droves of human cattle with the same looks, tastes, customs, possibilities, etc. . . .) Bosoum is a place that looks over a wide stretch of country, and as I stand here on a kind of terrace, made of red ochre-coloured laterite, gazing on the marvellous quality of the light and admiring the vast undulations of the ground, I ask myself what there is to attract me to any one point rather than to any other. Everything is uniform; there can be no possible predilection for any particular site. I stayed the whole day yesterday without the least desire to stir. From one end of the horizon to the other, wherever my eye settles, there is not a single point to which I wish to go. — *Travels in the Congo* (1929)

Rimbaud Having a Bad Day in Harar, Abyssinia

I still get very bored. In fact, I've never known anyone who gets as bored as I do. It's a wretched life anyway, don't you think — no family, no intellectual activity, lost among negroes who try to exploit you and make it impossible to settle business quickly? Forced to speak their gibberish, to eat their filthy food and suffer a thousand aggravations caused by their idleness, treachery and stupidity!

And there's something even sadder than that — it's the fear of gradually turning into an idiot oneself, stranded as one is, far from intelligent company.

— letter to his mother, 1886, in Geoffrey Wall, *Rimbaud*

V. S. Naipaul Disgusted by India

The point that one feels inescapable is the fact of India's poverty; and how deep is one's contempt for those Indians who, finding no difficulty in accepting one standard in India and another outside it, fail to realize this, and are failing to work night and day for the removal of this dreadful insult and humiliation . . . I wonder, wonder if the shitting habits of Indians are not the key to all their attitudes. I wonder if the country will not be spiritually and morally regenerated if people were only made to adopt the standards of other nations in the business of shitting . . .

So goodbye to shit and sweepers; goodbye to people who *tolerate* everything; goodbye to all the refusal to act; goodbye to the absence of dignity; goodbye to the poverty; goodbye to caste and that curious *pettiness* which permeates that vast country; goodbye to people who, though consulting astrologers, have no sense of their destiny as *men* . . . It is an unbelievable, frightening, sad country. Probably it all has to change. Not only must caste go, but all those sloppy Indian garments; all those saris and lungis; all that squatting on the floor, to eat, to write, to serve in a shop, to piss.

—letter to Moni Malhoutra, 1963, in Patrick French,
The World Is What It Is

Umberto Eco, Hyperbolic in San Luis Obispo

The poor words with which natural human speech is provided cannot suffice to describe the Madonna Inn. To convey its external appearance, divided into a series of constructions, which you reach by way of a filling station carved from Dolomitic rock, or through the restaurant, the bar, and the cafeteria, we can only venture some analogies. Let's say that Albert Speer, while leafing through a book on Gaudí, swallowed an overdose of LSD and began to build a nuptial catacomb for Liza Minnelli. But that doesn't give you an idea. Let's say Arcimboldi builds the Sagrada Familia for Dolly Parton. Or: Carmen Miranda designs a Tiffany locale for the Jolly Hotel chain. Or D'Annunzio's Vittoriale imagined by Bob Cratchit, Calvino's *Invisible Cities* described by Judith Krantz and executed by Leonor Fini for the plush-doll industry. Chopin's Sonata in B flat minor sung by Perry Como in an arrangement by Liberace and accompanied by the Marine Band. No, that still isn't right. Let's try telling about the rest rooms. They are an immense underground cavern, something like Altamira and Luray, with Byzantine columns supporting plaster baroque cherubs. The basins are big imitation-mother-of-pearl shells, the urinal is a fireplace carved from rock, but when the jet of urine (sorry, but I have to explain) touches the bottom, water comes down from the wall of the hood, in a flushing cascade something like the Caves of the Planet Mongo. — *Travels in Hyperreality* (1995)

Lord Byron on the Black Sea (the Euxine)

There's not a sea the passenger e'er pukes in,
Turns up more dangerous breakers than the Euxine.

— Byron, *Don Juan* (1818–24)

∽⚬ 20 ⚬∽
Imaginary People

I**T IS NOT FRIVOLOUS TO CONSIDER THE TRAVEL**
literature that describes men with tails, or one-eyed
people, or dragons. Such marvels are the reasons
the early travel books commanded attention. The Tang
Dynasty traveller Xuanzang, who was meticulous in his
topographical descriptions, often mentions the presence
of dragons. ¶ The many varieties of travel narrative
show what readers wish to find in travel — the strange,
the sexy, the disgusting, the amazing, the Other. Susan
Sontag analysed this fascination (and gullibility) in her
essay "Questions of Travel", where she wrote, "Books
about travel to exotic places have always opposed an 'us'
to a 'them' — a relation that yields a limited variety of
appraisals. Classical and medieval literature is mostly of

the 'us good, them bad' — typically, 'us good, them horrid' — sort. To be foreign was to be abnormal, often represented by physical abnormality; and the persistence of those accounts of monstrous peoples, of 'men whose heads / Do grow beneath their shoulders' (Othello's winning tale), of anthropophagi."

Those men whom Othello mentions having seen appear in *The Travels of Sir John Mandeville*, one of the most popular books of the Middle Ages. It was popular precisely because of the bizarre people and places it described. Mandeville claimed that he travelled the world from 1322 to 1356. The first known edition appeared in French in 1371, and in English translation in the early fifteenth century. It went through many editions, and was augmented and embellished as it was reprinted. Mandeville probably did not exist, or if he did exist as a fantasizing Frenchman of the fourteenth century, he may not have gone anywhere: many of Mandeville's strange tales also appeared in the books of other travellers of the time.

Such grotesque and outlandish accounts hold an enduring fascination, even though it was known (as Henry Fielding wrote) that there was a "vast pile of books which pass under the names of voyages, travels, adventures, lives, memoirs, histories, &c., some of which a single traveller sends into the world in many volumes, and others are, by judicious booksellers, collected into vast bodies in folio, and inscribed with their own names, as if they were indeed their own travels; thus unjustly attributing to themselves the merit of others."

We know from comparing parallel passages that Chaucer probably read Mandeville. Shakespeare certainly did. Some of the book represents accurate geography; other parts are distorted, fanciful, absurd, and freakish.

Mandeville's Marvels

THE ISLANDS NEAR JAVA

In that country and others thereabout there be wild geese that have two heads. And there be lions, all white and as great as oxen, and many other diverse beasts and fowls also that be not seen amongst us.

In one of these isles be folk of great stature, as giants. And they be hideous for to look upon. And they have but one eye, and that is in the middle of the front. And they eat nothing but raw flesh and raw fish.

And in another isle toward the south dwell folk of foul stature and of cursed kind that have no heads. And their eyen be in their shoulders.

And in another isle be folk that have the face all flat, all plain, without nose and without mouth. But they have two small holes, all round, instead of their eyes, and their mouth is flat also without lips.

And in another isle be folk of foul fashion and shape that have the lip above the mouth so great, that when they sleep in the sun they cover all the face with that lip . . .

And in another isle be folk that have horses' feet. And they be strong and mighty, and swift runners; for they take wild beasts with running, and eat them.

And in another isle be folk that go upon their hands and their feet as beasts. And they be all skinned and feathered, and they will leap as lightly into trees, and from tree to tree, as it were squirrels or apes.

And in another isle be folk that be both man and woman, and they have kind; of that one and of that other. And they have but one pap on the one side, and on that other none. And they have members of generation of man and woman, and they use both when they list, once that one, and another time that other. And they get children, when they use the member of man; and they bear children, when they use the member of woman.

And in another isle be folk that go always upon their knees full marvellously. And at every pace that they go, it seemeth that they would fall. And they have in every foot eight toes.

IN THE KINGDOM OF PRESTER JOHN

In that desert be many wild men, that be hideous to look on; for they be horned, and they speak nought, but they grunt, as pigs. And there is also great plenty of wild hounds. And there be many pop-injays, that they clepe psittakes their language. And they speak of their proper nature, and salute men that go through the deserts, and speak to them as apertly as though it were a man. And they that speak well have a large tongue, and have five toes upon a foot. And there be also of another manner, that have but three toes upon a foot, and they speak not, or but little, for they can not but cry.

DEFLOWERING

Another isle is there, full fair and good and great, and full of people, where the custom is such, that the first night that they be married, they make another man to lie by their wives for to have their maidenhead: and therefore they take great hire and great thank. And there be certain men in every town that serve of none other thing; and they clepe them cadeberiz, that is to say, the fools of wanhope. For they of the country hold it so great a thing and so perilous for to have the maidenhead of a woman, that them seemeth that they that have first the maidenhead putteth him in adventure of his life.

SEXUAL HABITS ON "ANOTHER ISLE" NEARBY

In that country they take their daughters and their sisters to their wives, and their other kinswomen. And if there be ten men or twelve men or more dwelling in an house, the wife of everych of them shall be common to them all that dwell in that house; so that every man may lie with whom he will of them on one night, and with another, another night. And if she have any child, she may give it to what man that she list, that hath companied with her, so that no man knoweth there whether the child be his or another's. And if any man say to them, that they nourish other men's children, they answer that so do over men theirs . . . And I asked them the cause why that they held such custom: and they said me, that of old time men had been dead for deflowering of maidens, that had serpents in their bodies that stung men upon their yards, that they died anon: and therefore they held that customs to make other men ordained therefore to lie by their wives, for dread of death, and to assay the passage by another [rather] than for to put them in that adventure.

Marco Polo's Human Oddities

Let me tell you next of the kingdom of Lambri [in present-day Sumatra], which also has a king of its own but professes allegiance to the Great Khan. The people are idolaters . . .

Now here is something really remarkable. I give you my word that in this kingdom there are men who have tails full a palm in length. They are not at all hairy. This is true of most of the men — that is, of those who live outside in the mountains, not of those in the city. Their tails are as thick as a dog's. There are also many unicorns [probably rhinos] and a profusion of wild game, both beast and bird.

— *The Travels of Marco Polo*, translated by Ronald Latham (1958)

Andaman is a very big island. The people have no king. They are idolaters and live like wild beasts. Now let me tell you of a race of men well worth describing in our book. You may take it for a fact that all the men of this island have heads like dogs, and teeth and eyes like dogs; for I assure you that the whole aspect of their faces is that of big mastiffs. They are a very cruel race: whenever they can get hold of a man who is not one of their kind, they devour him.

— *The Travels of Marco Polo*

࿆ 21 ࿆

Writers and the Places They Never Visited

F OR A WRITER TO DESCRIBE A PLACE HE OR SHE has not bothered to visit is not only self-deluded but deeply insulting to the people living there and to those travellers who actually troubled to go there. Laziness, indifference, contempt, fear of the place, fear of travel, fear of being disillusioned, and the novelist's natural instinct to fantasize — all are factors in the decision of a writer to stay home and invent the exotic, as Saul Bellow did, conjuring up an Africa he had never seen while sitting in his book-lined study in Tivoli, New York, without ever having to swat a tsetse fly. Even so, you know a writer's mind, and especially his or her fantasies, from the fiction. You know what they think of themselves, and other people, and of the world.

The results of such leaps of imagination can be odd, and bad karma seems to blight the fiction of faked countries, because none of these works has remained popular or widely read. Kipling's imagined Mandalay is an exception, and seems to have displaced the real city. The writers cooking up a country tend to overdo it: look no further than Bellow's *Henderson the Rain King* or the Tarzan novels. Joseph Conrad, who piloted a river steamer up the Congo River, and afterward wrote *Heart of Darkness*, about a man piloting a river steamer up the Congo River, is subtle, understated, and powerful.

David Livingstone claimed to have been the first to put Lake Nyasa on the map in 1859, but this was accomplished in 1846 by a Portuguese trader, Candido de Costa Cardoso. In the search for the source of the Nile, the Welsh explorer John Petherick (1813–1882) produced a map of Bahr-el-Ghazal in 1858 and described his travels in his *Egypt, the Soudan, and Central Africa* three years later. But his fellow explorer John Speke publicly disputed the map and the book, claiming that Petherick had lied about his travels, had not been that far south or west, and had concocted both the map and the trip from hearsay. The Nile explorer Samuel Baker wrote in his diary, "Petherick's pretended journey published in England was entire fiction . . . Petherick is a gross impostor."

Even the traveller, looking closely, often gets things wrong. Richard Henry Dana's Hawaiians in *Two Years Before the Mast* (1840), after months of sailing, mistook the island of Nantucket for the whole of the United States, because it was all they saw: the mainland is not visible from the island.

Here is another instance of travellers' ignorance, from Mary Kingsley's *Travels in West Africa* (1897). She writes, "Watch again a gang of natives trying to get a log of timber down into the river from the bank . . . No idea of a lever, or anything of that sort — and remember that, unless under white supervision, the African has never made an even fourteenth-rate piece of cloth or pottery, or a machine, tool, picture, sculpture, and that he has never even risen to the level of picture-writing."

Never mind the masterpieces of Benin bronzes, the magnificent carvings of the Chokwe people, whom she would have known from her travels in Angola. A little research would have revealed the Amharic script of Abyssinia, two thousand years of Nok sculpture, the immense variety of African pottery, or ancient examples of terracotta statuary. Yet she seems not to have taken any notice even in the places she claimed to know well: Gabon with its Punu and Fang masks and carvings, or the masterpieces of carving — Bamileke and others, and indeed elaborate pots — from Cameroon.

Yet I am fascinated by imaginary landscapes, what Dr. Johnson called "romantick absurdities and incredible fictions", that are retailed as the real thing, especially landscapes I have seen. I do not recognize the fictional Africas, and Kafka's America is one of the weirdest countries of all. As for the outrageous George Psalmanazar — he fooled almost every reader (except Jonathan Swift) in early-eighteenth-century England with his book about Formosa.

George Psalmanazar's Travels in Formosa

THE AMAZING THING about this impostor of travel was the completeness and credibility of his book. Drawing on Dutch accounts, and fantasizing, he created a whole Formosan landscape and culture and made up an entire language of gobbledygook that even years later was taken by some scholars to be an actual Asiatic tongue. The book, published in London in 1704, was a huge success.

George Psalmanazar (or Psalmanaazaar) also managed to conceal his real identity under this outlandish name (perhaps a version of the Assyrian king Shalmaneser in 2 Kings): his birth name and birthplace are unknown. He was probably French, and he may have been born around 1689. For a while he claimed to be an Irish pilgrim. He also at various times said he was Japanese or Formosan. He claimed to worship the sun and the moon, and he slept sitting upright in a chair ("Formosanstyle", he said), but he was more than the lovable eccentric who was later befriended by Dr. Johnson. "A great lover of penitents," Jeffrey Meyers writes in his biography *Samuel Johnson: The Struggle*, "Johnson reverenced Psalmanazar, who'd confessed his sins, reformed his character and become pious, endured prolonged hardship and — though an opium addict — died an exemplary Christian." But in his travel book, Psalmanazar played upon the anti-Jesuit animus current in the early eighteenth century; disparagements of Catholic missionaries are frequent in his book, something that would have found favour with the predominantly Catholic-hating English.

"The prevailing Reason for this my Undertaking was," he writes, "because the Jesuits I had found had imposed so many Stories, and such Gross Fallacies upon the Public, that they might the better excuse themselves from those base Actions, which brought upon them that fierce Persecution in Japan." The Japanese persecution of Catholics in the 1630s was a historical fact that was given a fictional retelling in Shusako Endo's 1966 masterpiece, *Silence*.

Psalmanazar's book is in two parts, the first, "An Historical and Geographical Description of Formosa, Giving an account of the Religion, Customs, & of the Inhabitants, Together with a Relation of what happen'd to the Author in his Travels; particularly his Conferences with the Jesuits, and others, in several Parts of Europe. Also the History and Reasons of his Conversion to Christianity, with his Objections against it (in defence of Paganism) and their Answers." The second part relates his travels: "An Account of the Travels of Mr. George Psalmanaazaar, a Native of the Isle Formosa, thro' several parts of Europe; with the reasons of his Conversion to the Christian Religion."

Discourses on religion aside, the book is highly readable, both for its narrative of abduction and its delineation of a colourful culture. George is taken, under protest, by Jesuits from his native land. He travels to the Philippines, then to Goa, then Gibraltar, where "very much indisposed by the change of Climates, Air and Diet," he needs to recuperate. Then on to Toulon, Marseille, and into Catholic Avignon and Lutheran Bonn and Calvinist Holland, where he becomes embroiled in theological arguments. He is ultimately converted to Christianity, becoming "a most faithful Member of the Church of England".

Having established his loyalty to his adopted country and rulers (William III, who ruled until 1702, when Queen Anne succeeded him), ingratiating himself with readers, he goes on to describe the island of

Formosa, with occasional allusions to Japan. This country is "one of the most Pleasant and Excellent of the Asiatic Isles, whether we consider the convenient Situation, the healthful Air, the fruitful Soil, or the curious Springs and useful Rivers, and rich Mines of Gold and Silver wherewith it abounds".

He chronicles the history, the monarchy, how the island was invaded by the emperor of Tartary and subdued, the arrival of the Dutch and the English traders, mayhem, mutinies, government, the more colourful of the laws. "Every man may have as many Wives, as his estate is able to maintain," he says, because children are highly valued. Adultery is severely punished; a man may lawfully kill his wife if she is unfaithful. "But this Law does not extend to Foreigners, to whom the Natives are wont to offer Virgins or Whores, to be made use of at their Pleasure, with Impunity."

No mention is made of Buddhism, which flourished in Formosa except for the forty years when the Dutch tried to sideline it. Psalmanazar explains Formosan religion as sun and moon worship, and "idolatry" that requires the sacrifice of oxen, rams, and goats. If "their God is not appeased by other Sacrifices", infants are killed — their hearts cut out and burned in the thousands. Meticulous illustrations are included in the book, showing where these human sacrifices are performed, where priests cut babies' throats "and pluck out their Hearts".

Because nothing seems to be excluded, the book has a convincing verisimilitude: superstitions, diseases, weapons, musical instruments, and the food of the islanders — roots that they make into bread, fruit, pigs, and "they eat serpents also". Formosans are not allowed to eat pigeons or turtles. They breed "Elephants, Rhinocerots [*sic*], Camels" to use as beasts of burden; and for their amusement, "Sea-Horses". In the countryside there are "Lyons, Boars, Wolves, Leopards, Apes, Tygers, Crocodiles".

Not everyone was taken in by George Psalmanazar's hoax. He was mocked even in his own time (he died in 1763), but the book remained popular, perhaps for the reason that travel books have always been popular, because the traveller (like Psalmanazar) claims to be an eyewitness to amazing sights. And the very barbarities in the book's details seemed to prove that it was a truthful account of a distant land.

Poe's Believable Landscapes

EDGAR ALLAN POE'S life was short, and not a travelling one, yet his fiction is full of foreign landscapes, among them believable Paris, Switzerland, Holland, and Norway, as well as nameless gothic moorlands, and even unearthly ones, such as the cold regions at the end of *The Narrative of Arthur Gordon Pym*. I read Poe as a teenager and was transported from my humdrum existence to his world of horror and mystery and freakishness.

Poe was born in Boston in 1809 to parents who were actors. His father had disappeared and his mother was dead by the time he was two years old. Adopted by the Allan family, from whom he got his middle name, he was taken abroad, and before he turned eleven he had seen Scotland and England. But after 1820 he merely shuttled from one American city to another — New York, Philadelphia, Baltimore, Richmond; and he was dead at forty. High-strung, quarrelsome, competitive, and alcoholic, Poe had an intensity and a belief in his own genius, which compelled his creation of real and imaginary worlds.

The gothic attracted him, as it attracts many, for its brooding landscape of crags and castles, haunted palaces, its "sense of insufferable gloom" and "shadowy fancies" ("The Fall of the House of Usher"), of moorland and howling wolves, plagues such as "the Red Death", crypts and catacombs ("A Cask of Amontillado"), and "gloomy grey hereditary halls" ("Berenice").

The gothic memory in "William Wilson" is emblematic: "My earliest recollections of a school-life, are connected with a large, rambling, Elizabethan house, in a misty-looking village of England, where were a vast number of gigantic and gnarled trees, and where all the houses were excessively ancient."

Or the lugubrious opening of "The Fall of the House of Usher": "During the whole of a dull, dark, and soundless day in the autumn of the year, when the clouds hung oppressively low in the heavens, I had been passing alone, on horseback, through a singularly dreary tract of country; and at length found myself, as the shades of the evening drew on, within view of the melancholy House of Usher."

In his detective fiction, macabre stories, and even his early science fiction, Poe shows himself to be a reader of travel, history, and the arcane — the Red Death, the Spanish Inquisition ("the horrors at Toledo"), the devil in the belfry in the Dutch borough of Vondervotteimittiss; "The Assignation" takes place in a believable Venice.

Now and then there's a serious geographical lapse, as in "Silence — A Fable", which takes place in a "dreary region in Libya, by the borders of the river Zaire . . . yellow ghastly river . . . hippopotami." Elsewhere, his work is distinguished by its exactitude. Poe had never been to France, yet the French loved Poe in Baudelaire's translations. Detective Auguste Dupin appeared in "The Purloined Letter", "The Mystery of Marie Rogêt", and also in "The Murders in the Rue Morgue", where he is here, walking with the narrator in Paris, part of a paragraph that is convincing in its precision:

> You kept your eyes upon the ground — glancing, with a petulant expression, at the holes and ruts in the pavement (so that I saw you were still thinking of the stones), until we reached the little alley called Lamartine, which has been paved, by way of experiment, with the overlapping and riveted blocks. Here your countenance brightened up, and, perceiving your lips move, I could not doubt that you murmured the word "stereotomy", a term very affectedly applied to this species of pavement.

Some corpses are found to be horribly mutilated, and this leads to the Rue Morgue, "one of those miserable thoroughfares which intervene between the Rue Richelieu and the Rue St. Roch". It turns out that the murderer is an enraged orang-utan with a razor, but Poe knows (as some other authors do not) that orang-utans come from Borneo.

The opening of his terrifying story "A Descent into the Maelström" is Poe's most impressive fictional representation of an actual landscape:

> "We are now," [the old man] continued, in that particularizing manner which distinguished him — "we are now close upon the Norwegian coast — in the sixty-eighth degree of latitude — in the great province of Nordland — and in the dreary district of Lofoden. The mountain upon whose top we sit is Helseggen, the Cloudy. Now raise yourself up a little higher — hold on to the grass if you feel

giddy — so — and look out, beyond the belt of vapour beneath us, into the sea."

I looked dizzily, and beheld a wide expanse of ocean, whose waters wore so inky a hue as to bring at once to my mind the Nubian geographer's account of the Mare Tenebrarum. A panorama more deplorably desolate no human imagination can conceive. To the right and left, as far as the eye could reach, there lay outstretched, like ramparts of the world, lines of horridly black and beetling cliff, whose character of gloom was but the more forcibly illustrated by the surf which reared high up against it, its white and ghastly crest, howling and shrieking for ever. Just opposite the promontory upon whose apex we were placed, and at a distance of some five or six miles out at sea, there was visible a small, bleak-looking island; or, more properly, its position was discernible through the wilderness of surge in which it was enveloped. About two miles nearer the land, arose another of smaller size, hideously craggy and barren, and encompassed at various intervals by a cluster of dark rocks.

The appearance of the ocean, in the space between the more distant island and the shore, had something very unusual about it. Although, at the time, so strong a gale was blowing landward that a brig in the remote offing lay to under a double-reefed trysail, and constantly plunged her whole hull out of sight, still there was here nothing like a regular swell, but only a short, quick, angry cross dashing of water in every direction — as well in the teeth of the wind as otherwise. Of foam there was little except in the immediate vicinity of the rocks.

This goes on for many more pages, with the revelation of the maelstrom, showing that Poe, a man who had hardly been anywhere — and certainly nowhere like this — was able to create a credible landscape out of his reading and his imagination.

Thomas Janvier, *In the Sargasso Sea*

JANVIER, WHO IS forgotten now, was born in 1849, educated in Philadelphia, lived in New York City, and travelled in Europe and Mexico. He wrote biography, history, and travel; he published a guidebook about

Mexico and short stories set in France; and with one exception he wrote directly from experience, describing places he'd been — Provence and Mexico.

In the Sargasso Sea (1898) was recommended to me by the humourist S. J. Perelman, who told me that this depiction of a man struggling on a sea of weeds was like a version of living and writing in Hollywood. Perelman might have been introduced to the book by his friend Nathanael West, who mentions Janvier in his powerful Hollywood novel, *The Day of the Locust*. Todd, West's main character, gets a glimpse of the place where movie sets are disposed of.

> He left the road and climbed across the spine of the hill to look down on the other side. From there he could see a ten-acre field of cockleburs, spotted with clumps of sunflowers and wild gum. In the centre of the field was a gigantic pile of nets, flats and props. While he watched, a ten-ton truck added another load to it. This was the final dumping ground. He thought of Janvier's "Sargasso Sea". Just as that imaginary body of water was a history of civilization in the form of a marine junkyard, the studio lot was one in the form of a dream dump.

The Sargasso Sea actually exists. It was first seen by Columbus, and described by Jules Verne (the *Nautilus* motored through it in *Twenty Thousand Leagues Under the Sea*). As a convergence of ocean currents, it is an elliptical "free-floating meadow of seaweed almost as large as a continent" (*Encyclopedia Britannica*), rotating slowly clockwise. Because it is adjacent to Bermuda it is part of the mystery associated with the Bermuda Triangle. A breeding place for eels, this sea within a sea is bordered by the Gulf Stream on the west. Its name is from the profusion of brown floating gulfweed (genus Sargassum) visible on its surface.

It was thought, mistakenly, that the Sargasso Sea trapped ships, and contributing to the vivid ship-swallowing myth, this is the conceit that Janvier uses to great effect in his novel.

> I had come out from the wheel-house and was standing on the steamer's bridge — which rose right out of the water so that I looked down from it directly on the weed-laden sea. As far as my sight would carry through the soft golden haze I saw only weed-covered

water, broken here and there by a bit of wreckage or by a little open space on which the pale sunshine gleamed. A very gentle swell was running, giving to the ocean the look of some strange sort of meadow with tall grass swaying evenly in an easy wind . . . So far as the world was concerned I was dead already — being fairly caught in the slow eddying current which was carrying my hulk steadily and hopelessly into the dense wreck-filled centre of the Sargasso Sea.

And later:

I had before me what I think must be the strangest sight that the world has in it for the eyes of man. For what I looked at was the host of wrecked ships, the dross of wave and tempest, which through four centuries — from the time when sailors first pushed out upon the great western ocean — has been gathering slowly, and still more slowly wasting, in the central fastnesses of the Sargasso Sea.

Janvier, a traveller, was widely read in his time, which was just a century ago. On his death, the appreciative *New York Times* obituary praised Janvier for his "suave irony, gentle aloofness", and went on, "His varied books of travel had the same combination of qualities — keen and close observation, with a curious sympathy of understanding and vividness of presentation."

Edgar Rice Burroughs: "I Can Write Better About Places I've Never Seen"

MANY PEOPLE, OF whom I am one, formed their first notions of Africa from the work of Edgar Rice Burroughs, specifically the Tarzan books — and films and illustrated comics. Even knowing this was fantasy adventure, readers, young ones especially, felt an incomparable thrill. Burroughs never set foot in Africa, though he knew something about roughing it — he'd been a cowboy, a soldier in the Seventh Cavalry, and a gold miner in Idaho.

He was one of those American writers who was so full of speculative schemes (Twain was another) that they worked their way into his fiction. Burroughs had been a poor student, a failed businessman, and somewhat desperate as a writer when, at the age of thirty-six, he published *Tarzan of the Apes* as a serial in *All-Story* magazine. He'd been fascinated by the ethnographic exhibits (native dances, grass skirts, African warriors) and zoo animals he'd seen in Chicago at the World's Columbian Exhibition in 1893. He'd read Burton and Stanley on Africa, as well as H. Rider Haggard adventures and Kipling's *Jungle Book*. He was asked many times how he came up with the idea of Tarzan. He claimed he didn't know (though Tarzan's upbringing can be compared with Mowgli's in Kipling, and Kipling mentions Tarzan approvingly in his own autobiography, *Something of Myself*), but said that the character helped him escape from the humdrum life he was leading. "My mind, in relaxation, preferred to roam in scenes and situations I'd never known. I find that I can write better about places I've never seen than those I have."

In *Tarzan of the Apes* (1914), Tarzan is John Clayton, the son of Lord Greystoke, whose wife has died while living in a remote cabin in West Africa. The female ape Kala, grieving for her own dead baby, kills Lord Greystoke and abducts young Clayton, whom she calls Tarzan ("white skin" in ape language), raising him as her own. Jane Porter, another castaway, also turns up in this first novel, along with a cast of sinister opportunists. Tarzan is not sure who he is, but his skills and his strength have made him Lord of the Jungle. The book was such a hit with readers that a year later he wrote *The Return of Tarzan* (featuring his marriage to Jane), and altogether twenty-five Tarzan books, other stories with an African setting, as well as a number of westerns and works of science fiction.

After a prolific career as a writer of adventure stories, quite wealthy, living in Hawaii and feeling neglected, Burroughs, at the age of sixty-six, witnessed the bombing of Pearl Harbor. He immediately signed up as a war correspondent and travelled throughout the Pacific. He remained in Hawaii until the end of the war.

It is obvious that as he continued to write the Tarzan books he mugged up on Africa. The setting for the Tarzan stories appears to be the Gabon of Du Chaillu's *Exploration and Adventures in Equatorial Africa*. He would have found Swahili in Burton, since Tarzan's Waziri people use accurate Swahili words, such as *Mulungu* for God, *askari* for soldier, and *shifta* for bandit. Tarzan becomes their chief after their own chief dies battling Arab slave traders. A lovely African girl in *Tarzan: The Lost Adventure* is named Nyama. This is the Swahili word for meat, as well as a generic word for game (and a slang word in East Africa for a low woman). But in all the books Africans are primitive (Tarzan usually mocks them) and not to be compared with the apes, Tarzan's real family. Civilized man is worse than any other — "more brutal than the brutes". The great apes, the Mangani, who are Tarzan's extended family, have a whole language to themselves, which Burroughs invented or contrived from travel book glossaries. One can easily see that Tarzan is the creation of an armchair traveller, a devourer of travel books.

Saul Bellow's Fairly Serious Fooling

BELLOW HAD NOT seen Africa before he wrote *Henderson the Rain King* (1959), his novel about the larger-than-life Eugene Henderson — war hero, pig farmer, ranter. Very tall and very strong and highly ingenious, Henderson describes himself as "a millionaire wanderer and wayfarer", and he adds, "A brutal and violent man driven into the world . . . A fellow whose heart said, *I want, I want.*"

This novel, Bellow's favourite, is his weakest, and perhaps because of that, his most revealing: slack writing is full of disclosure.

Bellow, henpecked, exasperated, in need of imaginative relief, felt cornered in an unhappy marriage when he conceived and wrote the book. The African setting, the freedom of Henderson to roam and rant, the transformation that fiction writing allows, were probably a consolation to Bellow. If he couldn't go to Africa and leave his miseries behind, at least he could fantasize about such an escape.

"I am just a traveller," Henderson says to King Dahfu. But to Chief Itelo he said, "Your Highness, I am really kind of on a quest." It seems to me that this is the crux of the matter: Bellow cannot imagine an Africa that is not full of marvels, odd customs, harems, wrestling matches, lion hunts, and the mystical rain ceremony that elevates Henderson to kingship among the Wariri, in the same way that Tarzan is elevated to chief of the similar-sounding Waziri in *The Return of Tarzan*.

In the imagined world of the non-travelling fiction writer there is usually a convergence of the grotesque and the stereotypical. A comparison of Henderson with Tarzan is not out of place. The difference is that Burroughs admitted he was writing pulp fiction, while the highly intelligent Bellow, self-conscious in this role as fabulist, often plays it for laughs. This novel — strained comedy, occasional farce, and sometimes outright clowning — is unconvincing to anyone who has lived in an African village, yet when Bellow won the Nobel Prize, *Henderson* was commended as his "most imaginative expedition".

Burton's *First Footsteps in East Africa* is invoked by Henderson. But the antiquated nature of the travel and Bellow's invented tribes make me think that (like Edgar Rice Burroughs) he was influenced more by Paul Du Chaillu's 1861 *Exploration and Adventures in Equatorial Africa*, in which Du Chaillu, an American of French descent, was made a king of the Apingi tribe in Gabon.

Du Chaillu wrote, "Remandji said, 'You are the spirit, whom we have never seen before. We are but poor people when we see you. You are of those whom we have often heard of, who come from nobody knows where, and whom we never hoped to see. You are our king and ruler; stay with us always. We love you and will do what you wish.' Whereupon ensued shouts and rejoicings; palm wine was introduced, and a general jollification took place, in the orthodox fashion at coronations. From this day, therefore, I may call myself Du Chaillu the First, King of the Apingi."

Henderson becomes the Rain King in a similar fashion. Challenged by an interviewer about the reality in his novel, Bellow replied, "Years ago, I studied African ethnography with the late Professor Herskovits. Later he scolded me for writing a book like *Henderson*. He said the subject was much too serious for such fooling. I felt that my fooling was fairly serious. Literalism, factualism, will smother the imagination altogether."

This seems to me a delusion on Bellow's part, yet another delusion of the non-travelling writer.

Arthur Waley: Not Madly Singing in the Mountains

DESPITE PUBLISHING MORE than twenty volumes of his translations from Chinese and Japanese, including *The Way and the Power, Tao Te Ching, The Analects* of Confucius, and Murasaki's *Tale of Genji*, Waley never travelled to China or Japan.

Waley claimed that he didn't want to risk being disappointed by seeing the real places so bewitchingly described in poetry and prose. Was this so? The Yale Sinologist Jonathan Spence wrote in the journal *Renditions*, "One can make all kinds of guesses concerning Waley's reasons for not going to Asia: that he didn't want to confuse the ideal with the real, or that he was interested in the ancient written languages and not the modern spoken ones, or that he simply could not afford the journey. Certainly we are safe in assuming that the trip would have been disconcerting."

Modern China would surely have disconcerted him. Waley was happier in his imagined Tang Dynasty. Here is one of his great translations, and a wonderful affirmation of nature, from the Tang poet Po Chu-i:

Madly Singing in the Mountains

There is no one among men that has not a special failing:
And my failing consists in writing verses.
I have broken away from the thousand ties of life:
But this infirmity still remains behind.
Each time that I look at a fine landscape,
Each time that I meet a loved friend,
I raise my voice and recite a stanza of poetry
And am glad as though a God had crossed my path.
Ever since the day I was banished to Hsun-yang
Half my time I have lived among hills.
And often, when I have finished a new poem,
Alone I climb the road to the Eastern Rock.
I lean my body on the banks of white stone:
I pull down with my hands a green cassia branch.
My mad singing startles the valleys and hills:
The apes and birds all come to peep.

Fearing to become a laughing-stock to the world,
I choose a place that is unfrequented by men.

V. S. Pritchett: A Lot of Verisimilitude, and a Howler

PRITCHETT WROTE *Dead Man Leading*, a novel set in Brazil, in 1937, years before he finally travelled there. The novel describes the quest of some explorers who have been lost in the jungle. Pritchett said that he was inspired by the Fawcett expedition of 1925, which vanished (probably massacred) while searching for a lost city deep in the Mato Grosso.

One of the reasons Pritchett's book is persuasive is that he makes imagery so familiar. He speaks of the brown of a Brazilian river resembling strong tea, and a sky like a huge blue house; the forest is faint, like "a distant fence", and the jungle at another point is bedraggled and broken, "as if a lorry had crashed into it". There is a creek "like a sewage ditch" and a bad rainstorm making "the intolerable whine of machines" and a forest odour "like the smell of spirits gone sour on the breath".

Much later, after he made a visit to Brazil, Pritchett concluded that he had invented the truth. But not entirely. One of the howlers in the book is the mention of "the gulping Lear-like laugh" of an orang-utan. There are no orang-utans in Brazil. They are found ten thousand miles away, in Borneo, and in any case they seldom make a sound.

A Truly Kafkaesque America

FRANZ KAFKA CANNOT be held accountable for the title of his novel *Amerika*. Left unfinished, it was published after his death by his friend and literary executor, Max Brod, who gave it this name. Kafka usually referred to it as *Der Verschollene* (*The Missing Person* or *The Man Who Disappeared*). The man in question went to America.

Though Kafka never got farther west from his home in Prague than France, in his letters to Brod he fantasized about travelling to distant places, among them South America, Spain, and the Azores. In affectionate letters he asked two women at the periphery of his life, Felice Bauer and Dora Diamant, to travel with him to Palestine, where he dreamed of abandoning writing, getting healthy, and landing a job as a waiter. This waiter fantasy occurred in 1923, the year before he died. Claiming that he suffered from "travel anxiety" (*Reiseangst*), Kafka did not go to any far-off places. His real fear was that by travelling — being away from his room, his desk, his books — he would put an end to his writing. His invented America is based on his reading, and he was said to have been influenced by *Amerika Heute und Morgan* (*America Today and Tomorrow*), by an itinerant Hungarian, Arthur Holitscher, who had travelled around the United States as a sceptical tourist. In this book, as in Kafka's *Amerika*, the misspelled name "Oklahama" occurs often.

The fictional result is surreal. In the first sonorous paragraph, the hero, Karl Rossmann, sails into New York harbour and sees the Statue of Liberty, "as if in a burst of sunlight. The arm with the sword now reached aloft, and about her figure blew the free winds." The sword instead of the torch is perhaps deliberate.

After the shock of a chaotic, unrecognizable New York City and an interlude with his uncle Edward Jakob, Karl spends some time with a wealthy Mr. Pollunder at a labyrinthine mansion outside the city. Not much countryside is described, yet we don't expect daffodils and shady glens from Kafka. We expect anxiety dreams, and predictably the narrative becomes like an anxiety dream, even to Uncle Jakob's suddenly sending Karl away, for no apparent reason. Karl looks for a job, hooks up with two tramps, and hits the road. Just outside the city they look back and see a bridge: "The bridge connecting New York to Boston hung delicately over the Hudson and trembled if one narrowed one's eyes. It appeared to bear no traffic, and a long smooth lifeless strip of water stretched underneath."

Karl becomes an elevator operator at the Occidental Hotel, in a large, Middle European–seeming city, and eventually reconnects with the two tramps, who are living with, and looking after, a very fat diva-prostitute named Brunelda (one of their tasks is to bathe her). The novel remained incomplete but is full of tantalizing fragments, including a brothel named Enterprise No. 25 and the Nature Theater of Oklahoma. In every sense, this America, the morbid dream of a tubercular genius in a room in Prague, is Kafkaesque.

❧ Travel Wisdom of ❧
EVELYN WAUGH

E velyn Waugh knew better than most people that there is a great
deal of pleasure to be derived from a travel book in which the
traveller is having a bad time — even better if it is an ordeal. Travel
gave him fame as a young man, and though he said (see below) he did
not travel to collect material, his fiction was enriched by his travel,
from *Black Mischief* at the beginning of his career to *The Ordeal of
Gilbert Pinfold* near the end. Many theorists of travel have claimed
that Waugh's travel writing represents the high-water mark of the
genre; this is demonstrably untrue, yet Waugh's travel is personal and
opinionated, with episodes of high comedy. It is surprising that a man
who cared for comfort and high society risked deep discomfort and low
company in Africa and South America, but that he was a much hardier,
more diligent, and fairer-minded traveller than he let on.

One does not travel, any more than one falls in love, to collect material. It is simply part of one's life. For myself, and many better than I, there is a fascination in distant and barbarous places, and particularly in the borderlands of conflicting cultures and states of development, where ideas, uprooted from their traditions, become oddly changed in transplantation. It is here that I find the experiences vivid enough to demand translation into literary form.

— *Ninety-two Days* (1934)

To have travelled a lot, to have spent, as I have done, the first twelve years of adult life on the move, is to this extent a disadvantage. At the age of thirty-five one needs to go to the moon, or some such place, to recapture the excitement with which one first landed at Calais.

— *When the Going Was Good* (1947)

I do not think I shall ever forget the sight of Etna at sunset; the mountain almost invisible in a blur of pastel grey, glowing on the top and then repeating its shape, as though reflected, in a wisp of grey smoke with the whole horizon behind radiant with pink light, fading gently into a grey pastel sky. Nothing I have seen in Art or Nature was quite so revolting.

— *Labels* (1930)

My own travelling days are over, nor do I expect to see many travel books in the near future. When I was a reviewer, they used, I remember, to appear in batches of four or five a week, cram-full of charm and wit and enlarged Leica snapshots. There is no room for tourists in a world of "displaced persons". Never again, I suppose, shall we land on foreign soil with letter of credit and passport (itself the first faint shadow of the great cloud that envelopes us) and feel the world wide open before us.

— *When the Going Was Good*

When we have been home from abroad for a week or two, and time after time, in answer to our friends' polite inquiries, we have retold our experiences, letting phrase engender phrase, until we have quite made a good story of it all; when the unusual people we have encountered have, in retrospect, become fabulous and fantastic, and all the checks and uncertainties of travel had become very serious dangers; when the minor annoyances assume heroic proportions and have become, at the luncheon-table, barely endurable privations; even before that, when in the later stages of our journey we reread in our diaries the somewhat bald chronicle of the preceding months — how very little attention do we pay, among all these false frights and bogies, to the stark horrors of boredom.

— *Remote People* (1931)

22

Travellers' Bliss

BLISS IS RARE IN THE TRAVEL NARRATIVE, where the usual theme is hardship and sometimes horror. Our happiness in print in any case always seems boastful and improbable, quite far from the human condition. But now and then the traveller arrives at the Great Good Place, gives thanks for his luck, and shows the reader that the travail which gave the word "travel" its form can result in an epiphany, like Doughty's triple rainbow or Vikram Seth's sight of the Potala Palace. The first traveller is William Bartram, who spent four years among Native Americans in the South and, contradicting all the reports of pugnacity and savagery, found only hospitality, goodwill, and wisdom. He described the people who were later expelled from their native land to travel westward on the Trail of Tears.

The Good Manners of the Muscogulges of the Creek Nation

A [Muscogulge] man goes forth on business or avocations, he calls in at another town, if he wants victuals, rest or social conversation, he confidently approaches the door of the first house he chooses, saying, "I am come." The good man or woman replies, "You are; it's well." Immediately victuals and drink are ready; he eats and drinks a little, then smokes Tobacco, and converses either of private matters, public talks or the news of the town. He rises and says, "I go." The other answers, "You do!" He then proceeds again, and steps in at the next habitation he likes, or repairs to the public square, where are people always conversing by day, or dancing all night, or to some more private assembly, as he likes; he needs no one to introduce him, any more than the black-bird or the thrush, when he repairs to the fruitful groves, to regale on their luxuries, and entertain the fond female with evening songs.

It is astonishing, though a fact, as well as a sharp reproof to the white people, if they will allow themselves liberty to reflect and form a just estimate, and I must own elevates these people to the first rank among mankind.

— William Bartram, *Travels Through North and South Carolina* (1791)

C. M. Doughty Sees a Triple Rainbow in Arabia

Late in the afternoon there fell great drops from the lowering skies; then a driving rain fell suddenly, shrill and seething, upon the harsh gravel soil, and so heavily that in a few moments all the plain land was a streaming plash . . .

After half an hour the worst was past, and we mounted again. Little birds, before unseen, flitted cheerfully chittering over the wet wilderness. The low sun looked forth, and then appeared a blissful and surpassing spectacle! A triple rainbow painted in the air before us. Over two equal bows a third was reared upon the feet of the first;

235

and like to it in the order of hues. — These were the celestial arches of the sun's building, a peace in heaven after the battle of the elements in the desert-land of Arabia.   — *Travels in Arabia Deserta* (1888)

Vikram Seth on the Potala Palace in Lhasa

When I next look out we are already in the broad valley of the Lhasa River — with fields of wheat and barley, tall trees, buildings of cement, and, from far away, the dominating vertical plane of the Potala palace, monolithic and of immense grandeur, white and pale pink and red and gold.

In this late afternoon light it is so beautiful that I cannot speak at all. I get up and stare at it, holding on to one of the supports at the back of the truck, and looking forwards in the direction we are travelling. The hill on which it rests, and its own thick, slightly slanting walls, combine to give it a powerful sense of stability; and the white and gold add an almost unreal brilliance to the vast slab that is its structure.

— *From Heaven Lake* (1983)

Flaubert Blissed-Out on the Nile

When we arrived off Thebes our sailors were drumming on their darabukehs, the mate was playing his flute, Khalil was dancing with his castanets: they broke off to land.

It was then, as I was enjoying those things, and just as I was watching three wave-crests bending under the wind behind us, that I felt a surge of solemn happiness that reached out towards what I was seeing, and I thanked God in my heart for having made me capable of such a joy: I felt fortunate at the thought, and yet it seemed to me that I was thinking of nothing: it was a sensuous pleasure that pervaded my entire being.

— *Flaubert in Egypt*, translated by Francis Steegmuller (1972)

Freya Stark at Peace in Hakkiari, Turkey

It was still far from daylight. The high dome of heaven was revolving with peacock colours and secret constellations among the outlined rocks. There was, of course, no sign of the muleteers. I sat there for over an hour, watching the moonlight retreat from the rocky bastions, a process of infinite majesty and peace. I felt, as Firdausi says, like dust in the lion's paw.   — *The Valleys of the Assassins* (1934)

⤖ 23 ⤖

Classics of a Sense of Place

S OME TRAVEL BOOKS ARE LESS ABOUT TRAVEL (that is, a specific itinerary and perambulation) than about an intense experience of a particular place. It could be a wilderness area (Thoreau's Maine), a river (Moritz Thomsen's Amazon), an American state (John McPhee's Alaska), or part of a state (Jonathan Raban's "bad land" of eastern Montana) — or the whole of Wales (Jan Morris), the whole of Spain (Pritchett), or India for half a lifetime (Chaudhuri). Carlo Levi was banished to southern Italy, exiled in the hill town of Aliano in 1935, for his anti-fascist views. He rambled around the town for a year, tended the sick (he was a doctor), and later wrote with feeling about it, and he is buried there. That, too, was travel. He said it was like being on the moon. I think of this as both an inner and an outer journey: what is illuminated is the landscape and the people — the place rather than the traveller or the trip. In most of the following cases the writers are in residence.

The Maine Woods *by Henry David Thoreau*

In 1846 in Maine, only a matter of days from his home in Concord, Thoreau found the wild place he was looking for. In the chapter "Ktaadn" he defines the essence of wilderness. "It is difficult to conceive of a region uninhabited by man," he begins modestly. Then comes his hammer stroke:

> Nature was here something savage and awful, though beautiful. I looked with awe at the ground I trod on, to see what the Powers had made there, the form and fashion and material of their work. This was that Earth of which we have heard, made out of Chaos and Old Night. Here was no man's garden, but the unhandselled globe. It was not lawn, nor pasture, nor mead, nor woodland, nor lea, nor arable, nor waste-land. It was the fresh and natural surface of the planet Earth, as it was made forever and ever.

The book was published posthumously, and based on three pieces that Thoreau had written, about three fairly short trips to the hinterland of Maine. Thoreau made his last trip in 1857. He was forty then, and you can see by his prose style that he is a different sort of traveller: humbler, affronted by the changes he sees in the eleven years since his first visit, no longer a quoter of Milton, or a praiser of lumberjacks, or a hyperbolic observer of the mystical Indian. He is now a denouncer of the logging industry and a clear-sighted diarist. Native Americans fascinated Thoreau, and this third trip in Maine offered him his best opportunity to study them.

> Once, when Joe had called again, and we were listening for moose, we heard come faintly echoing or creeping from far through the moss-clad aisles, a dull dry rushing sound, with a solid core to it, yet as if half-smothered under the grasp of the luxuriant and fungus-like forest, like the shutting of a door in some distant entry of the

damp and shaggy wilderness. If we had not been there no mortal had heard it. When we asked Joe in a whisper what it was, he answered, "Tree fall."

Thoreau was assertively American, in a manner of conspicuous non-conformity inspired by Emerson. Thoreau's passion was for being local, and that included being a traveller in America — to show how to care about the country, what tone to use, what subjects to address. Along the way, in adopting and refining these postures, he became our first and subtlest environmentalist. In Maine his subjects were, as he listed them in a letter, "the Moose, the Pine Tree & the Indian". The last words he spoke on his deathbed were "Moose . . . Indian."

The Spanish Temper *by V. S. Pritchett*

As a traveller in Spain, who hiked a large portion of it and wrote about it in his first book, *Marching Spain* (1928); as a journalist in the 1920s; and as a passionate reader of Spanish writing, V. S. Pritchett was well equipped to sum up this sunny, old-fashioned, and enigmatic country and its people. He was unhappy about his youthful book and so he wrote *The Spanish Temper* (1954) when he was middle-aged. It is to me the ultimate book about Spain — not a big book but a wise, enlightened one, epigrammatic and perceptive. As a short story writer (his story "The Evils of Spain" could be read along with this book), Pritchett was a master of compression. When writing on Spanish food, Franco, bullfighting, *Don Quixote,* and the many different landscapes of Spain, he is always original and challenging.

Speaking about the Spanish Civil War, he recounts the gore and violence and the mass executions. "The barbarian is strong in the Spanish people," he writes and immediately afterward alludes to the bullfight:

> The most damaging criticism of the Spanish taste for bullfighting is rather different: the bullfight suffers from the monotony of sacrifices, and it is one more example of the peculiar addiction to the repetitive and the monotonous in the Spanish nature. Many foreigners who have known Spain well have noted this taste for monotony. The

drama of the bullfight lies within the drama of a foregone conclusion . . . The fate of the bull is certain.

In another place, at Guadix in southern Spain, he marvels at a panorama of rock and mountain:

> It is a land for the connoisseur of landscape, for in no other European
> country is there such variety and originality. Here Nature has had
> vast Space, stupendous means, and no restraint of fancy. One might
> pass a lifetime gazing at the architecture of rock and its strange col-
> ouring, especially the colouring of iron, blue steel, violet and ochreous
> ores, metallic purples, and all the burned, vegetable pigments. These
> landscapes frighten by their scale and by the suggestion of furrowed
> age, geological madness, malevolence and grandeur.

The Matter of Wales *by Jan Morris*

A CULTURAL STUDY, a history, combining topography, language, national character, and travel, lovingly anatomized, Morris's 1984 book
describes "not only a separate nation, but a distinctly separate and often
vehement idea." Here is Morris's disquisition on Welsh rocks and stones:

> The substance of Welsh nature is largely rock, for some four-fifths
> of the surface of Wales is hard upland, where the soil is so thin that
> stones seem always to be forcing their way restlessly through, and
> it feels as though a really heavy rain-storm would wash all the turf
> away. The softness of the valleys, the calm of the low farmlands are
> only subsidiary to the character of the country: the real thing, the
> dominant, is hard, bare, grey and stony.
>
> This means that the truest Welsh places offer experiences as much
> tactile as visual, for everywhere there are stones that seem to invite
> your stroking, your rolling, your sitting upon or, if you happen to be
> a druid or a survivor from the Stone Age, your worshipping. There
> are thrilling clumps of jagged stones on hilltops, and stark solitary
> stones beside moorland roads, and stones gleaming perpetually
> with the splash of earth-dark streams, and stone walls which seem
> less like walls than masonry contour-lines, snaking away across the
> mountain elevations mile after mile as far as the eye can see.

The Saddest Pleasure *by Moritz Thomsen*

"IT HAS BEEN forty-five years since I took a trip whose object was pleasure," Moritz Thomsen writes before leaving his farm in the Ecuadorian coastal province of Esmeraldas (which he wrote about in *The Farm on the River of Emeralds*). He was an older Peace Corps volunteer — fifty when he joined — and a rare one: he never went home. He decided to travel down the Amazon, "because there is an emptiness in my life that needs to be filled with something fresh and moderately intense".

He makes rules for himself in the travel: "Dollar meals if I can find them; five dollar hotels, if they still exist. No guided tours, no visits to historical monuments or old churches. No taxis, no mixed drinks in fancy bars. No hanging around places where English might be spoken." He takes his time, floating from river to river, stopping at the Amazon ports of Manaus and Belém and finally reaching Bahia on the coast. After all the bad food and discomfort and illness, and his witnessing the distress and poverty and the fallen world that is Amazonia, he concludes, "There are no solutions any more; the continent will never recover." In his oblique and humane and self-deprecating way, he is the ideal guide. Though he credits me as the source of his title (a line from my novel *Picture Palace*), the quotation is actually from Madame de Staël, in *Corinne, ou l'Italie* (1807): "Travel is one of the saddest pleasures of life."

Coming into the Country *by John McPhee*

FIRST PUBLISHED IN 1977, even thirty-odd years later this book about Alaska is still the best one ever written about that enormous piece of land and its tiny population. McPhee (b. 1931) was in the hinterland, paddling the rivers and streams, before trails were blazed and the road beside the Trans-Alaska Pipeline was open to the public. The book is part wilderness experience — McPhee travelling with a group of scientists and environmentalists — and part social experiment — his meeting new Alaskans and indigenous people, and examining the fantasies and contradictions. What is most impressive is how deeply McPhee penetrates to the heart of the country. Though he is always dour in manner, literal-minded, factual, resistant to any levity, allowing his narrative to sprawl, this is probably why the book has endured. McPhee's feet are always on the ground, even when faced by a grizzly bear (twelve pages of suspense and information).

Speaking of the provincialism of Alaska, he writes:

> In Alaska, the conversation is Alaska. Alaskans, by and large, seem to know little and to say less about what is going on outside. They talk about their land, their bears, their fish, their rivers. They talk about subsistence hunting, forbidden hunting, and living in trespass. They have their own lexicon. A senior citizen is a pioneer, snow is termination dust, and the N.B.A. is the National Bank of Alaska. The names of Alaska are so beautiful they run like fountains all day in the mind. Mulchatna. Chilikadrotna. Unalaska. Unalakleet. Kivalina. Kiska. Kodiak. Allakaket. The Aaniakchak Caldera. Nondalton. Anaktubvuk. Anchorage. Alaska is a foreign country significantly populated with Americans. Its languages extend to English. Its nature is its own.

Bad Land *by Jonathan Raban*

"WHAT I FELT all the way was like a scale model of immigrants to America," Raban once said, describing this book. "It was the story of America written in one particular landscape." In the beginning of *Bad Land* (1996) he describes himself as an emigrant, "trying to find my own place in the landscape and history of the West". He chose an unlikely and pretty much unwritten-about place, the dry, flat expanses of eastern Montana. This is a book about a part of America that no American could have written: we don't have Raban's objectivity, his passion, or his sense of alienation. He is also widely read and intensely curious — curious in the way of an intelligent foreigner in America: "Bred to looking at a landscape as if it were a picture, to the posted scenic viewpoint, I was responding to the prairie like a shut-in taking his first walk across a blinding city square. It was all periphery and no centre."

Travel, history, biography, and autobiography, this highly original portrait of prairie America, published in 1996, is also about the people who travelled there and who learned to adapt to the rigours of the weather, the stubborn soil, the great oceanlike emptiness that inspires Raban to view the landscape as an inland sea, in which the emigrants are like solitary voyagers. Intensely observant, curious to the point of nosiness, Raban gets to know them, examines their family histories, their dreams, the images that have been painted of the land, the photographs, the guidebooks, and he describes the journey itself — the emigrant train, filled with distinct individuals, whom we come to know, confronted by a new climate.

Dreadful though the cold could be, it was not the most destructive element in Montana's repertoire of violent weather. In summer, the air over the northern plains is turbulent: it moves in swirls and gyres, with fierce rip currents and whirlpool-like tornadoes. Here the north-westerly air stream, blowing from Alaska and the Arctic Circle, collides with warm southeasterlies blowing from the Gulf of Mexico and the southern U.S. interior. The exposed, treeless prairie, baking in the sun by day and cooling rapidly during the afternoons, intensifies the aerial commotion.

This is magnificent thunderstorm territory. The only time in my life when I have been seriously afraid of lightning was in eastern Montana on a dirt road miles from anywhere . . . The distant storm winked and winked again. Like photo-flashes going off in the face of some celebrity on the far side of a city square, these blips of white light seemed no business of mine, and I drove on . . . Closer now, the lightning flashes were like the skeletal inverted leaves of ferns, and when the thunder came I took it for some gastro-enteritic flare-up in the car engine — a blown gasket or a fractured piston . . .

Then the lightning shafts were stabbing, arbitrarily, at the bare ground, and much too close for comfort . . . A slight but audible interval opened up between the lightning strikes and the rockslides of thunder, and in the lee of the storm came hail, crackling against the windshield and sugaring the road. It lasted just a minute or two. Then the lost sun returned, the prairie was rinsed and green, tendrils of steam rose from the grass, and the dark thundercloud rolled away eastward into North Dakota.

The Traveller's Tree *by Patrick Leigh Fermor*

WHAT IS IMPRESSIVE about this book is its completeness, its humane assessment of the Caribbean islands and their people, and its elegance — an evocative as well as droll appreciation of a vast area. The book is now sixty years old, and so it is also an album of pretty pictures about places that are different, some of them much changed, many of them no longer pretty at all. Haiti comes to mind. In Leigh Fermor's view, Haiti is old-fashioned and proud, lovable, beauteous, cultured, a bit severe — a far cry from the hellishly poor and devastated country of today, the victim of dictatorships, hurricanes, famine, disease, and most recently one of the worst earthquakes in human history.

So *The Traveller's Tree* is dated ("Negroes", "aerodrome", "luncheon"), but all the more valuable for that, because it is in the nature of a travel book, especially an expansive one like this, to serve as a history of a region, noting manners and customs, language and cuisine. He travelled in Trinidad in 1947–48, when V. S. Naipaul was a high school student, before Graham Greene went to Haiti, and around the time Ian Fleming became resident in Jamaica. For many travel writers, Patrick Leigh Fermor is everything a travel writer ought to be — urbane, well read, witty, forgiving, well travelled, and a meticulous observer. His writing is magical, his eye is unerring, and so is his ear — for human speech, for music, for the sound of the sea and birdsong, for the feel of a place. And his barbs tend to be elegant: "Hotel cooking in the island [Trinidad] is so appalling that a stretcher may profitably be ordered at the same time as dinner."

Here, having just landed in a Haiti that is no more, Leigh Fermor is travelling up the main road toward Port-au-Prince in an old wagon. "These black and obsolete vehicles are drawn by horses on the point of death and driven by very old men." He goes on:

> The cane-field and savannah turned into the outskirts of the capital.
> Thatched cabins straggled into the country under the palm trees, and
> multiplied into a suburb, through which the road ran in a straight,
> interminable line. For the first mile or so, the town consisted entirely
> of rum shops and barbers' saloons and harness makers. Hundreds
> of saddles were piled up in the sunlight. Bits and bridles and saddle-

bags hung in festoons. There were horses everywhere. Our equipage churned its way upstream through a current of horses and mules ridden by Negroes who straddled among bulky packages, all heading to their villages with their purchases for Christmas. One or two were singing Haitian *meringues*, and several were carrying game cocks under their arms, lovingly stroking their feathers as they trotted past. Old women, puffing their pipes, jogged along side-saddle. They had scarlet and blue kerchiefs tied round their heads in a fortuitous, rather piratical fashion, half covered by broad-brimmed straw hats against the sun. The sides of the road pullulated with country people chattering, drinking rum, playing cards and throwing dice under the trees. The air was thick with dust, and ringing with incomprehensible and deafening Creole. I felt I might like Haiti.

Italian Hours *by Henry James*

"VENICE WAS ONE of the greatest topographical love affairs of James's life," Leon Edel, his biographer, wrote. For Henry James, Venice was everything he wished for in a distant city — villas facing onto the canals, churches crammed with Renaissance masterpieces, great food, voluble people, and in his time not expensive. He called it "the repository of consolations". A number of his fictions are set in Venice, *The Aspern Papers* among them, and he wrote several of his novels there, notably *The Portrait of a Lady*, which is set in England and in Rome and Florence. *Italian Hours* (1909) sums up James's love of Italy, and particularly Venice, as in this dense and appreciative paragraph:

One may doubtless be very happy in Venice without reading at all — without criticizing or analysing or thinking a strenuous thought. It is a city in which, I suspect, there is very little strenuous thinking, and yet it is a city in which there must be almost as much happiness as misery. The misery of Venice stands there for all the world to see; it is part of the spectacle — a thoroughgoing devotee of local colour might consistently say it is part of the pleasure. The Venetian people have little to call their own — little more than the bare privilege of leading their lives in the most beautiful of towns. Their habitations are decayed; their taxes heavy; their pockets light; their opportunities few. One receives an impression, however, that life presents itself to them with attractions not accounted for in this meagre train of advantages, and that they are on better terms with it than many people who have made a better bargain. They lie in the sunshine; they dabble in the sea; they wear bright rags; they fall into attitudes and harmonies; they assist at an eternal *conversazione*. It is not easy to say that one would have them other than they are, and it certainly would make an immense difference should they be better fed. The number of persons in Venice who evidently never have enough to eat is painfully large; but it would be more painful if we did not equally perceive that the rich Venetian temperament may bloom upon a dog's allowance. Nature has been kind to it, and sunshine and leisure and conversation and beautiful views form the greater part of its sustenance. It takes a great deal to make a successful American, but to make a happy Venetian takes only a handful of quick sensibility. The Italian people have at once the good and the evil fortune to be conscious of few wants; so that if the civilization of a society is measured by the number of its needs, as seems to be the common opinion to-day, it is to be feared that the children of the lagoon would make but a poor figure in a set of comparative tables. Not their misery, doubtless, but the way they elude their misery, is what pleases the sentimental tourist, who is gratified by the sight of a beautiful race that lives by the aid of its imagination. The way to enjoy Venice is to follow the example of these people and make the most of simple pleasures. Almost all the pleasures of the place are simple; this may be maintained even under the imputation of ingenious paradox. There is no simpler pleasure than looking at a fine Titian, unless it be looking at a fine Tintoretto or strolling into St. Mark's, — abominable the way one falls into the habit, — and resting one's light-wearied eyes upon the windowless gloom; or than floating in a gondola or than hanging over a balcony or than taking one's coffee at Florian's. It is of such superficial pastimes that a Venetian day is composed, and the pleasure of the matter is in the emotions to which they minister. These are fortunately of the finest — otherwise Venice would be insufferably dull. Reading Ruskin is good; reading the old records is perhaps better; but the best thing of all is simply staying on. The only way to care for Venice as she deserves it is to give her a chance to touch you often — to linger and remain and return.

The Autobiography of an Unknown Indian
by Nirad C. Chaudhuri

AT THE AGE of fifty, a scriptwriter for All-India Radio, not having published any book, Chaudhuri was possessed by a revelation. "It came in this manner," he wrote. "As I lay awake in the night of May 4–5, 1947, an idea suddenly flashed into my mind. Why, instead of merely regretting the work of history you cannot write, I asked myself, do you not write the history you have passed through and seen enacted before your eyes?" That enlightenment came three months before India's independence. He set about immediately, struggled with some chapters, then hit his stride; and the result is a masterpiece, *The Autobiography of an Unknown Indian* (1951) — a man in a particular place and time.

No better book has been written about India. That Chaudhuri was from the town of Kishorganj, in East Bengal, makes it all the more valuable. He was born in 1897, the year of Queen Victoria's Diamond Jubilee, and died in 1999, in England — a long life in which he was an eyewitness to the most dramatic changes in India. But the book is filled with the details of life — food, caste, religion (a shocking description of animal sacrifice at a Kali temple), life in the provinces and in the cities: Chaudhuri lived in both Calcutta and Delhi. Far from being a serene book, it is argumentative, critical, sometimes denunciatory, as Chaudhuri was in his subsequent books. But he was that rare bird, a traveller in his own country, with a feel for the people and the land and the seasons. Then, as now, East Bengal was famous for its rain and its floods.

If the picture on the river during the rainy season at Kishorganj was the Deluge and the Ark made homely, gregarious, and sociable, we were no less steeped in the spirit of water on land. Everything was wet to the marrow of the bone. Neither we nor our clothes were ever properly dry. When we were not slushy we were damp. The bark of the trees became so sodden that it seemed we could tear it up in handfuls like moss. We could not walk from the hut which was our bed- and living-room except on a line of bricks laid at intervals of about two feet or on a gangway made of bamboos, and the meals were more often than not held up by unseasonable showers. Little rills were running off the road, cutting miniature ravines in its side. Our servants were always wet, and their brown skins were always shining.

The tremendous drenching power of the rain was brought home to us by the dripping coming and going of our father and of our visitors, but above all by the sight of the birds. The ludicrously pitiable appearance of the crows in the rainy season is so notorious that the phrase "bedraggled crow" has become a figurative synonym in the Bengali language for an untidy and dishevelled person . . .

But one of the most attractive and engaging sights of the season was to be seen in the inner courtyard of our house, when there was a heavy downpour. The rain came down in what looked like closely packed formations of enormously long pencils of glass and hit the bare ground. At first the pencils only pitted the sandy soil, but as soon as some water had collected all around they began to bounce off the surface of water and pop up and down in the form of minuscule puppets. Every square inch of ground seemed to receive one of the little things, and our water-logged yard was broken up into a pattern which was not only mobile but dizzily in motion. As we sat on the veranda, myriads of tiny watery marionettes, each with an expanding circlet of water at its feet, gave us such a dancing display as we had never dreamt of seeing in actual life.

Christ Stopped at Eboli *by Carlo Levi*

THIS IS ONE of those important books that, after I'd read it, compelled me to go and see the place for myself. I visited Aliano (Levi calls it Gagliano) in Lucania, in southern Italy, when I was on my around-the-shore-of-the-Mediterranean trip. It was a detour from the coast, but a memorable one. I wrote about it in *The Pillars of Hercules.* "He wasn't Italian," an old man told me in the town, speaking in Italian. "He was a foreigner — a Russian." I questioned this. " *'Breo,'* " the man said. At first I didn't understand, and then I guessed at the word, *Ebreo,* a Jew. So everything Levi experienced in 1935, and wrote about in 1943, was still true in 1995: these people were remote, mentally and geographically, off the map in every sense.

The book describes the oddity of this educated Florentine among the peasants of a remote village in the deep south of Italy — a forgotten people, hardly Christian. Christ didn't get to Aliano, they explain to him; Christ stopped miles away, at Eboli. "We're not Christians," they say. They are superstitious, violent, passionate, mercurial, secretive, with a greater belief in dragons than in any saint.

> I was struck by the peasants' build: they are short and swarthy with round heads, large eyes, and thin lips; their archaic faces do not stem from the Romans, Greeks, Etruscans, Normans, or any other invaders who have passed through their land, but recall the most ancient Italic types. They have led exactly the same life since the beginning of time, and History has swept over them without effect.

Among other things, this is one of the great studies of modern European peasant life, written by a highly intelligent and sympathetic alien, resident in a rural village. There is one toilet in the village, "and probably there was not another one within a radius of fifty miles". Werewolves lurk nearby, the villagers say. Unwritten but arcane laws govern the behaviour of men and women. When Levi's sister visits, she is forbidden to live with him; no man can be left alone with a woman who is not his wife. Levi spends his time in the village painting, writing, and healing the sick.

> Christ never came this far, nor did time, nor the individual soul, nor hope, nor the relation of cause to effect, nor reason, nor history. Christ never came, just as the Romans never came, content to garrison the highways without penetrating the mountains and forests, nor the Greeks . . . No one has come to this land except as an enemy, a conqueror, or a visitor devoid of understanding. The seasons pass today over the toil of the peasants, just as they did three thousand years before Christ; no message, human or divine, has reached this stubborn poverty.

Before he died in 1975, Levi gave instructions that he be buried in the cemetery of Aliano. And there he rests, in the dust among the pines.

A Moveable Feast *by Ernest Hemingway*

THERE ARE TWO *Moveable Feast*s — the first one published in 1964, heavily edited and cobbled together by his widow, and fourth wife, Mary; the second, edited by his grandson Sean Hemingway, published in 2009, is truer to Ernest Hemingway's surviving manuscript (some pages are reproduced) and subtitled "The Restored Edition". It was the last book that Hemingway wrote; he committed suicide not long after finishing it. Both editions are worth reading. The first seems better structured and more organized — though this organization was imposed. The restored edition is longer, more ruminative, but kinder to various of the characters — Scott Fitzgerald especially, but also Hemingway's second wife, Pauline, who comes off badly in the 1964 edition.

The subject is Paris in the 1920s. Hemingway knew the city well — he arrived with wife Hadley late in 1921 and lived there off and on until 1928, when he left to take up residence in Key West with his new wife, Pauline. The themes of this memoir of Paris are being hard-up and happy, the love that Hemingway has for Hadley and his son, and his passion for writing. Being poor, hungry much of the time, Hemingway constantly reverts to the subject of food — flavours, aromas, simple food, good wine; the pleasures of eating and drinking. It is a book about physical sensation, and the intensity of such physicality in Paris.

"Then there was the bad weather," the book begins. "It would come in one day when the fall was over. You would have to shut the windows in the night against the rain and the cold wind would strip the leaves from the trees in the Place Contrescarpe."

Streets are mentioned so often they become familiar, as do parks and churches and people's apartments. The book is filled with restaurants, bistros, and bars, and their specialties in food and drink. The result is that, reading *A Moveable Feast*, especially the fuller version, we are able to make a map of Paris in our imagination and to follow the comings and goings of Hemingway and the literary lions who stalk its pages — James Joyce, Ford Madox Ford, Fitzgerald, Ezra Pound, Gertrude Stein, and others. Its fault and its virtue is that it is dated: Paris is no longer as

THE TAO OF TRAVEL

Hemingway describes it, but this is a vivid portrait of the city as it looked and smelled and tasted in the twenties.

At one point, Hemingway, a close observer of the life of the city, takes on travel writers:

> Travel writers wrote about the men fishing in the Seine as though they were crazy and never caught anything; but it was serious and productive fishing. Most of the fishermen were men who had small pensions, which they did not know then would become worthless with inflation, or keen fishermen who fished on their days or half-days off from work . . . I followed it closely and it was interesting and good to know about, and it always made me happy that there were men fishing in the city itself, having sound, serious fishing and taking a few *fritures* home to their families.
>
> With the fishermen and the lie on the river, the beautiful barges with their own life on board, the tugs with their smokestacks that folded back to pass under the bridges, pulling a tow of barges, the great plain trees on the stone banks of the river, the elms and sometimes the poplars, I knew that I could never be lonely along the river.

The End of the Game *by Peter Beard*

ALMOST FIFTY YEARS ago, Peter Beard went to Africa and found himself in a violated Eden. Africa possessed him as it does anyone who has wondered who we once were, as humans at our most heroic, thriving as hunters. The Africa he saw was the Africa that transformed me a few years later — and transformed many others. "Before the Congo I was a mere animal," Joseph Conrad wrote. Beard's landmark account of his awakening, *The End of the Game* (1965), with its unforgettable images, gives fresh meaning to the word "prescience", and it remains one of the classics of unambiguous warning about humans and animals occupying the same dramatic space: "The tragic paradox of the white man's encroachment. The deeper he went into Africa, the faster life flowed out of it, off the plains, and out of the bush and into the cities."

East Africa is not a pretty place in the usual sense of that twinkling word. The elemental and powerful landscape, ranging around the Rift

Valley, is one of the earth's monuments to vulcanism, showing as great plains, steep escarpments, and deep lakes. The Africa Beard saw, even then, in the almost undetectable early stages of corruption, was teeming with animals, thinly populated, hardly urbanized, and self-sufficient. Years later, the pressures of human population on animal life and the land itself became apparent in an Africa faltering and fragile, as though after the Fall. Beard's improvisational safari to the edge of Somalia in 1960 was a piece of unrepeatable history. He understood very early that the "harmonies and balances" in East Africa had been deranged, and this dramatic crease in the greenest continent was on the wane.

Mingling personal history with African history, Beard vividly evoked the building of the Mombasa–Nairobi Railway. "A railroad through the Pleistocene," Teddy Roosevelt called it in his *African Game Trails*, playing up the primitive. Roosevelt, a sort of evil twin to the biblical Noah, hunted down and killed two (and sometimes as many as eighteen) of every species of animal that could be found from the Kenyan coast to the swamps of southern Sudan (total bag, 512 creatures). He wrote, "The land teems with beasts of the chase, infinite in number."

"Infinite" is the kind of hyperbole that affects many deluded travellers in Africa. The powerful message of *The End of the Game* was that the animals were finite, that urbanization was a creeping blight, that a free-for-all was imminent. Most of what Beard predicted came to pass, but even he could not have imagined what an abomination the cities of East Africa became — sprawling, dense with slums, so crime-ridden as to be almost uninhabitable.

The End of the Game is less a wildlife book than a book about human delusion, as important now as it was when it first appeared. Rare among visitors to Africa, Beard went simply to learn and grow. Because he was essentially an observer, patient and keen-sighted, not a ranter, with no agenda, he was able to see a process at work that many had missed, in the convergence of people and animals. One of his book's great virtues, and its lasting value, is that it takes no notice of politics. It is single-mindedly concerned with the living and the dead, predators and prey. Beard was true to what he saw — and the truth of it has made it prophetic.

The Rings of Saturn *by W. G. Sebald*

IN 1992, AS he tells us on the first page of his book, W. G. Sebald, a German teacher-writer living in England, decided to strap on his rucksack and circumambulate the flat, featureless, not very large county of Suffolk. The result was *The Rings of Saturn*, a ruminative work full of free association and arcane lore, with the subtext "Not a lot of people know this!" Sebald claims that the book was "prose fiction" (Chatwin made the same claim about his *Songlines*) and inspired by Sir Thomas Browne's *Urn Burial*, but though this is self-serving, the stitched-together anecdotes do have a point, perhaps unintentional, but forceful nevertheless.

To write about what one sees in Suffolk would be a work of topography or social history, but rambling describes what Sebald does — on foot and on the page. What do we find in Lowestoft? Not much. Joseph Conrad had a seafaring connection to Lowestoft, and from this slender link Sebald develops a whole historical reverie that involves Conrad, King Leopold of Belgium, the hellish Congo, Roger Casement, and Casement's sensational diaries. This is pretty much the structure of the book, except that a bigoted note occurs when he speaks of the Congo and Belgians, whom Germans (though Sebald doesn't say why) particularly abominate. "And, indeed, to this day one sees in Belgium a distinctive ugliness, dating from the time when the Congo colony was exploited."

Does he mean a metaphorical ugliness? No. "At all events, I well recall that on my first visit to Brussels in December 1964 I encountered more hunchbacks and lunatics than normally in a whole year. One evening in a bar in Rhode St Genèse I even watched a deformed billiard player who was racked with spastic contortions." And so forth.

He comes to Dunwich. Dunwich hardly exists, most of it having been overwhelmed by the sea. And so what Sebald provides is nothing less than the history of the town, the name of every sunken church, the monastery, and a detailed account of the storms that reduced Dunwich to a pathetic settlement.

But here is the point: the native of a place seldom sees what the alien sees, seldom remarks on what he or she takes for granted. Sebald describes how the passengers in the first train he takes, from Norfolk to

Lowestoft, are so silent "that not a word might have passed their lips in the whole of their lives". This is empty hyperbole. English people, and in particular the provincial English, seldom yammer on public transport. Without saying so, the German is comparing the English to Germans. Still, the originality of the book arises from the remarks that only a foreigner would make, and such observations, even when they are misapprehensions and distortions, have value.

ଓ 24 ଓ

Evocative Name,
Disappointing Place

A PLACE NAME CAN BEWITCH THE TRAVELLER. The name "Singapore" cast a spell on me until I lived there for three years in the 1960s without air-conditioning. But the village of Birdsmoor Gate, in the west of England, near where I lived after Singapore, was just as lovely as its name. California names, such as Pacific Grove, Walnut Creek, and Thousand Palms, seemed to beckon. But in Philadelphia, the corner of Kensington Avenue and Somerset Street — music to the ears of the average Anglomaniac — is a dangerous slum area and the busiest drug-dealing site in an otherwise salubrious city. ¶ In *Remote People*, Evelyn Waugh talks about the deception of names. "How wrong I was, as things turned out," he says, "in all my preconceived notions about this journey. Zanzibar and the Congo, names pregnant with romantic suggestion, gave me nothing, while the places I found most full of interest were those I expected to detest — Kenya and Aden."

Here are some place names that have misled the credulous traveller.

Shepherds Bush: A grey, malodorous, overpopulated district, the opposite of its name, in west London. The traveller not wise to the truth of this squints and mutters, "Where is it?" gazing at the greasy cafés, kebab shops, Australian mega-pubs, cut-price emporiums, and honking traffic. Shepherds Bush is noted for its shopkeepers, who, when it's not raining, stand at their doorways voluptuously scratching themselves.

Casablanca: "Casablanca is an anonymous cluster of high-rises, and modern roads so straight and thin there'd be no room for Sidney Greenstreet there" (Pico Iyer).

Baghdad: "Celebrated as the city of the *Arabian Nights*," James Simmons writes in *Passionate Pilgrims*, "Baghdad 1,000 years before had been one of the great cities of Asia, a centre of art, literature and learning. Richard Burton called it 'a Paris of the ninth century.'"

Simmons goes on: "Baghdad disappointed the Blunts, as it has virtually all modern travellers. Freya Stark called it 'a city of wicked dust'. And Robert Casey, who visited Baghdad in 1930, dismissed it as 'a dust heap — odorous, unattractive, and hot. Its monuments are few, its atmosphere that of squalor and poverty.'" And this was before the invasion, the fall of Saddam Hussein, and all the bombs.

Mandalay: An enormous grid of dusty streets occupied by dispirited and oppressed Burmese, and policed by a military tyranny.

Tahiti: A mildewed island of surly colonials, exasperated French soldiers, and indignant natives, with overpriced hotels, one of the world's worst traffic problems, and undrinkable water.

Timbuktu: Dust, hideous hotels, unreliable transport, freeloaders, pestering people, garbage heaps everywhere, poisonous food.

Marseille: Just a short walk from the pretty harbour are sullen neighbourhoods of public housing, tenements, refugees, and bewildered immigrants, with no one saying *bienvenu*.

Samarkand: Not the Silk Road fantasy of minarets and domes but a stinking industrial city in Uzbekistan, known for its chemical factories, fertilizer plants, and out-of-control drunkenness.

Guatemala City: A place that has continually been flattened by earthquakes and badly rebuilt. The majority of the population are slum dwellers, many of whom are eager to emigrate from their failed state.

Alexandria: Almost all my life I had dreamed of Alexandria. Most of life's disappointments begin in dreams. At one time, like the greatest cities in the world, Alexandria, Egypt, belonged to everyone who lived in it. And, as Lawrence Durrell wrote in *Justine*, it was shared by "five races, five languages, a dozen creeds: five fleets turning through their greasy reflections behind the harbour bar. But there are more than five sexes." Yet today Alexandria is a monoglot city of one race, Arabic-speaking Arabs, and one creed, Islam, and is puritanical.

Kunming: Once a small, self-contained agricultural town in the rural south of China, ancient, visually bewitching, known for its serene parks, Kunming is now a huge horrendous city, overrun by cars and buses, concrete and tenements, and one of the main routes of the drug trade from Burma.

São Paulo: Like Bombay, Tokyo, and Los Angeles, which are known for their ugly buildings, their bad air, and their twenty-million-plus populations, São Paulo (lovely, saintly name) has to be seen and suffered through to be understood as one of the worst city-planning disasters on earth. Or rather, "No planning," the São Pauleano says, "just" — and lifts his hand and makes the money sign.

Biarritz: Apart from the tiny corniche and the picturesque — but grotesquely overpriced — Hôtel du Palais, this is a crowded French city of cement bungalows, labyrinthine roads, mediocre restaurants, and a stony beach of cold and dangerous surf.

❧ Travel Wisdom of ❧
PAUL BOWLES

The Paul Bowles (1910–1999) of stereotype is the golden man, the enigmatic exile, elegantly dressed, a cigarette holder between his fingers, luxuriating in the Moroccan sunshine, living on remittances, occasionally offering his alarming and highly polished fictions to the wider world. This portrait has a grain of truth, but there is much more to know. Certainly Bowles had style, and success with one book, *The Sheltering Sky*. But a single book, even a popular one, seldom guarantees a regular income. And, apart from money, Bowles's life was complicated emotionally, sexually, geographically, and without a doubt creatively. ¶ A resourceful man — as the exile or expatriate tends to be — Bowles had many outlets for his imagination. He made a name for himself as a composer, writing the music for a number of films and stage plays. He was an ethnomusicologist, an early recorder of traditional songs and melodies

259

in remote villages in Morocco and Mexico. He wrote novels and short stories and poems. He translated novels and poems from Spanish, French, and Arabic. So the louche, languid soul of the stereotype turns out to have been a busy man, highly productive, verging on a drudge. ¶ He was handsome and hard to impress, watchful and solitary, and he knew his own mind. His mood of acceptance, even of fatalism, made him an ideal traveller. He was not much of a gastronome — as his fiction shows, the disgusting meal (fur in the rabbit stew) interested him much more than haute cuisine. He was passionate about landscape and its effects on the traveller. Bowles was fortunate in writing at a time (not long ago, but now gone) when travel magazines still welcomed long, thoughtful essays. ¶ He wrote for the American *Holiday*, the frivolous name masking a serious literary mission. The English fiction writers V. S. Pritchett and Lawrence Durrell also travelled for this magazine; so did John Steinbeck after he won the Nobel Prize, when he criss-crossed the United States with his dog. Bowles wrote a piece for *Holiday* about hashish, another of his enthusiasms, since he was a lifelong stoner. ¶ He knew what he enjoyed in travel, and what bored him: "If I am faced with the decision of choosing between visiting a circus and a cathedral, a café and a public monument, or a fiesta and a museum, I am afraid I shall normally take the circus, the café, and the fiesta." The following quotations are from *Their Heads Are Green and Their Hands Are Blue* (1963).

Each time I go to a place I have not seen before, I hope it will be as different as possible from the places I already know. I assume it is natural for a traveller to seek diversity, and that it is the human element which makes him most aware of difference. If people and their manner of living were alike everywhere, there would not be much point in moving from one place to another.

There are probably few accessible places on the face of the globe where one can get less comfort for his money than the Sahara. It is still possible to find something flat to lie down on, several turnips and sand, noodles and jam, a few tendons of something euphemistically called chicken to eat, and the stub of a candle to undress by at night. Inasmuch as it is necessary to carry one's own food and stove, it sometimes seems scarcely worth while to bother with the "meals" provided by the hotels. But if one depends entirely on tinned goods, they give out too quickly. Everything disappears eventually — coffee, tea, sugar, cigarettes — and the traveller settles down to a life devoid of these superfluities, using a pile of soiled clothing as a pillow for his head at night and a burnous as a blanket.

Perhaps the logical question to ask at this point is: Why go? The answer is that when a man has been there and undergone the baptism of solitude he can't help himself. Once he has been under the spell of the vast, luminous, silent country, no other place is quite strong enough for him, no other surroundings can provide the supremely satisfying sensation of existing in the midst of something that is absolute. He will go back, whatever the cost in comfort and money, for the absolute has no price.

∂✷ 25 ✷∂

Dangerous, Happy, Alluring

Dangerous Places

"WHAT GIVES VALUE TO TRAVEL IS FEAR," Albert Camus wrote (*Notebooks, 1935–1942*). "It is the fact that, at a certain moment, when we are so far from our own country . . . we are seized by a vague fear, and the instinctive desire to go back to the protection of old habits. This is the most obvious benefit of travel. At that moment we are feverish but also porous, so that the slightest touch makes us quiver to the depths of our being. We come across a cascade of light, and there is eternity. This is why we should not say that we travel for pleasure. There is no pleasure in travelling."

Stirring stuff, but the first thing to say to this is that Camus, a timid traveller, never travelled very far. Camus was afflicted with motorphobia, a morbid fear of riding in cars. The irony of this is that he died in a car crash. His publisher, Michel Gallimard, asked Camus to accompany him to Paris from Provence in his expensive sports car, a Facel Vega, insisting it would be the quickest way to get there. Speeding through the village of Villeblevin, Gallimard lost control of the car, killing himself and Camus, in whose pocket was his unused train ticket to Paris. Camus was that singular pedant, a theorist of travel, rather than a traveller. But his argument is a good one: a place's aura of danger can cast a spell.

I was once on a TV show with the self-appointed chronicler of such places, the Canadian traveller and journalist Robert Young Pelton, who made his name with his first book, *The World's Most Dangerous Places*. Quite different from his public image as Danger Man, in person he was likable and eager to please, though he wagged his finger as he told horror stories of his travels. Yet most of his stories were about places I'd been to and hadn't found horrible. I agreed that Algeria was somewhere to avoid for its frequent massacres, also Chechnya and Abkhazia — as though anyone would want to go to those bombed-out places. When he droned on about Cambodia, Colombia, Pakistan, Zimbabwe, and the Philippines ("Don't be fooled by the modern veneer of the Philippines. It is a have and have not country where outsiders are spared much of the brutality and injustice," he says on his website, ComeBackAlive.com), I said, "Robert, we are on the outskirts of Newark!"

Newark, with its adjacent and stagnant wetlands, seemed dank and cut off and ominous, like a city in a swamp. It was at the time advertised as "New Jersey's homicide capital" by its own newspaper, the *Star-Ledger*: more than a hundred murders a year. Pelton conceded that point, and my next one, which was that countries are not violent, people are, some more than others, and parts of Newark were possibly as dangerous as parts of Chechnya.

On Pelton's ominously titled "Could Be Your Last Trip" list are Afghanistan, Iraq, Somalia, Pakistan, Mexico, the whole of Russia, New Guinea, Burma, Sri Lanka, and Sudan.

I do not quibble with his listing Iraq and Afghanistan, both of which are war zones. Somalia has no government and exists in a state of anarchy managed by tribal chiefs, warlords, and pirates. But by taking care I have had a wonderful time in Cambodia, Mexico, Burma, Sri Lanka, Russia, and even Sudan (see my *Dark Star Safari*), which Pelton describes as "a big, bad, ugly place with a belligerent, extreme Islamic government hell-bent on choking the entire country under Islam's shroud". Yes, the Sudanese government is bad and ugly, but from village to village I met only friendly folk.

The Philippines is one of the world's most underrated travel destinations, hospitable and very beautiful. I would advise the traveller to be cautious in certain areas of Mindanao, in the way I would advise caution in certain areas of Camden, New Jersey, seventy-three miles from Newark, named the number one most dangerous city in the USA.

One list of the top ten most dangerous cities in the world, based on their murder rate (number of murders per 100,000), has Ciudad Juárez at the top (130 murders per 100,000). The other cities on this list include Caracas, New Orleans, Tijuana, Cape Town, San Salvador, Medellín, Baltimore, and Baghdad. Other lists include Mogadishu, Detroit, St. Louis, Rio de Janeiro, and Johannesburg.

I have had nothing but safe travel experiences in South Africa, and yet the official statistics are very scary. In a one-year period (the twelve months from April 2007 to March 2008) South Africa reported 18,148 murders, and many had presumably gone unreported. The number of reported sex crimes, including rapes and assaults (according to a *New York Times* report in 2009), was 70,514. The violence in South Africa is increasing. This news does not deter safari-goers, soccer fans, bird watchers, or the many oenophiles who seek to sample the dessert wines and Pinot Noirs of the Western Cape.

Apart from some obvious hellholes — Mogadishu, Baghdad, Kabul — every city has its high-risk neighbourhoods. It is in the nature of a city to be alienating, the hunting ground of opportunists, rip-off artists, and muggers. I once asked a concierge in a large hotel near Union Square in San Francisco for directions to the Asian Arts Museum. Though it was within walking distance, he begged me to take a taxi, to speed me past the streets of panhandlers, homeless people, decompensating schizos, and drunks. In the event, I walked — briskly — and was not inconvenienced.

Afghanistan and Pakistan were — not even that long ago — delightful places to travel in. And they may be again. India is full of terrorist groups, not just the pro-Kashmiris who shot up Bombay, but the more violent Maoist Naxalites who regularly set off bombs, derail passenger trains, and have killed more than six thousand people in the past dozen years in the so-called Red Corridor, a stripe running along the right-hand side of India. But in spite of its violence and disorder, India is still one of the most attractive destinations in the world.

At various times in my life, soldiers or militiamen at roadblocks in parts of Africa have pointed rifles at me and demanded money. I have been shot at by shifta bandits in northern Kenya. But in these places I was off the map and expected to be hassled.

As for my own top ten dangerous places, I have felt conspicuously alien, vulnerable, unsafe, and tended to walk fast in

Port Moresby, Papua New Guinea: One of the most dangerous, crime-ridden cities in the world, inhabited by drifters and squatters, locally known as "rascals", and career criminals, many of whom, wearing woolly hats, come from the Highlands and are looking for prey.

Nairobi: Downtown, muggers galore, even in daylight.

East St. Louis, Illinois: One of the poorest, most beat-up, most menacing-looking cities in the United States.

Vladivostok: A clammy-cold harbour city of vandalized buildings, scrawled-upon walls, underpaid sailors, and confrontational drunks and skinheads.

England: On Saturday afternoons, among the hoodlums, after soccer matches.

Rio de Janeiro: At the reeking periphery of the Carnival mobs, among prowlers and drunks and aggressive celebrants.

Addis Ababa: In the Merkato bazaar, which abounds with pickpockets and thieves.

Solomon Islands: The smaller, hungrier islands, noted for their xeno-
phobia, some of whose locals demand large sums of money from any
outsider who lands on the beach.

Kabul: Just outside the city, at a village where walking alone, I was spotted by about a dozen women who, unprovoked by me, began throwing
stones at my head.

Newark: Stuck overnight, having missed a plane, I had to walk in the
evening from my dreary hotel to find a place to eat, and at one point,
dodging traffic, stepping over a dead dog, I was confronted by hostile
boys yelling abuse and heckling me.

Happy Places

Are there truly happy places? I tend to think that happiness is a particular time in a particular place, an epiphany that remains as a consolation
and a regret. Fogies recall many a happy time, because fogeydom is the
last bastion of the bore and reminiscence is its anthem. Ordering food
in a restaurant in the 1950s, William Burroughs said, "What I want for
dinner is a bass fished in Lake Huron in 1927."

There is a well-publicized list of happy places, which includes Den-
mark at the top, followed in descending order by Switzerland, Austria,
Finland, Australia, Sweden, Canada, Guatemala, and Luxembourg.

With the exception of small, threadbare Guatemala, what do these
countries have in common? They are the world's most developed, urbanized, bourgeois, and (so it seems) the smuggest and teeniest bit boring. I
seriously doubt that they are as happy as advertised. Cold, dark Finland
in January is not a place one associates with jollification. Finland, in
fact, is quite high on the "Countries with the Most Suicides" list, and one
doesn't think of Austria as the Land of Smiles.

Tonga's archipelago is informally known as the Friendly Isles. Captain
Cook initiated the idea, but with the passing years this has seemed more
and more like a frivolous sobriquet to beguile visitors, in the manner of
bestowing the name Greenland on the land of snow and ice. Tongans are
hierarchical, class-obsessed, rivalrous, and, like most islanders, territo-
rial and rightly suspicious of strangers who wash ashore.

The very word "friendly" is loaded, and it is usually just a tourist-industry come-on. I wrote in *Fresh Air Fiend*, "In my experience, the friendliest people on Pacific islands are those who have the greatest assurance that you are going to leave soon."

"The real enemy, the destroyer of our happiness, is within ourselves," the Dalai Lama once said in a homily. Likewise, the true creator of our happiness is within us. There are contented people in the world, whose easy manner and good cheer persuade the traveller that he or she is in a happy land. Happy times are unforgettable, and sometimes they last for more than a moment. I have had joyful experiences in many places, at particular times. I agree with Burroughs's fish story: happiness is usually retrospective.

There is also another factor, not "I'd like to live here" but "I wouldn't mind dying here." Here are ten instances:

Bali: I travelled there in the 1970s and after a week in Ubud wanted to quit my job, summon my wife and two children from Singapore, and spend the rest of my life on that fragrant island. My little family resisted.

Thailand: My recurring fantasy is dropping out and spending the rest of my days in a rural village in northern Thailand, as a paying guest, among hospitable villagers.

Costa Rica: On a bay in the rural north-western province of Guanacaste I felt strongly: I will build a house with a veranda and sit there scribbling like O. Henry in Honduras.

The Orkney Islands: Small, proud, remote, self-contained. Hard-working and well built, with Neolithic ruins and traditional pieties. I went there once and never stopped dreaming about these islands and their fresh fish.

Egypt: Not Cairo but somewhere else. Maybe I'd live on a houseboat, moored on the upper Nile, toward Aswan.

The Trobriand Islands: The people are uncompromising but I would make peace, settle on a small outer island, and sail around Milne Bay, as I did in the early 1990s.

Malawi: I have rarely been happier than I was in the Shire Highlands of rural southern Malawi in 1964, the year of *ufulu*, independence. I had a little house, a satisfying job as a teacher, and the goodwill of my neighbours in nearby villages. Later, I thought, If everything goes wrong in my life, I can always return to Malawi.

Maine: I think of the coast of Maine as coherent, lovely, well assembled by nature, populated by some of the most decent and reliable people I have ever known.

Hawaii: Perhaps it really is the tourist paradise of the brochures. I have lived in Hawaii longer than anywhere else in my life, and often when I am with a local person, and it's a beautiful day — the pure air, the fragrance of flowers, the surf up, the usual rainbow arching in the sky — this person will smile and say, "Lucky we live Hawaii."

Alluring Places

In my mind is a list of places I have never seen and have always wanted to visit. I read about them, look at maps, collect guidebooks and picture books. My imagination is full of appealing images — a great thing. The idea of unvisited places, future travel, enlivens the mind and promises pleasure. Here are ten out of many.

Alaska: Huge and thinly populated, one of the last true wilderness areas in the world, with Denali National Park and North America's highest mountain, Denali, at 20,320 feet. I imagine paddling along the coast, taking ferries to the annual Great Aleutian Pumpkin Run, seeing the small towns and the empty places.

Scandinavia: I have never been to Norway, Sweden, or Finland. I'd like to see them in their winter darkness, at their gloomiest and most suicidal, and also go cross-country skiing. Then another trip in the summer, reliving Ingmar Bergman's *Smiles of a Summer Night* in Sweden, picking cloudberries in northern Norway, and visiting the Lapps.

Greenland: With widely scattered and diverse indigenous populations, many of whom have retained their traditional skills, Greenland (Kalaallit Nunaat) is inviting. Fridtjof Nansen skied across it in 1883, the first recorded crossing. He stayed among the Greenlanders and recounted how, housebound in the depths of winter, they sat naked, perspiring around a fire. I would also like to see Scoresby Sund, the largest fjord in the world, and hear the patter of the drum made from a polar bear's bladder.

Timor: There is liberated, independent, and chaotic East Timor and the Indonesian province of West Timor. I want to see them both, go from one to the other, talk to people, eat their fermented rice and steamed fish, go bird watching.

Angola: The Portuguese landed in Angola in 1575, colonized it, converted some people, plundered it for minerals — diamonds in particular — settled the coast, and ignored the hinterland. The Chokwe people in the interior, who now have their own political party, are among Africa's finest artists, carvers, and dancers. For almost thirty years Angola was engaged in a civil war, but now it is rebuilding, and with its oil reserves it has the money to be independent and prosperous. I would like to see the country before prosperity takes hold.

New Britain Island: A large island off Papua New Guinea, with a small population of indigenous people, secret societies, rare birds, and balmy weather. And if that doesn't work out, I'd travel in the area, to Manus Island (written about by Margaret Mead) and New Ireland.

Sakhalin: I could just make it out, grey and flat, over the windswept channel, from the northernmost port in Japan, Wakkanai. I could have taken a ferry, but I had to travel south, so I filed this away in my mind as a place I wished to see. Once a prison colony, Sakhalin was visited in 1890 and written about by Chekhov. What's the attraction for me? The challenge of bleakness, no city to speak of, hardy people, and a railway.

The Darien Gap: I have travelled around but not overland through this section of jungle that lies between Panama and Colombia. The road is not reliable, and the fact that it is a geographical bottleneck, not to say a barrier, makes it inviting as a place in which I would happily disappear.

The Swat Valley: Once, long ago in Peshawar, I met some locals — tribals — who offered to take me upcountry into Swat, and to see the surrounding area — Taxila and ruined Buddhist monasteries, which comprised ancient Gandhara and its Hellenic art. I said, "Some other time." Now it is the haunt of the Taliban, but perhaps one day . . .

The American South: I have had the merest glimpse, a long drive around the entire Gulf Coast, from Florida to New Orleans. But that glimpse, and the people I met, made me want to take a trip of six months or so, in rural Mississippi, Alabama, Georgia, and Louisiana, through Tennessee and the Carolinas — off the highways, into the pinewoods, down the red clay roads.

❧ 26 ❧
Five Travel Epiphanies

NOW AND THEN IN TRAVEL, SOMETHING UN-
expected happens that transforms the whole nature of the trip and stays with the traveller. Burton
travelled to Mecca in disguise, considering it a lark, but
when at last he approached the Kaaba this sceptic was
profoundly moved. It sometimes seems to me that if
there is a fundamental quest in travel, it is the search
for the unexpected. The discovery of an unanticipated
pleasure can be life-changing. ¶ Here are five epipha-
nies that I have experienced in travel, unforgettable to
me, and for that reason they have helped to guide me.

One

I WAS IN Palermo and had spent the last of my money on a ticket to New York aboard the *Queen Frederica*. This was in September 1963; I was going into the Peace Corps, training for a post in Africa. The farewell party my Italian friends gave me on the night of departure went on so long that when we got to the port, a Sicilian band was playing "Anchors Aweigh" and the *Queen Frederica* had just left the quayside. In that moment I lost all my vitality.

My friends bought me an air ticket to Naples so that I could catch up to the ship there the next day. Just before I boarded the plane, an airline official said I had not paid my departure tax. I told him I had no money. A man behind me in a brown suit and brown Borsalino said, "Here. You need some money?" and handed me twenty dollars.

That solved the problem. I said, "I'd like to pay you back."

The man shrugged. He said, "I'll probably see you again. The world's a small place."

Two

FOR THREE DAYS in August 1970 I had been on a small cargo vessel, the MV *Keningau*, which sailed from Singapore to North Borneo. I was going there to climb Mount Kinabalu. While aboard, I read and played cards, always the same game, with a Malay planter and a Eurasian woman who was travelling with her two children. The ship had an open steerage deck, where about a hundred passengers slept in hammocks.

It was the monsoon season. I cursed the rain, the heat, the ridiculous card games. One day the Malayan said, "The wife of one of my men had a baby last night." He explained that the rubber tappers were in steerage and that some had wives.

I said I wanted to see the baby. He took me below, and seeing that newborn, and the mother and father so radiant with pride, transformed the trip. Because the baby had been born on the ship, everything was changed for me and had a different meaning: the rain, the heat, the other people, even the card games and the book I was reading.

Three

THE COAST OF Wales around St. David's Head has very swift currents and sudden fogs. Four of us were paddling sea kayaks out to Ramsay Island. On our return to shore we found ourselves in fog so dense we could not see land. We were spun around by eddies and whirlpools.

"Where's north?" I asked the man who had the compass.

"Over there," he said, tapping it. Then he smacked it and said, "There," and hit it harder and said, "I don't know, this thing's broken."

Darkness was falling, the April day was cold, we were tired, and we could not see anything except the black deeps of St. George's Channel.

"Listen," someone said. "I hear Horse Rock." The current rushing against Horse Rock was a distinct sound. But he was wrong — it was the wind.

We kept together. Fear slowed our movements, and I felt sure that we had no hope of getting back that night — or ever. The cold and my fatigue were like premonitions of death. We went on paddling. A long time passed. We searched; no one spoke. This is what dying is like, I thought.

I strained my eyes to see and had a vision, a glimpse of cloud high up that was like a headland. When I looked harder, willing it to be land, it solidified to a great dark rock. I yelped, and we made for shore as though reborn.

Four

WE WERE DRIVING in western Kenya under the high African sky, my wife beside me, our two boys in the back seat. It was not far from here that I had met this pretty English woman and married her. Our elder son had been born in Kampala, the younger one in Singapore. We were still nomads, driving toward Eldoret. Years before, as a soon-to-be-married couple, we had spent a night there.

The boys were idly quarrelling and fooling, laughing, distracting me. My wife was saying, "Are you sure this is the right road?" She had been travelling alone for three months in southern Africa. We were in an old rental car. Cattle dotted the hills, sheltering under the thorn trees. We were just a family on a trip, far away.

But we were travelling toward Eldoret, into the past and deeper into Africa, into the future. We were together, the sun slanting into our eyes, everything on earth was green, and I thought: I never want this trip to end.

Five

JUST BEFORE INDEPENDENCE Day in 1964, when Nyasaland became Malawi, the minister of education, Masauko Chipembere, planted a tree at the school where I was teaching in the south of the country. Soon after this, he conspired to depose the prime minister, Dr. Hastings Banda. But Chipembere himself was driven out.

Time passed, and when I heard that Chipembere had died in Los Angeles ("in exile", as a CIA pensioner), I thought of the little tree he had shovelled into the ground. Twenty-five years after I left the school, I travelled back to Malawi. Two things struck me about the country: most of the trees had been cut down — for fuel — and no one rode a bicycle any more. Most buildings were decrepit too. Dr. Banda was still in power.

It took me a week to travel to my old school. It was larger now but ruinous, with broken windows and splintered desks. The students seemed unpleasant. The headmaster was rude to me. The library had no books. The tree was big and green, almost forty feet high.

❦ 27 ❦
The Essential Tao of Travel

1. Leave home

2. Go alone

3. Travel light

4. Bring a map

5. Go by land

6. Walk across a national frontier

7. Keep a journal

8. Read a novel that has no relation
to the place you're in

9. If you must bring a cell phone,
avoid using it

10. Make a friend

Acknowledgements

FOR SUGGESTIONS, IMPROVEMENTS, and moral support, I would like to thank Jin Auh, Larry Cooper, Roger Ebert, Patrick French, Forrest Furman, Harvey Golden, Ted Hoagland, Pico Iyer, Tim Jeal, Joel Martin, Geoffrey Moorhouse, Jan Morris, Dervla Murphy, Jeffrey Meyers, Simon Prosser, Jonathan Raban, Mort Rosenblum, Oliver Sacks, Andrea Schulz, Nicholas Shakespeare, Alexander Theroux, Joseph Theroux, Louis Theroux, Marcel Theroux, Juliet Walker, and Andrew Wylie. And special thanks, with love, to my wife, Sheila.

Index of People and Places